THE
UNKNOWN
THOMAS HARDY

By the same author

The World of Victorian Humor (ed.) (Appleton-Century-Crofts, 1961)

Six Essays in Nineteenth-Century English Literature and Thought (ed.) (University of Kansas Press, 1962)

Thomas Hardy's Epic-Drama: A Study of 'The Dynasts' (University of Kansas Press, 1963)

Thomas Hardy's Personal Writings: Prefaces, Literary Opinions, Reminiscences (ed.) (University of Kansas Press, 1966; Macmillan, 1967)

The Development of William Butler Yeats, 1885–1900 (University of Kansas, 1968)

British Poetry 1880–1920: Edwardian Voices (ed.) (Appleton-Century-Crofts, 1969)

The Nineteenth-Century Writer and His Audience (ed.) (University of Kansas Press, 1969)

English Romantic Poets and the Enlightenment: Nine Essays on a Literary Relationship (Voltaire Foundation, 1973)

Irish History and Culture: Aspects of a People's Heritage (ed.) (Regents Press of Kansas/Wolfhound Press, 1979)

The Final Years of Thomas Hardy, 1912–1928 (Macmillan/Regents Press of Kansas, 1976)

The Dynasts, by Thomas Hardy, New Wessex Edition (Macmillan, 1978)

The Scottish World (ed.) (Thames and Hudson/Harry Abrams, 1981)

Rudyard Kipling: Interviews and Recollections (Volumes 1 and 2) (ed.) (Macmillan/Barnes and Noble, 1983)

Victorian Literary Critics: George Henry Lewes, Walter Bagehot, Richard Holt Hutton, Leslie Stephen, Andrew Lang, George Saintsbury, Edmund Gosse (Macmillan/St. Martin's, 1984)

The Literary Achievement of Rebecca West (Macmillan/St. Martin's, 1985)

The Victorian Short Story (Cambridge University Press, 1986)

THE UNKNOWN THOMAS HARDY

Lesser-Known Aspects of Hardy's Life and Career

HAROLD OREL

University Distinguished Professor of English
University of Kansas

St. Martin's Press
New York

© Harold Orel, 1987

First published in the United States of America in 1987

Printed in Great Britain

ISBN 0-312-00538-5

Library of Congress Cataloging-in-Publication Data

Orel, Harold, 1926–
    The unknown Thomas Hardy.

    Bibliography: p.
    Includes index.
    1. Hardy, Thomas, 1840–1928.   2. Hardy, Thomas,
1840–1928—Knowledge and learning.   3. Authors,
English—19th century—Biography.   I. Title.
PR4753.074   1987   823'.8   87-4653
ISBN 0-312-00538-5

To George and Carol Worth

Contents

Acknowledgements

Special thanks are due to the editors of the American periodical *English Literature in Transition 1880–1920,* and to Macmillan and Weidenfeld & Nicolson (England) for permission to reprint material incorporated within longer essay-chapters of this book. Much of this material has been revised.

I am also grateful to the Thomas Hardy Society of England, whose members have done so much to make more widely known the achievements of Hardy's creative work.

Owing to the accident of his being an architect's pupil in a county-town of assizes and aldermen, which had advanced to railways and telegraphs and daily London papers; yet not living there, but walking in every day from a world of shepherds and ploughmen in a hamlet three miles off, where modern improvements were still regarded as wonders, he saw rustic and borough doings in a juxtaposition peculiarly close. To these externals may be added the pecularities of his inner life, which might almost have been called academic—a triple existence unusual for a young man—what he used to call, in looking back, a life twisted of three strands—the professional life, the scholar's life, and the rustic life, combined in the twenty-four hours of one day, as it was with him through these years.

(Florence Emily Hardy, *The Life of Thomas Hardy 1840–1928,* London, Macmillan, 1962, pp.31-2)

Introduction

Towards the end of the twentieth century it has become clear that Thomas Hardy's high reputation, established during his lifetime and lasting for a full fifty years after his death, has undergone two major sea-changes. In this book I discuss unfamiliar aspects of his life and career, but for the moment let us consider these two transformations of public attitude toward Hardy the man.

The harsh reception given by a relatively small number of reviewers to the publication of *Jude the Obscure* (from 1895 on) turned Hardy to the production of occasional pieces: short stories, a surprising number of letters to editors of various periodicals, *The Dynasts* in three volumes and eight volumes of collected poems. Most of those authors who belonged to Hardy's generation had died or given up writing creative fictions by the end of the first decade of this century. Hardy's singular staying-power meant that, increasingly, he was seen as a Grand Old Man of English letters, a survivor and (the epithet was more than once applied) the 'last Victorian'.

Looking back on the last three decades of Hardy's long life—born in 1840, Hardy died in 1928—we can appreciate the fact that the reading public, vast though it was, knew very little of a personal nature about him. Hardy was, after all, determinedly private and granted journalists and fellow-writers permission to visit him at Max Gate only infrequently; hid from a curious public behind countless scotch pines planted on the grounds of his home, Max Gate on the Wareham Road; and maintained that his poems were 'in a large degree dramatic or personative in conception' (Preface to *Wessex Poems,* 1898). In his preface to *Time's Laughingstocks and Other Verses* he insisted that the poems in that

1

volume should be regarded 'in the main, as dramatic monologues by different characters'. In the General Preface to the Wessex Edition, printed in 1912, he even denied that he wrote on the basis of a consistent philosophy: 'The sentiments in the following pages have been stated truly to be mere impressions of the moment, and not convictions or arguments.'

Decorum is often considered to be a hallmark of Victorianism. Hardy's public image was that of a dignified, quiet and thoroughly unremarkable human being who had managed, somehow and without clear explanation, to triumph over the isolation of his childhood in Dorset (the least populated county of England), his relatively few years of formal schooling, the obscurity of his five years (1862–7) in London and the commercial craftiness of his earliest publishers. He did not travel extensively. He never belonged to a literary school, and he rejected numerous opportunities to become the leader of one. Indeed, he came to the literary profession rather late, after the age of 30. He debated the possibilities of devoting himself to a life of acting, or of service to the Church of England, rather than architecture, in which he worked full-time between 1856 and 1872. His first novel, *Desperate Remedies,* was published in 1871. (The first one he had written, *The Poor Man and the Lady,* completed three years earlier, did not win a publisher's contract, and he cannibalized portions of it for subsequent novels.) At the turn of the century he was regarded widely, and justly, as a professional bookman, but how he had turned into one when all the circumstances of his early life and environment were so unpromising was not fully understood then—or, for that matter, to this day. Like many Victorians, his life was shrouded in decent obscurity. Hardy's first marriage to Emma Lavinia Gifford turned into a disappointment, but the problems of the relationship in Emma's final years were not widely known even within literary circles, and the publication of Hardy's passionate love-poem sequence, 'Poems of 1912–13' as part of the larger collection, *Satires of Circumstance: Lyrics and Reveries, with Miscellaneous Pieces* (1914) stilled gossip in most quarters. Even the marriage, little more than a year later, to Florence Emily Dugdale, his secretary-amanuensis, seemed too personal an affair to deserve public scrutiny.

There is no need to review here all the problems created by those who sought to protect Hardy's right to privacy. They wrote accounts of his family background, education, circle of friends and relationships with publishers and editors that suggested, all too often, that here was a new candidate for a pantheon of blameless literary heroes. The net effect, however, seemed to be that Hardy's amazing talent for invention was continually being patronized. Biographers often assumed that Hardy saw as his primary duty the transcription of what he saw around him; that he wrote a kind of fictionalized journalism (of a high calibre, admittedly) rather than genuine creative fictions. Hardy was often invoked as an authority on the woman's question, the hiring of agricultural labourers or the state of affluence of a small market-town like Dorchester (i.e. Casterbridge). The 'originals' of his settings and characters became all-absorbing issues for a large number of commentators, many of whom compiled catalogues of walks in and around 'Wessex'—a term that Hardy had resurrected from desuetude. In brief, he was treated as a social historian who had lived a placid, blameless existence in a remote corner of England, and his writings indicated that Dorset deserved to be better known.

The emphasis of these biographically-oriented studies fell primarily on matters of demonstrable fact that became all the more interesting because Hardy had chosen to fictionalize them. The few troublesome issues that surfaced—Hardy's plagiarism of some important passages in A.B. Longstreet's *Georgia Scenes* (1835) when he came to the writing of *The Trumpet-Major,* or his bitter gibes at reviewers and readers of circulating-library novels, or his denial that he held mordantly pessimistic views about the President of the Immortals—were explained away as being less illustrative of character than they appeared to be. Moreover, for several decades the view that Hardy had betrayed his true vocation (the writing of novels) when he turned to poetry reigned unchallenged, despite Hardy's oft-repeated comments that he rated poetry much higher than prose fiction, and that he wanted to be judged by, and remembered for, his poems.

Carl Weber's discreet biography (1940) followed some fifty books of hushed and reverential treatment; it used as its base a number of works on Hardy's knowledge of topography and folklore. The quality of insight contained in the books written by Lionel Johnson (*The Art of Thomas Hardy,* 1894, notable mostly for its being early on the scene), F.A. Hedgcock's *Essai de critique: Thomas Hardy, penseur et artiste* (1911), a book that incensed

Hardy because of its misstatements of fact), Lascelles Abercrombie (*Thomas Hardy: A Critical Study,* 1912, a shorter version of which became the entry used in the *Encyclopaedia Britannica* for fully half a century), Harold Child (*Thomas Hardy,* 1916), H.C. Duffin (*Thomas Hardy: A Study of the Wessex Novels,* 1921), S.C. Chew (*Thomas Hardy: Poet and Novelist,* 1921), Joseph Warren Beach (*The Technique of Thomas Hardy,* 1922), Ernest Brennecke (*Thomas Hardy's Universe: A Study of a Poet's Mind,* 1924, another work that Hardy found deeply offensive), H.B. Grimsditch (*Character and Environment in the Novels of Thomas Hardy,* 1925), Clive Holland (*Thomas Hardy, O.M.: The Man, His Works, and the Land of Wessex,* 1933), A.P. Elliott (*Fatalism in the Works of Thomas Hardy,* 1935), A.C. Chakravarty (*'The Dynasts' and the Post-War Age in Poetry,* 1938), and W.R. Rutland (*Thomas Hardy,* 1938)—all varied in emphases and interpretations. Even so, it is fair to say that Hardy's 'philosophy', consisting of his views on man's relation to the Immanent Will (Hardy's name for God in the modern world), marriage and divorce, capital punishment, and so on, provided the major materials for analysis, rather than the basic data of his life. Taken altogether, these secondary works did less to illuminate Hardy's art than to keep his name academically respectable while scores of books debunked the reputations of other prominent Victorian artists and writers.

But Weber's *Hardy of Wessex,* (1940) appeared in the same year as the *Southern Review's* Thomas Hardy Centennial Edition, a gathering of essays that looked lovingly, and with admirable intelligence, at Hardy's total achievement. Hardy the artist, for the first time, became the primary concern of poets (W.H. Auden's 'A Literary Transference' acknowledged a profound debt to Hardy), university dons, professional bookmen and general readers. The *Southern Review* issue became a landmark in the history of Hardy criticism and helped to usher in a second stage of commentaries. In the 1940s Hardy turned into a writer of singular merit, perhaps the one Victorian novelist and poet whose attitudes towards ethical and moral problems were recognizably modern. Inevitably, the interest of investigators turned towards the human being behind the fictions. Victorian decorum no longer seemed sufficient reason to ignore a large quantity of hitherto ignored or unassembled evidence. The Toucan Press Monographs, edited and published by J. Stevens Cox (collected in 1970–1) ran to more than seventy titles and included interviews with a large number of men and women who remembered encountering Hardy, sometimes in surprising circumstances. Gertrude Bugler, who took the role of Tess in a production of the Hardy Players, was consulted; so was Norman Atkins, who as Alec d'Urberville, ruined her life in the same drama; and so were Hardy's barber, gardener, parlourmaid, driver, secretary, musical accompanist, cook and numerous residents of Dorchester. The Toucan Monographs also gave wider currency to a series of sensational charges contained in books written by Lois Deacon and her followers, notably Frank Southerington.

J.O. Bailey, in *The Poetry of Thomas Hardy: A Handbook and Commentary* (1970), a fine reference work, also publicized—somewhat trustingly—elaborate theories about Hardy's alleged affair with Tryphena Sparks, and even the existence of an illegitimate child. Robert Gittings, in *Young Thomas Hardy* (1975), printed in an appendix 'Hardy and Tryphena Sparks', an incisive analysis (originally published in *The Times Literary Supplement*) of all the reasons why the 'affair' was much less than Lois Deacon had supposed. Love-making could not have taken place out-of-doors because 1867 had been a wet year, 'with a rainfall above the average, and a bad summer'. Beyond this service (i.e. setting the meteorological record straight) Gittings significantly altered the perceptions of a large number of readers who had assumed, perhaps too casually, that Hardy's family background, as described in the *Life* he had prepared for Florence Emily, had been truthfully rendered. Gittings's research, much of it conducted for the first time, identified an alarming number of lies and artful misstatements in Hardy's account. Gittings may have over-emphasized the 'peasant' roots of that past; he implied more than was necessary about Hardy's interest in an endless parade of women (in the second volume of his biographical study, *The Older Hardy*, 1978, he went so far as to print photographs of 'Hardy's four ladies of fashion in the 1890s' on a single page); he stressed Hardy's unpleasant behaviour towards each of his wives; and his characterization of Hardy as a cranky, mean-spirited recluse who chose not to waste his money on charity or good works baffled many who wondered how such a paradigm of disagreeable behaviour could possibly have written so many large-hearted works of fiction about down-trodden, unhappy human beings.

It was inevitable, therefore, that Gittings's Hardy immediately became a controversial image on both sides of the Atlantic, and that, in the third stage of biographical studies, scholars attempted to refute or modify its harsher elements. A sampling of these works includes Denys Kay-Robinson's *The First Mrs Thomas Hardy* (1979), a spirited defence of a woman whose 'character was stronger than Hardy's'; Desmond Hawkins's *Hardy: Novelist and Poet* (1976), which emphasizes regionalism in the fiction and poetry, and maintains stoutly that 'Hardy had a surer grasp of the elements of tragedy that any other English novelist in the last century'; F.E. Halliday's 'Thomas Hardy: The Man in his Work', in Lance St John Butler's anthology, *Thomas Hardy after Fifty Years* (1977), which declares—as if Gittings had never written—'I mention these things to show how much Hardy meant to me fifty years ago, and to suggest how much he still means, not only because he was a great writer but also because he was a great and lovable man'; and, recently, Michael Millgate's biography, *Thomas Hardy* (1982). Though not yet the definitive biography, it reviews available evidence in a fair-minded and intelligent fashion. Bias shows up primarily in the treatment of Emma and Florence, who seem to be treated ungenerously so that Hardy's Job-like patience in the face of an Uncomprehending Womankind can be dramatized.

I have left out a great deal in this review of books dealing with Hardy's life, but beg forgiveness. The term 'growth industry', applied to Hardy scholarship, is surely appropriate. W. Eugene Davis and Helmut E. Gerber, in their preface to *Thomas Hardy: An Annotated Bibliography of Writings about Him, Volume II 1970–1978* (1983), identified some 5,000 items of value to Hardy researchers appearing in less than a decade, and predicted that a third volume would have to be prepared in less than another decade. (The equally bulky first volume, with relatively few omissions—and those inadvertent—had covered a full century, the years between 1870 and 1969.) There is simply not time to debate all the issues of interpretation raised by the reading of the evidence in the volumes written either by Gittings or Millgate. Moreover, the massive volumes of collected letters of Thomas Hardy, edited by Richard L. Purdy and Michael Millgate, are introducing new materials for our understanding of Hardy the man (five have been printed, another three are on the way).

Nevertheless, the cyclical appearance and disappearance of certain fashions in the writing of 'lives' must be taken for granted. The current concern of biographers with Hardy's relations to women, although understandable, has left in shadow a number of equally interesting and noteworthy elements of a great Victorian's life. I want to treat, in this book, a number of less familiar aspects. Taken together, they suggest new ways of thinking about Hardy's contribution to English literature.

Why does it matter? Why, after all that has been printed about him, is there still something more to learn that is worth learning? In both England and the United States he is the second most popular writer of fiction who lived during the entire nineteenth century; only Dickens's novels enjoys greater sales today. All his works are in print. His readers may be found in all classes, doing all kinds of work, at all levels of income. (Davis and Gerber found their materials in twenty languages, but Hardy's works have been translated into more than twice that many.) The Thomas Hardy Society of Japan, founded by Professor Mamoru Osawa in 1957, has almost a thousand members, most of whom teach English at the university level, and recently published *A Thomas Hardy Dictionary* (1984), an extraordinary linguistic undertaking that defines all Hardy's dialect words as well as thousands of archaic, obsolete, rare, literary or poetic lexical items. Hardy is the most widely-read English novelist in the People's Republic of China; I recently visited the University of Nanjing and was escorted round the campus by two graduate students who, like their peers, had read most of his novels in English and wanted to know why Hardy was so 'melancholy'. And Hardy is the best-known and best-liked English novelist in India.

A book that really tells us something new about Hardy's life will be of interest to many, and not only in English-speaking countries. The needed information is not necessarily recorded in the thinly-disguised autobiography that he dictated, in the third person, to his second wife, Florence Emily. Researchers and biographers have devoted an astonishing amount of energy to the task of deciphering the elements of truth in this *Life*. In some ways they have helped us to see Hardy more plainly. It is no disservice to their work—or to those who have edited Hardy's architectural and literary note-books, reviewed the textual histories of Hardy's novels and poems, and studied Hardy's correspondence—to suggest that several major elements in Hardy's life remain unfamiliar to the general public, and even to many Hardy scholars.

Hardy once described himself as 'a time-worn man'. Others have described him as a hermit who shut himself up in his home at Max Gate, Dorchester, in Dorset, who had a limited circle of acquaintances, and no genuine friends; who paid little attention to current events in his home county or in the world because he preferred to muse on the years of his childhood; and who was suspicious of literary experiments and new schools of writing. There is some truth in these stereotypes—but not much.

It seems appropriate to begin with a consideration of the importance that Hardy attached to architecture even after he had renounced the profession as a means of making a living. His first publication, 'How I Built Myself a House', fictionalized in a flattering way the Arthur Blomfield for whom he was working in London. His first three novels used architect-heroes. All his fictions, and many of his poems, illustrated an attention to architectural detail that only the trained eye could provide. But he did not simply transfer insights from one field to another. He designed the house-plans for Max Gate, with mixed success (as both his wives knew). Several idiosyncracies in its appearance and livability were due directly to his bias for specific periods of architectural history. Moreover, on his frequent assignments for the Society for the Protection of Ancient Buildings, he provided an expert's advice, and some of his most poignant comments, contained in brief addresses and various essays, identified what he regarded as his sins in restoring churches during the 1850s and 1860s.

This chapter is followed by a discussion of Hardy's interest in the theatre. It was life-long and intense. Hardy knew a great deal about actors, playwrights, producers and the conditions of the contemporary stage. He adapted several of his novels and short stories for the theatre, and consulted with others who wanted to write plays or operas based on his fictions. He served as godfather to the Hardy Players of Dorchester and encouraged their efforts while holding them to the highest standards. He developed a theory of theatrical minimalism that finally led to the writing of *The Queen of Cornwall*, and to a number of observations about the value of mumming in both the writing and acting of plays. (Elements of this theory may be found in the stage-directions for *The Dynasts*.)

Several of his forays into public controversy, which grew from his commitment to free expression, attacked the censorship of plays. Hardy enjoyed enduring friendships with a number of writers: William Barnes, the lexicographer and dialect poet who, from the beginning, served as a father-figure; Horace Moule, the journalist, poet and essayist who influenced Hardy's crucial decision to give up the secure profession of architect in favour of the riskier world of literary endeavour; George Meredith, the famous novelist who rejected Hardy's first novel when it was submitted to the publishing firm for which he served as reader; Algernon Charles Swinburne, who (like Hardy) had more than a fair share of notoriety; Leslie Stephen, editor and essayist; and Edmund Gosse, biographer and encourager of Hardy when hostile reviews dismayed the 'man from Wessex'.

I go into fuller detail about Hardy's friendships with two very popular Victorian novelists: Rudyard Kipling, who appreciated the support that Hardy offered when he returned to England in 1889; and H. Rider Haggard, who shared much more with Hardy than most contemporaries realized. The network of these friendships has never been traced in full detail, and the relationships between Hardy and Kipling and Haggard have not been defined by any previous biographer.

The Dynasts, which Hardy called an epic-drama, was (in his view) the culmination of his poetical career. Since he regarded poetry as being of a higher order than the prose novel, it becomes doubly strange that so important a work in the canon has been misjudged since the years of its original appearance (1903–8), and has been underestimated by critics from the very beginning. Entire volumes devoted to Hardy's career mention it in passing, or not at all. I have already published a book noting its indebtedness to Homer and Milton, *Thomas Hardy and the Epic Tradition: A Study of 'The Dynasts'* (1963), and do not want to repeat the insights recorded there. But I do want to review the reasons why this work has been dismissed for insufficient cause. Its effort to re-define a genre, or more precisely to create a new genre, was heroic. It contains the fullest exposition to Hardy's philosophy, which treats man's insignificance in relation to the Immanent Will; no novel contains more of what Hardy believed about the unsuitability of anthropocentric religion for the modern world. *The Dynasts* employs more than thirty verse-forms, indicating that it is deliberately experimental. It has been an important influence on twentieth-century English poetry, acknowledged as such by dozens of poets. It was dramatized for the BBC as a patriotic document during two world wars, and scenes from it have been selected for several stage presentations. Not least of the elements marking it for reconsideration is the fact that it is the most important single treatment, by any major creative writer in England, of the Napoleonic Wars.

I next discuss Hardy's interest in human law (as opposed to divine law), and the dispensing of justice within law-courts. This is a very ill-understood aspect of Hardy's life, barely mentioned in any of the biographies written during the past decade. Nevertheless, Hardy sat in court at least thirty-eight times as a magistrate and served at least sixteen times on juries for the Assizes. He was friendly with a large number of judges, solicitors and barristers; he fictionalized legal problems that consistently demonstrate a sophisticated knowledge of courtroom procedure; and he had a number of fascinating experiences as a magistrate in the courts of Dorchester. Indeed, he knew a great deal about real criminals and prison-sentences even before he began to write fiction. When the Borough Petty Sessions met on 16 January, 1928, five days after Hardy's death, I believe that the magistrates stood in silence as a mark of respect to a fellow-magistrate (rather than to a world-renowned author).

The last topic is Hardy's concern with the pagan and Roman past of England. It was something more than 'antiquarianism'. I try to explain the reasons why Hardy brooded so often about the past. Because English archaeology was grossly amateurish in the years before General Pitt-Rivers systematized the science of digging, Hardy's acquaintance and growing friendship with the General indicate that his use of archaeological information is more extensive and more scientifically accurate than similar treatments in practically all other Victorian novels. We can hardly assess the full power of such a scene as that of the penultimate chapter of *Tess of the d'Urbervilles* unless we know what generations of Englishmen thought they knew about Stonehenge.

None of these essay-chapters provides a reader with the key that will unlock, once and for all, the mysteries of genius (a difficult task at best, since Hardy's genius materialized in Dorset as unexpectedly as that of Keats earlier in the century). Moreover, materials coming into print in recent years suggest that even more can be said about the unknown Thomas Hardy. We need to re-examine the relationships between Hardy and his various publishers. We still do not have a full-scale investigation of Hardy's knowledge of music, musical instruments, and musical history. And what Hardy knew about the art of Victorian illustration, meant to accompany short stories and serialized novels in periodicals, deserves an up-to-date assessment. These and other problems have not received their due attention, and they affect our understanding not only of Hardy the man, but of his creative work. My hope is that this book, in its own way and to a satisfying degree, will clarify our sense of the kind of man Thomas Hardy was, and send us back, refreshed, to his fiction and to his poetry.

1

An Architect's Eye

The most important of all the ways in which Hardy continued his ties to the profession of architecture—long after he had cut free from John Hicks of Dorchester, G.R. Crickmay of Weymouth, Arthur Blomfield and T. Roger Smith of London—was the design and construction of Max Gate, on the Wareham Road. This major project called on all of Hardy's knowledge of the compromises made, of necessity, between architects and builders, between workmen and the would-be home-owner. A full century later, it also affords an opportunity to look back on Hardy's decision to foresake his career, and to speculate (still one more time) on the reasons why he decided in the early 1870s to pursue the far more risky profession of author. He had already published *Under the Greenwood Tree* (1872) and *A Pair of Blue Eyes* (1873) was under way when he found himself forced to choose between careers. T. Roger Smith had offered to hire him again—one of the school designs which Hardy had helped draw up had won acceptance, and Smith could use his talents. Did Hardy foresee years of helping one architect after another, each senior to him, each a more firmly-established architect that himself? Did he suffer with a bone-tightening fear of his own mediocrity, and of his certain failure to win recognition among his peers if he continued in this field? Did he sense a need for more money than he could reasonably borrow for the establishing of his own firm, with his own assistants? Had he become uneasy about the probability that he would need to mingle with churchmen? Were his own inadequacies as a religious believer compounded by doubts of his mastery of social graces? (Blomfield's father was a former Bishop of London who died shortly before Hardy went to work in London, but churchmen were in and out of

Blomfield's office all day long. If any single theme dominated the pages of Hardy's early fiction, it is that of antagonism between social classes; the bitterness of merit unrecognized by those with more money and higher social status than the young heroes Hardy delineated.)

To be sure, Emma encouraged Hardy to make the break, and in later years she basked in Hardy's recognition of the support she had provided at a critical juncture of his life. Hardy might have become a commercial fiction-writer even if she had been neutral on the matter. We know that he entertained a low opinion of many stories that he read in current periodicals and believed that he could do better; we also know that he was realistic about the unlikelihood that his best poetry would find an interested audience, and knew that he would have to write novels if he wanted to earn a decent living. Nevertheless, Emma held consistently to her conviction, formed at a surprisingly early stage, that Hardy could do better as an author than as an architect's assistant, and Hardy certainly listened to her enthusiastic remarks about his writing abilities. A question inevitably comes up: did she harbour serious doubts about his fitness for the profession of architecture?

Max Gate, then, is the house that Hardy designed after he had acquired a decent income and prospects for the future, and it becomes a litmus test of his abilities as an architect to provide decent accommodation for Emma, and to give himself respectable working space. It is worth looking at in some detail.

One mile east of Dorchester, the property on which Max Gate was built stood close to a weatherbeaten tollgate-house. In it had lived, for several decades, a married couple named Mack; in later years Hardy was to speak with light irony of how his home had altered the name of Mack's Gate to suit Hardy's purpose. (Mack was alive when Hardy was growing up.) The ground was leasehold and belonged to Fordington Field, an area of some 3,000 acres. Hardy purchased 1.5 acres from the office of the Duchy of Cornwall in London, and a conveyance of the freehold was executed in September 1886. (Hardy does not stress the point, but no part of this land had been sold to a private individual for several generations prior to his own purchase.) Some forty years later he was to add another half-acre.

At the time Hardy was negotiating the purchase of his lot, he was 44 years of age. Construction began on 26 November 1883 and was undertaken by Thomas Hardy, Sr, then in his middle seventies, and his son Henry, Thomas's brother, for the sum of 1,000 pounds. (The father, being rheumatic, may not have done too much of the work. Henry assumed responsibility for the quality of the workmanship; within three years of the completion of construction, part of the ceiling in the dining-room collapsed, and he had to repair it.) Hardy referred to himself in the *Life* as 'constantly overlooking operations'. He moved into his house on 29 June 1885.

Max Gate, newly finished, was red-brick, heavy-set, and raw-looking. It sat on a piece of property that had not yet been landscaped with the small trees (mostly Austrian pines) that Hardy was to plant almost immediately. The front looked towards the south, towards Conquer Barrow, a prehistoric earthwork. At the west end a square turret topped the front (Hardy, much later, was to add another turret at the east end), but he had exerted little effort to match elements of architecture (e.g. the windows on different levels). Hardy did not worry excessively about the convenience of his servants. The kitchen and scullery seemed to have been placed an unnecessarily long distance from the dining-room on the ground floor, and more than one visitor during the first decade remarked on the smallness of the rooms and (as the pines grew) the darkness and isolation of the structure as a whole. Why Hardy felt an obligation to include a carriage house and provisions for a stable that could accommodate two horses when, in practice, he hired traps and horses for special occasions, has not been established beyond the fact that, as a prudent man, he may have thought it was less expensive to build everything all at once rather than dribble out substantial sums of money on afterthoughts.

'Undistinguished and ill-designed', one biographer has written of Max Gate.[1] His view is representative of many others. Hardy devised a spare bedroom that could sleep only a single visitor; he mixed Gothic and neo-classical ingredients in an unappealing way (no one style served as an arbiter of taste); he failed to make provision for running hot water and omitted a bathroom from his plans. He also seems to have been a little unsure as to how to use the space set aside for a garden; it was later subdivided into a lawn, an orchard, and a kitchen garden, and the lawn itself was to be further subdivided into two lawns.

On the other hand, Hardy was determined not to let costs of

building get away from him; he always remembered what had happened to the finances of Sir Walter Scott. Perhaps the primary thing he did while supervising construction was to pinch pennies, to the point where his father and brother felt seriously constrained in what they could include. Within a decade Max Gate turned into something 'cottage-like and lonely', in Hardy's words, but that was the inevitable consequence of growing a miniature forest on the major part of the cleared space, constructing a brick wall taller than himself to keep out unwelcome visitors and choosing dark woods for the interior when lighter decorating elements would have been both appropriate and more cheering. Yet there was something right about all this, too: Hardy wanted his home to be taken seriously, to have its own *gravitas*. Almost immediately the home assumed some of his own coloration. Sir James George Frazer, writing in *The Magic Art*, recorded a telling quotation. Hardy said he had been told that the reason why some of his trees in front of his house at Max Gate did not thrive was because he looked at them before breakfast on an empty stomach.[2]

Was Max Gate really a cramped and unfriendly house, as so many newspaper interviewers said? Doubtless they expected something grander from one of England's best-known and most successful novelists. The house could not be said to offer, either to the casual visitor or to the trained architect, a parade of distinctive architectural details; the layout of the drawing-room, dining-room, central hall and bedrooms was conventional to the point of triteness; and Hardy kept changing his mind about one of the key elements of his plan, namely where he should locate his study. The first study, in which he wrote *The Woodlanders*, was placed above the drawing-room. The second, in which he composed *Tess*, was at the back of the house. He finally settled into his third version of a study on the floor-level over a new kitchen.

On the other hand, Hardy was not by nature ostentatious, and he had a great deal of steady writing to do to earn a living even in 1883 and 1884. (On 31 December 1885, he debated the possibility that building this house had not been 'a wise expenditure of energy'.) He had ensured his comfort, and Emma's convenience, by making sure that drainage and sewage met more than minimal requirements. Even if he had not kept up with what was available in the way of more modern and convenient arrangements for plumbing, heating and lighting, there is no record of Emma's dissatisfaction with the amenities that he did pay for. Moreover, Hardy, within his limits, was willing to buy some unusual 'extras': the window-frames were made of oak, the window-sills were built of Portland stone, and the windows had leaded panes. The anomalous west turret—so often scoffed at by those who believed that Hardy's architectural training should have ensured a more distinctive façade, or more elegant trim—held narrow windows that enabled Hardy and Emma, whenever they desired, to look out over a most handsome view of the surrounding countryside. Indeed, Hardy's sense of the importance of windows led him to build them large, to place them at varying heights from the floor and to trap the maximum amount of light from either the sun or moon. His third study, for example, had a rather large window that faced east: 'and the full moon rising over the tops of the dark pines was a familiar sight'.[3]

An illustration to *Wessex Poems* shows Hardy's concept of a sundial, but the sundial made in Dorchester from his design was not to be affixed to the east turret until after his death, and its value as an aesthetic element of the appearance of Max Gate could not be appreciated by those who came to visit him during his lifetime.

It is hard to believe that Hardy deliberately made the façade of his house unattractive, or that he believed he was severely, unreasonably cramping the dimensions of his floor-plan. He may well have designed the house from the inside outwards, as Michael Millgate has suggested. 'first deciding upon the number, function and size of the rooms and then contriving to fit those requirements within a reasonably coherent over-all structure, at whatever cost in terms of external symmetry.'[4] This rationalization of how Hardy proceeded, though plausible, may not ease the suspicion that Hardy did as well as he could, and spent his money as intelligently as he could for personal comfort and convenience, without making Max Gate into a particularly handsome or striking edifice, and without stamping on it the mark of a distinctive architectural talent. Victorian England lost an ordinary architectural assistant when Hardy decided to reject T. Roger Smith's offer of renewed employment, and gained a distinctive story-telling voice. Hardy, in the mid-1870s, a full decade before he designed Max Gate, must have known that it was so.

The first architect to appear in Hardy's fiction —a Mr Penny, in 'How I Built Myself a House'—turned up in the first piece he submitted for publication to a periodical. *Chambers's Journal*, which published the story in its issue of 18 March 1865, when Hardy was 25, did not run it with Hardy's name. The amiable nature of the sketch was such that its author probably never entertained illusions about the quality of its literary content. Years before he drew up his plans for Max Gate, Hardy imagined what it might be like for a young man and his wife to consult with an architect about an ideal house, costing 1,800 pounds, that would take the place of the unbearable 'Highly Desirable Semi-detached Villa' in the London suburb where they were currently living.

Perhaps not enough is told us about Mr Penny, the architect whose name was later to grace another character in *Under the Greenwood Tree*, Hardy's second published novel. But then, we also learn very little about the hero and his wife, Sophia. The cost of the home is soon exceeded by alterations, or 'extras', not included in the original estimate. The hero of the story does not resent Mr Penny, who apparently has not restrained him firmly enough from changing the plans by which the builder must abide. Mr Penny, though his physical appearance is not specified, appears to be a courteous gentleman, very professional in his concerns and a specialist 'in designing excellent houses for families of moderate means'. The young man tells him his needs:

> Sitting there with him in his office, surrounded by rolls of paper, circles, squares, triangles, compasses, and many other of the inventions which have been sought out by men from time to time, and perceiving that all these were the realities which had been faintly shadowed forth to me by Euclid some years before, it is no wonder that I became a puppet in his hands. He settled everything in a miraculous way. We were told the only possible size we could have the rooms, the only way we should be allowed to go upstairs, and the exact quantity of wine we might order at once, so as to fit the wine-cellar in his head.

Mr Penny, in short, deals politely and firmly with his client; his opinions are 'propelled by his facts'. His calculations are so exact that he can bring in an estimate of costs at 1,870 pounds: 'Very satisfactory, in my opinion.' At a later stage, responding to a complaint from the young man that the plans have omitted a porch, Mr Penny responds (as Hardy doubtless heard his employer, Arthur Blomfield, respond to more than one client): 'A porch or no porch is entirely a matter of personal feeling and taste, so, of course, I did not put one without its being mentioned.' Mr Penny then proceeds to cite both the advantage and disadvantage of having one added to the plans. At a later time he sets right the problem confronted by the young man and his wife, who are almost suffocated by the smoke created by a study-fire: he simply recommends that they open the register.

A fountain-head of common sense, Mr Penny has learned his trade thoroughly, and how to handle problems of design and cost that frighten clients. Now it is entirely right that Hardy should have so regarded a successful practitioner of the profession for which he had signed away his years in London. But it is equally striking that in his first published volume of verse, *Wessex Poems* (1898), he dedicated 'Heiress and Architect' to 'A.W. Blomfield'. The poem had been written three decades earlier, in the last year that Hardy worked for Blomfield. Its mood, grimly determined that the heiress (and heroine of the poem) shall know the painful limits of human existence, seems to have been affected by Hardy's growing knowledge of the problems created not only for architects, but for themselves, by over-demanding clients. The 'arch-designer' of this poem, like Mr Penny, is of 'wise contrivance', and 'deeply skilled/In every intervolve of high and wide'. He is an architect, and tells her immediately that he cannot thwart 'the law of stable things'; that his plans must be drawn up 'in true accord with prudent fashionings'. He will not yield to her hopes that he will accommodate her plans for 'high halls with tracery/And open ogive-work'. He insists that the walls be closed in, 'for winters freeze'. He rejects her desire to live in a structure that will exhibit her laughter and her light. Some day, he tells her, the soul will become 'sick of glee' and want to hide from the world. Nor can she have a little chamber to which her Love may come. 'An hour will come', he sternly reminds her,

> when sight of such sweet nook
> Would bring a bitterness too sharp to brook,
> When brighter eyes have won away his look;
> For you will fade.

Finally, she cannot even count on the architect's being willing to design for her a loft where she might grieve alone. He is relentless in his onslaught on this 'last dear fancy'. She must remember that a winding turret is impractical:

Give space (since life ends unawares)
To hale a coffined corpse adown the stairs;
For you will die.

For the book, Hardy contributed his own drawing of a difficult attempt to transfer a coffin from a higher level of the house to a lower; the stairway is so narrow that there exists a serious danger of a rapid, undignified descent if the coffin should escape from the grips of those holding on to its sides.

We need not ascribe to Hardy Mr Penny's views about the need to behave prudently during the building of a private home, or an architect's more sinister remarks about the swift passing of human beauty and love given as advice to an heiress; these opinions, after all, are delivered by dramatically imagined figures whose judgements on matters within their purview have been requested by clients. But the point to be made is that Hardy's free and easy use of terms such as 'intervolve', 'ogive-work' and 'engrailed' reflect his own professional interests. As John Summerson once remarked, 'The sensibility to architectural forms and devices shown on some of these pages is a thing which, once acquired, can never be lost. Hardy had it and no study of him as man, novelist and poet can be complete without recognition of this fact.'[5] Hardy's technical vocabulary may be found in literally dozens of poems (the 'cusps' of the moon at 'demilune', in 'Once at Swanage'; firelocks that are 'heavy as putlogs', and 'architraves of sunbeam-smitten cloud', both in *The Dynasts*; and the 'mullioned windows worn and old' of 'Architectural Masks'). Hardy tells us a great deal about homes and buildings in his novels: where Bathsheba lives is lovingly detailed, and so are Overcombe Hill, Knapwater House and Endelstow House. No reader who enjoyed *Far from the Madding Crowd* can soon forget Hardy's description of both the interior and external features of the great barn. Melbury's house, Oxwell Hall and Overcombe Mill, Christminster (with its 'lichened colleges'), Stancy Castle, High-Place Hall, Mount Lodge, Melchester Cathedral, the Mellstock church and Tess's home are individualized by a novelist who began his working career as a trained architect.

Some critics misunderstand the continuity of a life when they discuss Hardy's art as if it began in his fourth decade and was unaffected by memories of the profession he had renounced. An odd circumstance of Hardy's first three novels (one of which, to be sure, never was published) is that the hero of each one—*The Poor Man and the Lady, Desperate Remedies* and *A Pair of Blue Eyes*—is an architect. Will Strong, protagonist of the first, was evidently a young man of genius (his name suggests an inner strength), and the use of much of this material in 'An Indiscretion in the Life of an Heiress' has enabled literary detectives to imagine, or to reconstruct, much that was lost when Hardy cannibalized his original manuscript, using portions of it in *Desperate Remedies* (the descriptions of Kingston Maurward House), *Under the Greenwood Tree* (at a very minimum, the tranter scenes), *A Pair of Blue Eyes* (Hardy's comments on London society), *The Hand of Ethelberta* (we are not quite so sure what Hardy used here) and 'The Poor Man and the Lady' a poem in *Human Shows* (published only three years before Hardy's death). Since the manuscript for this novel has completely disappeared, the fact that Hardy changed the name of the hero (to Egbert Mayne, which may remind some readers of 'Will Strong') and his line of work (to that of schoolmaster) makes inadvisable any stress on Hardy's belief in an architect's inherent wisdom or sensitivity.

Still, *Desperate Remedies* deals with Ambrose Graye, a young architect ('handsome, frank and gentle') who specializes in humour, picturesqueness and poetry; whose major flaw is too great a forgetfulness of the wickedness of the world. Hardy gives us not merely one architect; he provides two more (the lover Edward Springrove and the brother Owen Graye) and a number of details (Owen's drawing 'views' to kill time in an architect's office because there is no vacancy, Owen's taking responsibility for the rebuilding of a church not very far from Weymouth, Edward's having once written poetry and Edward's deep-rooted knowledge of Shakespeare). All of these have autobiographical resonances. The novel, sensationalized, dealing with dangerous subject-matter (an unmarried, propertied woman has an illegitimate child) and bitter in its social commentary, is not to be counted as one of Hardy's major works; but it illustrates Hardy's effort, one more time, to exploit his knowledge of a profession from which he was attempting, however cautiously, to disengage himself.

A Pair of Blue Eyes attempts to exorcise the theme of *The Poor Man and the Lady*, which for some eight years had dominated his imagination. Hardy had ample cause not to forget his resentment at a class system that was not open to talents; he had but recently learned, in Cornwall, that Emma's father regarded him as an unworthy match for his daughter. Perhaps, as Hardy once claimed, he saw more of himself in the character of Henry Knight than in that of Stephen Smith. Hardy, at any rate, here puts to good use his memorable first encounter with Emma. Endelstow vicarage is only a thinly disguised St Juliot rectory, and Smith's plans to 'restore' the dilapidated aisle and tower of the parish church are essentially those which Hardy prepared in Cornwall. The fact that Smith took longer than his employer had anticipated to draw up the plans ('Old H.' claims that he could have done it all in three hours) is explainable in that he has been smitten by Elfride's charms; but Smith, as Hardy portrays him, is a handsome representative of the architectural profession. Some day he may even become a partner of Mr Hewby, or so Mr Swancourt informs him.

The charms and technical failings of these early fictions have been justly assessed by early as well as late critics. Even so, at the beginning of his fiction-writing career Hardy depended heavily for subject-matter, imagery and characterization on those aspects of architecture that he had personally observed. Though he came to distrust the impulse which had led him to rely so heavily on his memories of architects and architects' apprentices in his earliest novels, he respected his craft long years after he abdicated his position as a young man in London who might reasonably entertain 'prospects'. He used only a few representatives of the profession in later fictions. They are worth identifying. Andrew Jones of 'Fellow-Townsmen', in *Wessex Tales*, designed the house that Mr Barnet gave to his wife at Fort-Bredy (she renamed it Château Ringdale), as well as the tomb for Mrs Downe that Mr Downe finally reduced to a modest headstone. The assorted architects of *A Laodicean* include Bowles, Knowles and Cockton, the assistants of George Somerset, who—in his intellectual concerns and his willingness to follow the intricacies of the debates on Paedobaptism—reminds us, inevitably, of Hardy during the 1860s. The unethical Mr Havill and William Dare are professional rivals of George Somerset, and their competitive impulses lead to serious consequences for Stancy Castle. Perhaps no novel is more heavily indebted to Hardy's knowledge of the atmospherics of architecture than *Jude the Obscure*, though it characterizes, for the most part, stone-masons rather than architects. The novel records a number of fascinating and perceptive analyses of the relation of details to the overall impressions that large, imposing edifices provide. Within its pages one may also find the Oldbrickham contracting firm, Biles & Willis, engaged in church restoration (Jude is given the task of relettering the Ten Commandments). Perhaps as striking as any other evidence of the influence left behind by this work between 1856 (the year in which he was articled to a Dorchester architect) and 1874 (the year in which he married and decided to stake everything on his chances for succeeding in the brutally competitive field of commercial fiction) is 'The Abbey Mason', a poem that he dedicated to John Hicks.[6]

A lengthy poem, it dramatizes the invention of the Perpendicular style of Gothic architecture. For Hardy, this development in cathedral structure represented the major, perhaps single, contribution of native English genius to an art already well-developed on the Continent. He visited Gloucester Cathedral in December 1911, and there saw what the master-mason in his poem sees: icicles changing the lines of his 'lame designs', forcing him to look more closely at the design possibilities inherent in 'accessory cusping-marks'. Hardy was mistaken in believing that the Perpendicular style could be precisely located 'in the screen between the south aisle and the transept'.[7] He paid no attention to similar, and earlier, developments at Old St Paul's and St Stephen's Chapel; he did not engage in serious architectural research before he sketched a romance of the mason who solved the 'ogive riddle', who answered the question of how to connect the ogees 'to give the flexures interplay'. But his artistic instinct was sound. The devising of this new style of construction was so happy a development in the history of ecclesiastical forms that it must have seemed to be—in the fifteenth century—divinely inspired. Moreover, the reprimand of the abbot, directed to the mason who has become swelled with pride by his own creation, provides Hardy with an opportunity to emphasize the need for humility in artistic creation. The canon insists that the mason has copied, and has not created:

> Surely the hand of God it is
> That conjured so, and only His!

The mason meekly accepts the rebuke.

> I feel the abbot's words are just,
> And that all thanks renounce I must.
>
> Can a man welcome praise and pelf
> For hatching art that hatched itself?
>
> ....
>
> So, I shall own the deft design
> Is Heaven's outshaping, and not mine.

The mason so vigorously protests his minor role in the creation of Perpendicular that he is 'at length believed', and as the cathedral at Gloucester grows higher and more massive, finally he is forgotten; he wears in death 'no artist's crown'. Thomas Horton (who served as abbot between 1357 and 1377) is given the insight that the mason, whose name has vanished from memory,

> did but what all artists do,
> Wait upon Nature for his cue.

It is a conceit, of course; Hardy could not have known from which source the mason responsible for the invention of Perpendicular derived his inspiration, or whether, indeed, only one mason was responsible for the solving of several tricky technical problems. Those responsible for keeping records determine whose names shall be written down, and conventions governed these things on the Continent as well as England; engineers and architects simply were not accounted as significant contributors to the glory of a completed cathedral, and their names have almost uniformly escaped memorialization. But Hardy here is expounding Ruskinian doctrine (that those who worked in Gothic forms derived their pay from the pleasures of their work), and it pleased him to think that the mason who had made possible

> The ogee arches transom-topped,
> The tracery-stalks by spandrels stopped,
>
> Petrified lacework—lightly lined
> on ancient massiveness behind—

had chosen, deliberately, to 'renounce fame's fairest fee'.

Hardy's attitude towards Gloucester Cathedral is in itself a statement of haunting and singular humility, recorded in a poem written when he had passed his own three-score and ten. More important, perhaps, than the curious invention of a myth (one that embodies an attitude towards over-generous commercial reward for artistic effort dedicated to the service of God) is Hardy's continuing love of the forms of ecclesiastical architecture. He began with an admiration of ceremony, liturgy and music; he was churchy, by his own admission; he contemplated (however briefly) taking orders. Though he denied the existence of a God personally concerned with his problems or his welfare, he paid homage to the lovelier features of the many houses of God in which he worked as an architect. He understood the full extent of the desecration worked by church-restorers (his own firms in Dorchester and London among them).

This brings us to a matter of permanent concern in Hardy's life, a sense of guilt that, while a practising architect, he had not fought strenuously enough against the damage done to churches by his professional colleagues. It is not quite clear why Hardy should have felt so personally culpable, or why his uneasy conscience should have persisted for so many years. Strictly speaking, Hardy, who never practised on his own, was not an architect but an intelligent and hard-working architect's assistant, a generalist with a far-ranging curiosity about the countless details of specialised work. He had only fitful contact with the Arts and Crafts movement, which cannot be said to have influenced his thinking when he supervised work away from Crickmay's office; and even then, he could not be held personally responsible for the decisions that he requested his employer (by mail) to make for his work at St Juliot, Hawkchurch and Slape House (Netherbury). It is not easy to assess Hardy's contributions to the Society for the Protection of Ancient Buildings (he belonged to it between 1881 and the year of his death, 1928); he has practically nothing to say about it in his autobiography, though he does allude to the paper that he asked Colonel Eustace Balfour to read to its members at the twenty-ninth annual meeting (June 1906). That paper—which I shall summarize in a moment—is brutally frank in its analysis of the harm committed by restorers, but the number of assignments Hardy actually carried out in this field is quite limited. Only three churches figure prominently in Hardy's *Notebook:* Stinsford,

St Juliot and West Knighton. He had no responsibility for the Stinsford restoration of 1842, as analysed in his notes; he prepared the drawings for St Juliot in 1870, and these were approved by Crickmay for the restoration of 1871–2; but he did take charge of the work on West Knighton in 1893–4, conducted in the same years that he busied himself with a number of literary projects. (C.J.P. Beatty, who has edited the *Notebook,* gives high professional marks to the work performed at West Knighton, but is not wholly satisfactory in his answer to the question why Hardy, who regretted having participated in badly-executed church restorations during his younger years, assumed the same kind of responsibility at West Knighton).

In fact, however, Hardy's interest in church restoration never went dormant. In a letter to Charles George Vinall, written on 20 October 1881, Hardy volunteered to help the surveyor in his scheme for rebuilding portions of the Minster Church of St Cuthburga, Wimborne.[8] He wrote to Thackeray Turner, the secretary to the Society for the Protection of Ancient Buildings, about the need for repairing (rather than tearing down) the church of the village of Stratton, a short distance from Dorchester.[9] As a consequence of his expression of interest, he was asked to attend a meeting of the Committee to consider how best to rebuild; he offered his views on how to save the chancel arch and the hagioscopes, the old windows and even the level of floor. Though the walls had decayed, Hardy was insistent that 'almost every stone could be put up again in its old place'.[10] These efforts—which Hardy modestly claimed had been exerted on behalf of the Society rather than as an expression of his own strong preferences—proved largely successful. In another letter to Turner, written on 28 September 1897, he made a strong case for carrying out the work needed to keep upright the tower of East Lulworth Church. 'This tower', he began as prologue to his detailed itemization of necessary tasks, 'is one of exceptional grace and artistic proportions, in curious contrast to the customary local architecture of so late a date. The upper part shows several unusual features; and when in its prime, with pinnacles and statuary complete, it must have been of extraordinary beauty.'[11] On 14 October 1900 he commented, in a letter to Nelson Moore Richardson, the honorable secretary of the Dorset Natural History and Archaeological Field Club, that he would gladly write an invited paper on Cerne Abbey if only he knew more about the plan and position of the abbey buildings. More could be learned by digging, but, Hardy added, 'this I should not be prepared to undertake even if permission were given'.[12] He felt sufficiently concerned about Jem Feacey's proposed alteration of the tower of Fordington St George Church that he resigned, in a muted protest, from the restoration committee he had joined some two years earlier, adding a grim afterthought, 'I wonder if I, or anybody, ever told you that its (i.e. the Tower's) proportions were so much admired by Sir Gilbert Scott that he sent a man to measure & make an exact drawing of it for preservation'.[13] In a letter written the next day, responding to the committee chairman's polite acknowledgement of his resignation, Hardy referred once again to the turret (the proposed changes in which he found extremely disagreeable), and added 'The fact is, architects do go on rather in a high-handed manner even nowadays, when they have had so many lessons!'[14] Hardy's interest in this church included a guinea subscription to help replace north aisle arches with stone Gothic ones, and a letter (dated 11 November 1906) defending stoutly the preservation of a substantially-built chancel that was threatened with demolition, perhaps merely to make room for a '20th century imitation Gothic replacement.[15]

The first extant letter from Mrs Henniker to Thomas Hardy (who had tried, early in their relationship, to educate her on how to date ecclesiastical architecture) acknowledges the receipt of 'Memories of Church Restoration', sent as a token of friendship. Mrs Henniker claimed that she could not agree with Hardy's objection to restoration, and added, 'And as to the Georgian pews—I think they *had far better go,* in spite of some interesting associations. They would have greatly disgusted the first builders, and it seems to me are more of an eyesore than some other innovations would be?'[16] Hardy agreed to disagree with her, remarking quietly that he loved 'the high old Georgian pews'.[17]

Hardy, who entertained strong views about the general superiority of medieval church builders to his professional contemporaries, could not resist expressing views about what might improve a church. Once he wrote to a distant relative, the Reverend Henry Hardy, rector of St Serf, Burntisland, Fife, that he had sent to the rector of Trinity Church, Dorchester (as reported in *The Times,* 6 September 1906) a rough outline of a tower that might be added in order to improve, or bring out, its 'external dignity'.[18] At West Knighton he broke into the west wall of the tower with an 'early English' window, and he took special measures to ensure the uniformity of both north side windows. Yet only a year later he was protesting to Hugh Thackeray Turner, secretary to the Society for the Protection of Ancient Buildings, that a fund-raising campaign on behalf of St Mary's, South Perrot, Dorsetshire, was proposing to destroy an old West Gallery, '*possibly* of Queen Anne date', in order to bring in 'choir & clergy stalls' that might never have been there in previous centuries.[19] He was not always able to choose the ideal course of action; the choice between desecration of sound materials and needed repairs of what had aged badly was not always simple. Perhaps as good an example as any of his wondering how to proceed is the case of St Catherine's Chapel, Abbotsbury, which stood 'in a fearfully exposed situation', and would soon become a ruin unless corrective measures were taken. He added, in a postscript to still another letter written to Turner, 'My impression is (though this is only a guess) that to prevent it falling, the alternatives are the Scylla & Charybdis of putting in new stones, or cementing over the old ones, exposure having crumbled them a good deal'.[20]

In many, if not a majority, of these situations, Hardy was being asked to serve as a consultant for the Society, and to give advice on how to preserve the churches he was assigned to visit. 'Speaking generally of what is called ''Church restoration'' ', he wrote to the Stinsford Church Restoration Committee (25 April 1909), 'it should be borne in mind that the only legitimate principle for guidance is to limit all renewals to repairs for preservation, and never to indulge in alterations'.[21] There follow a number of specific recommendations for repairs (the building, for multiple reasons, appealed to Hardy's tribal memories); admiration of the original craftsmanship evidenced by the oak pews, ancient stone work and Transition arches of the nave; and a desire to undo damage done by damp in the north aisle, the destruction of the sixteenth-century waggon roof with its bosses, the elimination of the west gallery and the installation of heating apparatus in an appropriate location. Because Hardy did not consider himself 'a practical man', he did not want to supervise repairs for a church he had known 'for many years'. It was 'an interesting building, and one very easy to injure beyond remedy'.

Hardy's recommendations for the Stinsford Church—coming as they did from a local burgher, a respected authority (though Hardy once referred to himself as 'an awful imposter' in the profession) and a representative of a prestigious society dedicated to preservation—were acted on favourably. But he did not always succeed in preventing the destruction of architectural features that he believed, in their original conception and execution, were infinitely superior to what was used as replacements. He became agitated, in one notable instance, at the rumours that the chancel at the Church of St Mary, Puddletown, was to be pulled down, and that its late Perpendicular waggon roof and seventeenth-century woodwork were to be destroyed. In their place, wrote Hardy to Alfred de Lafontaine, owner of Athelhampton Hall, would be put 'a bran new erection which will have no historic or religious associations whatever. And yet people are blamed for not going to church. I wonder if this is really to be done?' But it *was* done, and this despite everyone's knowledge that the edifice had been immortalized as Weatherbury Church in *Far from the Madding Crowd* and possessed great intrinsic interest to visitors because of its associations with a popular novel written by Thomas Hardy.[22]

Perhaps the fact that the congregation at Puddletown Church seldom filled even half the seats weighed heavily with the authorities as a reason for feeling free to tamper with the dimensions of the chancel. But Hardy was correct in noting that enlargement for the sake of more sitting room could not be, and was not, argued as a serious proposition, since it seemed at odds with the statistics on attendance in the first decade of this century. Hardy shook his head sceptically at the announcement that the foundations of a longer chancel had been discovered; he had personally examined the present chancel (though not recently) and had found no traces of its existence. He rejected the prediction that a chancel would benefit 'artistically or ecclesiastically' from being made larger. Seeking the sanction of promises made in a not irretrievable past, he recalled that the owner of the estate on which the church was located had once pledged not to allow the church to be altered during his lifetime, and had kept his promise. Moreover, Hardy quoted Arthur Blomfield, 'though a restorer', to the effect that 'this particular church was one which ought not to be touched'.[23] He concluded a letter to Thackeray Turner with a request that the Society for the Protection of Ancient Buildings 'exert itself' and even urged that a letter to *The Times* be sent, exploiting the connections of Puddletown Church with the church he had described in *Far From the Madding Crowd*—which, in itself, was a highly unusual request, for it meant that his name would be used in the kind of publicity campaign that ordinarily he shunned.

Hardy's sense of anguish (it cannot be termed less intense) culminated in a cry of outrage to Turner some eight months later. He had passed Puddletown Church towards the end of September 1910 and seen—to his horror—that not only had the chancel been pulled down as well as the east wall of the north aisle, but the adjoining arch, in danger of falling, had been propped up. 'Gravestones had been removed from the churchyard, and extensive clearing made & foundations dug; & window tracery & other Gothic details lay scattered about the churchyard'.[24] Nor, when the restoration work had further advanced, could Hardy characterize it as anything other than 'appalling'.[25]

The key document in any review of Hardy's opinions of what he and his fellow architects had been doing during the Queen's reign (altogether a period of some seven decades) is, of course, 'Memories of Church Restoration'. The essay, replete with examples of the damage done by pulling down and putting up, shifting of tombstones, trashing of vital elements of church interiors and 'improving' of small details at the expense of overall integrity, has often been read as a *mea culpa*. But Hardy, who sincerely believed that the passion for 'restoring' had wrought more damage than good, was also seeking to define common ground for those who shared his alarm at the same time that they appreciated the legitimate concerns of those who willingly underwrote the expenses of such work. Millions of pounds had been expended, but the results of attempts at preservation were mixed at best and disastrous in numberless cases. The Society for the Protection of Ancient Buildings, founded by Sir Gilbert Scott (1811–78), or 'Scott the Second', as Hardy facetiously named him, laboured strenuously to mitigate the damage, but the task went beyond the resources of any single organization. Perhaps, Hardy mused, the problems created by church restoration all over Great Britain would not diminish to a significant degree until 'all tampering with chronicles in stone be forbidden by law and all operations bearing on their repair be permitted only under the eyes of properly qualified inspectors'.[26] The proposal had no serious chance of acceptance, as Hardy well understood.

The problem confronted by the Society was, basically, how best to balance the claims of the antiquarian, historian and lover of human associations sanctified by centuries, against those of the parish that needed to use the church building for religious purposes. Hardy saw no way to implement an ideal solution, the enclosing of a venerable but 'ruinous' church in a crystal palace while a new church might be constructed alongside for services: 'Even a parish entirely composed of opulent members of the Society would be staggered by such an undertaking'.[27] In practical terms, there had to be compromises betweeen 'users and musers'.

Hardy's distaste for the excesses of restorers was based on personal experience as well as a delight in anecdotal lore, and as we have seen, Hardy often visited sites to report on the advisability or inadvisability of contemplated alterations. (He was meticulous in his accounting of expenses incurred while on this official business.) It is worth noting, however, that Hardy blamed builders far more severely than architects for the damage done in the name of restoration. True, his paper was running a bit long; perhaps, as he claimed, he might dwell upon the mistakes of members of his profession if he had had more time; but his presentation of the case against contractors and the more innocent patrons and patronnesses who paid them for their time was very severe in its indictment of their sins. Architects, Hardy conceded, had much to answer for. 'Yet one cannot logically blame an architect for being an architect—a chief craftsman, constructor, creator of forms—not their preserver'.[28] This amounts to a defence, even a glorification, of the architect's role, for Hardy had already written, in what was rapidly turning into a peroration,

> The true architect, who is first of all an artist and not an antiquary, is naturally most influenced by the aesthetic sense, his desire being, like Nature's, to retain, recover, or recreate the idea which has become damaged, without much concern about the associations of the material that idea may have been displayed in. Few occupations are more pleasant that that of endeavouring to re-capture an old design from the elusive hand of annihilation.[29]

Hardy, after 1874, would not have undertaken any work as a church restorer even if he had returned to the profession; he had witnessed too much, and recorded too many mistakes committed in the name of church restorations, to be able to work out a satisfactory compromise between a desire to hand on or modify an abstract form (something new) and a desire to extend the antiquity of its embodiment (something old). Who, then, might be trusted with what so many Englishmen and women perceived as a necessary obligation? For all Hardy cared, 'a retired tinker or riveter of old china, or some ''Old Mortality'' from the almshouse, would superintend the business better'.[30] But his conclusion really praised most of all 'indifferentism', which in several notable cases had preserved churches best. 'The policy of ''masterly inaction''—often the greatest of all policies—was never practised to higher gain than by these, who simply left their historic buildings alone. To do nothing, where to act on little knowledge is a dangerous thing, is to do most and best'.[31]

Hardy's disgust was aimed at 'the craze for indiscriminate church-restoration' (so he described it in his 1895 preface to *A Pair of Blue Eyes*) that had spread throughout England. Along the coast, the 'wild and tragic features' of the terrain had combined with the 'crude Gothic Art' of various church buildings to throw into 'extraordinary discord all architectural attempts at newness there'. He was thinking of St Juliot, where a local builder had razed to the ground tower, north aisle and transept, and replaced a venerable chancel-screen with ' a new and highly varnished travesty'. (The builder had felt generous: 'I won't stand on a pound or two while I'm about it', he told an astonished Hardy in 1870, 'and I'll give 'em a new screen instead of that patched-up old thing'.)[32]

St Juliot—despite its romantic associations with the sea; despite Hardy's appreciation of having met Emma there, and lost his heart to her—was too far gone. G.R. Crickmay's designs for 'improving' it could not undo damage already inflicted; nor do we really know how deeply involved Hardy was. Did he contribute ideas to Crickmay's 1870 elaboration of John Hicks's 1867 proposed south elevation and plan of the church? Suffice it to say that Hardy's repentance for having participated, in however small a degree, in vandalism of some of England's smaller and more helpless church edifices seems to have been connected (in later years) with a general regret over the loss of youthly energies, the remembered beauty of Emma, the knowledge of missed opportunities and an abiding curiosity over what might have ensued had he taken an alternative path into the future.

He did not feel this way about cathedrals, some of which (in England) were undergoing similar kinds of improvements, and sometimes on a much larger and more imaginative scale, than churches like St Juliot and Stinsford could afford. His interest in cathedrals may be traced back to his training in Gothic architecture. One amiable letter to James Reymond de Montmorency Abbott, dated 29 March 1913, praised his friend for not dropping architectural tours. 'I think them most cheering: cathedrals form an objective in a journey that does not disappoint as some others do'.[33]

We remember Hardy's generous tribute to the Gothic art-principle in which he had been trained:

> the principle of spontaneity found in mouldings, tracery and such like—resulting in the 'unforeseen' (as it has been called) character of his metres and stanzas, that of stress rather than of syllable, poetic texture rather than poetic veneer; the latter kind of thing, under the name of 'constructed ornament', being what he, in common with every Gothic student, had been taught to avoid as the plague.[34]

Some critics have attempted to extend Hardy's admiration of Gothic architecture to analyses of the general design of his novels, as if one key might serve to unlock the massively hinged door that opens inward on Hardy's art. (I am thinking of Kenneth Marsden's analysis, in *The Poems of Thomas Hardy: A Critical Introduction,* 1969. Others have been irresistibly drawn to Hardy's identification of a connection between his own poetical work and 'the Gothic art-principle'.)

Hardy used what was available, and drew his inspiration from all the arts, not only architecture. Joan Grundy, in *Hardy and the Sister Arts* 1979,[35] has several chapters on 'pictorial arts', 'theatrical arts', 'cinematic arts', 'music and dance' and 'the composite muse', the last-named devoting only a few pages to Hardy's interest in architecture. Susan Dean's *Hardy's Poetic Vision in The Dynasts* (1977) begins with a helpful analysis of 'the dioramic vision', 'a visual exhibit, carefully limited, proportioned, and aligned to balance with other components in a fully imagined whole'.[36] To summarize Hardy's architectural training manifests itself in two primary ways: first, Hardy lavishes detailed descriptions on all kinds of buildings and sees them as total structures or, alternatively, as a number of salient features; and second, he regards the human associations of buildings as being more important than the fineness of their design.

'The Two Houses' illustrates the significance of the second point. Houses bear the imprint of those who have inhabited them. A new house—a 'smart newcomer'—derides the age of a nearby house:

> New comer here I am
> Hence haler than you with your cracked old hide,
> Loose casements, wormy beams, and doors that jam.

What does modern architecture amount to? The case presented in the poem emphasizes 'hangings fair of hue', windows that open 'as they should' and water-pipes within. This catalogue omits babes newly born, 'lank corpses', 'dancers and singers', a bridegroom and bride, and countless others who exist as phantoms—Presences from an earlier time, held forever inside the walls of the older house. The newer house is 'awestruck' by the older house's listing of 'shades dim and dumb', and wonders whether it will also serve as the host of any comparable company. 'That will it, boy', answers the venerable 'pile' (the word did not seem offensive to Hardy):

> Such shades will people thee,
> Each in his misery, irk, or joy,
> And print on these their presences as on me.

Hardy was *literally* haunted by the knowledge that others had used the furniture of any house that he and Emma had to rent; that their thoughts and glances had 'imprinted' themselves in rooms where he sought to relax, or work.[37]

This idea turns up in the *Later Years,* more than once; it may also be found in 'The Strange House', a rather curious poem in which Hardy imagines what tenants of Max Gate might say to each other in the year *AD* 2000. Inevitably, they will remember former tenants. Hardy is thinking of himself and Emma; Emma's love of the piano is alluded to in the first stanza. A piano plays despite the fact that the present tenants have no piano:

> 'Their old one was sold and broken;
> Years past it went amiss'.

In a dialogue that records a conversation between a rational voice (its owner can see no figure on the stair) and a voice of someone able to sense undertones, hear piano-playing, see wraiths and intuit 'what once happened here', Hardy speaks of 'two love-thralls' who may have 'imprinted/Their dreams on its walls'.

The theme is orchestrated, again, in 'A House with a History', also printed in *Late Lyrics and Earlier*. The 'mere freshlings' who move into a house with 'their raw equipments, scenes, and says' are ignorant of the former voices that beat 'from ceiling to white hearthstone' in earlier times. The blankness of brow of newcomers does not mean that the past is no longer alive, simply that they are oblivious to what happened in the house years before. The poem is not Hardy's best statement of his abiding concern, but its opening lines encapsulate a view that we must take seriously as Hardy's own:

> There is a house in a city street
> Some past ones made their own . . .

In Chapter 4 of *The Woodlanders* Hardy writes of the Melbury house: in its reverberations 'queer old personal tales were yet audible if properly listened for'. And, in 'Memories of Church Restoration', Hardy underscored his deepest conviction on the matter: associative qualities—those created by human association—far outranked aesthetic qualities, and the vandalism wrought by insensitive architects did more damage to memories of what people had done within church walls than to the walls themselves.

I think the damage done to this sentiment of association by replacement, by the rupture of continuity, is mainly what makes the enormous loss this country has sustained from its seventy years of church restoration so tragic and deplorable. The protection of an ancient edifice against renewal in fresh materials is, in fact, even more of a social—I may say a humane—duty than an aesthetic one. It is the preservation of memories, history, fellowship, fraternities. Life, after all, is more than art, and that which appealed to us in the (may be) clumsy outlines of some structure which had been looked at and entered by a dozen generations of ancestors outweighs the more subtle recognition, if any, of architectural qualities. The renewed stones at Hereford, Peterborough, Salisbury, St Albans, Wells and so many other places, are not the stones that witnessed the scenes in English Chronicle associated with those piles. They are not the stones over whose face the organ notes of centuries 'lingered and wandered on as loth to die . . .'[38]

Of one thing Hardy was certain. Architectural fashions made impossible the drawing of hard and fast lines against any single style as permanently blessed or permanently damned. *A Laodicean* is generally recognised today as one of Hardy's lesser novels, mostly, perhaps, because its writing took place under very difficult circumstances, when Hardy's illness prevented him from taking full care of the manuscript from the fourteenth chapter onwards (instalments having been promised to *Harper's New Monthly Magazine*). Hardy could not develop a number of his crucial ideas relevant to Victorian engineering, refine his plot or satisfactorily relate his memories of the small talk of architectural service to a larger theme of architectural ethics and responsibilities. Yet there may be more autobiographical material in this unsatisfactory novel than Hardy was willing to let stand in any other novel. From the perspective of some three decades after its original publication in 1881, Hardy, in his preface of 1912 written for the Wessex Edition, noted with muted irony that many architectural details in the novel had become 'the baseless fabrics of a vision'. The first chapter introduces the reader to George Somerset, 'a summer traveller from London sketching mediaeval details in these neo-Pagan days', at a time when English Gothic architecture, beloved by Hardy because it gave respectability to the principle of spontaneity, had fallen into disrepute. George Somerset had observed the fall from grace of 'the great English-pointed revival under Britton, Pugin, Rickman, Scott and other mediaevalists'. He refused to succumb to the mania for 'the French-Gothic mania' which immediately succeeded it, and admired Palladian and Renaissance styles; but when Jacobean, Queen Anne 'and kindred accretions of decayed styles' came into favour he became 'quite bewildered on the question of style' and concluded that architecture as a living art had become extinct. 'Somerset was not old enough at that time' Hardy wrote with restrained grimness, 'to know that, in practice, art had at all times been as full of shifts and compromises as every other mundane thing; that ideal perfection was never achieved by Greek, Goth or Hebrew Jew, and never would be; and thus he was thrown into a mood of disgust with his profession'. Later, recalled from despair by the failure of his poems to win the favour of publishers and by his father's hint that 'unless he went on with his legitimate profession he might have to look elsewhere than at home for an allowance', Somerset returned to the

Gothic school which had been so important in his early years. The 'surprising instability of art ''principles'' had depressed him; but after taking time to reflect, he understood that 'This accident of being out of vogue lent English Gothic an additional charm'. Its very unfashionableness, in brief, appealed to him.

Hardy's determination to think his own thoughts about the transience of fashions in architecture and the follies of church restoration, and the permanence of human associations attached to all kinds of buildings, served him in good stead for all his years as an author. He never closed his architect's eye.

2

Hardy's Interest in the Theatre

Let us imagine that we are attending a dinner at the home of some gracious host and that the host introduces us to an elderly gentleman who begins to reminisce, quietly, about his lifelong love-affair with the theatre. He tells us that as an adolescent he learnt to enjoy the reading of dramatic literature. As a young man he wanted to try a year's experience as a supernumerary in order to gain the background needed for the writing of blank-verse dramas. He eagerly listened to gossip about the players of the past century and wanted, on every possible occasion, to see the great players of his own century. Several times he adapted his novels and short stories to dramatic form. He encouraged others to write operas based on his fictions. He entertained strong opinions about the standards of playwriting and spoke out often about the baleful influence of censorship on the contemporary London stage. He luxuriated in the knowledge that a group of actors and actresses had named themselves, informally, after himself, and that they wanted to be known as his 'Players'. For them he wrote no less than six scripts. He was largely responsible for their colourful adaptation of one of his novels, which turned into their biggest hit. He contributed significant elements to the writing and production of another seven plays during a sixteen-year period. After such a conversation, would we not be justified in concluding that we have had the privilege of speaking to a novelist who, but for the grace of God, might well have become an actor or dramatist?

Thomas Hardy, at a very early age, admired the ethical orientation, firmness of moral purpose and consistency of tone of the Greek dramatist. Aeschylus was a special favourite, if only because his *Agamemnon* contained, in the song of the choristers, a line that bit deeply into his consciousness, 'Ælinon, Ælinon! but may the good prevail'. These words, he grew to believe, formed the refrain of 'all really true literature'.[1] He agreed with Aeschylus that the higher passions must subordinate the lower. Morality took precedence over even the intellectual faculties and 'aspirations, affections, or humours' were more important to the true-thinking artist than any delineation of 'man's appetites'.

From Aeschylus to Shakespeare: the line included all masters of imaginative creation. 'The President of the Immortals'—the phrase with which Hardy concluded *Tess of the d'Urbervilles*—was borrowed from the *Prometheus.* Other allusions to Aeschylean drama may be found in *The Return of the Native, The Dynasts,* the poem 'Compassion' and *Jude the Obscure.* As for Sophocles, the influence of *Oedipus Tyrannus* on *The Mayor of Casterbridge* was major; Hardy annotated carefully his copies of the text of the *Antigone* and the *Trachiniae;* he greatly admired the structure of Sophocles' plays and even wrote a poem 'Thoughts from Sophocles' (unpublished during his lifetime) in which he brooded on 'the good of knowing no birth at all'. In his *Literary Notes* Hardy asked himself the question, 'What is fatality?' and answered, 'Sophocles made it clear that the characters of men constitute their fatality'. He was reacting to a passage in John Addington Symonds's *Studies of the Greek Poets,* Second Series (London, 1876). Hardy's enjoyment of the Greek drama derived from his appreciation of 'their firm grasp upon the harmony of human faculties in large morality', and not from his knowledge of (or even interest in) seeing actual productions. All the more remarkable, therefore, that Hardy wanted—and was able—to see, on 1 July 1924, the Balliol Players perform the *Oresteia* on the lawn of Max Gate. Hardy had originally suggested that the performance be given at Maumbury Rings: 'To be sure', he wrote in a letter of 17 June, 'it is not Greek, but it is almost certainly Roman, and the crimes that have been committed within its circle would I think match in horror those of the house of Atreus'.[2] But because he warned the players in advance that he could not attend a performance at Maumbury Rings, and because his invitation to the players to come to Max Gate for a second performance was couched in a particularly winsome manner, it proved unnecessary for him to stir abroad. The Granville-Barkers were among his guests; among the players, Hardy listed the name of Anthony Asquith (who played Cassandra). The play, retitled *The Curse of the House of Atreus,* was performed in windy and chilly weather but everybody enjoyed the occasion, particularly Hardy. 'Always sympathetic to youth, and a lifelong admirer of Greek tragedy, he fully appreciated this mark of affection and respect'.[3]

It is true that Hardy read Euripides less intensely, and quoted his plays less often, than he did either those of Aeschylus or Sophocles, but he owned a set of Euripides. He wrote in the first volume both Swinburne's damaging remark—'It is far easier to overtop Euripides by the head and shoulders than to come up to the waist of Sophocles or the knee of Aeschylus'—and a vigorous rebuttal, 'An old opinion but not true'.[4] (Swinburne had written his opinion in a private letter to Edmund Gosse in 1876; Gosse may have shown Hardy the letter.) Hardy also marked carefully his copies of English translations of *The Trojan Women* and the *Hippolytus* (the Bohn volumes).

As a young man in London, Hardy volunteered for a walk-on role in the pantomime *Ali-Baba and the Forty Thieves; or, Harlequin and the Genii of the Arabian Nights!,* written by Gilbert à Beckett. The play enjoyed modest success, a run of several weeks. In a scene entitled 'Oxford and Cambridge Boat Race', Hardy performed in the role of a 'Nondescript'. The play opened the day after Christmas 1866 and came after Hardy addressed inquiries about the theatre as a way of making a living to both Mark Lemon (the editor of *Punch,* a successful playwright and a moderately talented actor) and Mr Coe, who managed stage productions at the Haymarket. Their advice (and Hardy's personal experiences as a supernumerary) must have been discouraging. Moreover, any reasonably alert young man might swiftly come to the conclusion (on his own) that novel-writing would prove more lucrative than the writing of blank-verse plays.

Hardy paid frequent visits to the two-shilling pit seats of Drury Lane. He held in his hand a copy of the Shakespearian play that Samuel Phelps was declaiming on the stage (a severe enough test for the actors, if in fact they noticed his monitoring of their speech, as Hardy recorded in his autobiography).[5] He admired Phelps as Othello, Falstaff and Macbeth. He decided that he preferred Phelps to Charles Kean. Letters published in the *Dorset County Chronicle* in 1902 indicate that Hardy (who was writing about Edmund Kean's appearance in Dorchester in 1813) was an eager student of the history of the theatre. He attended, as often as possible, the dramatic readings by Charles Dickens at the Hanover Square Rooms. He knew a good deal about how Arthur Wing Pinero corrected actors at rehearsal, and James Barrie's relations with actors. His poem 'A Victorian Rehearsal', written after attending a gloomy run-through of Barrie's drama *Mary Rose,* is an observer's shrewd commentary on the unprepossessing nature of actors and actresses in a half-shaped production:

> Mutterings, crossings, and reversings
> Done by a queer little group dull-dressed,
> As 'twere some children's game unguessed;
> Town dwellers who affect them clowns,
> Or villains fierce with oaths and frowns;
> Among them being the leading lady,
> Whose private life is whispered shady,
> But who's to divorce her spouse, they say,
> Adding, 'it should be the other way'.

Hardy knew Ibsen's plays well and joined George Meredith and George Moore in support of the Independent Theatre Association's efforts to produce them; close friends—William Archer and Edmund Gosse, among others—kept him posted on developments in Scandinavian drama. (Gosse took him to an afternoon performance of *Hedda Gabler,* which he had translated, at the Vaudeville Theatre, 20 April 1891.) He was a devoted follower of the acting styles of Mrs Patrick Campbell and Henry Irving. On one occasion—for a matinée performance on 23 July 1890, given to raise money for a Holiday Fund for City Children— Hardy wrote 'Lines' delivered as an epilogue by Ada Rehan, an actress he much admired. Though a sultry afternoon reduced attendance, approximately a hundred pounds were added to Mrs Jeune's charitable cause, and Hardy professed himself pleased with the results. He was much less gratified by *The Globe's* comment that he had written 'poor stuff, poetically', and characterized the newspaper's criticism as 'extremely ungenerous'.[6]

Hardy thought that Ada Rehan, an American actress, distinguished herself particularly as 'the Shrew', a role she played on the opening night of [Augustin] Daly's Theatre in Leicester Square (1893).[7] Hardy's enthusiasm for her misled at least one reporter, a 'Literary Gossip' columnist for *The Globe,* who wrote that Hardy had recently convinced himself that his future lay in playwriting. When Hardy wrote to Daly about Ada Rehan's 'fine piece of acting' (28 June 1893) he may have meant no more than he enjoyed himself and that he admired her good looks. He was always susceptible to a woman's proud sense of assurance on a stage, and even more so to an attractive figure. Some three decades later the attention that he paid to Gertrude Bugler, a beautiful young Tess recruited for a Dorchester production, excited the jealousy of Florence and led to some mildly scandalized gossip. Hardy by this time was over 80. It seems a little hard to characterize his courteous behaviour as 'an infatuation', but more than one biographer has noted that it was consistent with the flowers and flattery that he bestowed on other lovely actresses.

He was titillated by the thought that Mrs Patrick Campbell lived only a block away from a flat that he had taken in Ashley Gardens, near Westminster Cathedral, in 1895. She was, at the time, interested in playing the role of Tess, and Hardy wrote to Emma that her proximity might 'be convenient for the work'.[8] Though an English production of *Tess* with Mrs Campbell as star did not work out, Hardy went faithfully to most of her later appearances on the London stage. He loved the talents of Eleanor Duse and Sarah Bernhardt, and sent to 'the divine Sarah' a French translation of *Tess* (June 1901) so that she might decide for herself whether she wanted to dramatize and produce it in French, 'because', as he wrote her, 'I feel that the chief character could be so finely rendered by yourself'.[9]

What he thought of Henry Irving in the role of Othello (which he saw in June 1906) we shall never know, for as a general rule he did not commit to paper his impressions of the rightness or wrongness of dramatic interpretations of famous roles. But he was (perhaps unsurprisingly) well-informed about a number of developments in contemporary drama. He attended the first performance of William Butler Yeats's play, *Where There Is Nothing* (26 June 1904). As an established writer he benefited from the courtesy shown him by other writers who solicited an opinion of their plays. For example, in 1905 Frederic Harrison sent him the script of *Nicephorus,* a play about a Byzantine emperor, and must have been delighted by Hardy's reaction: 'The drama would make a gorgeous spectacle, & the story is clearly exhibited; briskly too, so that an audience who should know nothing whatever of the tragedy as history (which of course would be the general condition), would have no difficulty in following its action'.[10] Lady Gregory's *Seven Short Plays,* in 1909, evoked the pleasant—but restrained—encomium, 'The stones you bring to your cairn, though you deprecate their fewness, all help to build it nevertheless'.[11] He received many more invitations to play-readings than he cared to accept, turning down, as one illustration, Henry Arthur Jones's kind request to attend a run-through of *The Tempter* (1893). He was an inveterate first-nighter so long as his health held up, braving, on one typical occasion, a heavy rain to be present at the first performance of *All the Comforts of Home,* by William Gillette and Ellen Terry (21 January 1891). He enjoyed being invited by James Barrie, a friend of long standing, to see *Walker, London,* in June 1893, and even more the opportunity to visit behind the scenes, where John Lawrence Toole, an actor in the play, entertained his visitors with 'hock and champagne . . . in his paint, wig & blazer, as he had come off the stage, amusing us with the drollest of stories about a visit he and a friend paid to the Tower some years ago: how he amazed the custodian by entreating the loan of the crown jewels for an amateur dramatic performance for a charitable purpose, offering to deposit 30/- as a guarantee that he would return them—&c &c &c'.[12]

That there was much wrong with the late Victorian theatre and its practices, he knew as early as the controversy that engulfed him when Arthur Wing Pinero's 'version' of *Far From the Madding Crowd,* namely *The Squire,* was first staged in late December 1881. He detested unethical actors, managers and playwrights, and perhaps encountered more than a fair share of the members of each category. But he held more important objections to the ways in which plays were staged. So far as Hardy was concerned, art was less important in the plays available to Londoners than artifice and accessories. His response was to advocate destruction of the conventional *mise-en-scène.* Scenery would be useful as backdrop only (a mere curtain at that); and the rounded stage would be surrounded on three sides by spectators. An 'arena' would eliminate the 'cumbersome' boxlike arrangement of an ordinary theatre.

To Florence Henniker, to whom he often wrote candidly about literary opinions, he confessed (1 December 1893) that he preferred writing novels to plays partly because they were more remunerative 'in the long run' and constituted a higher form of art: 'What is called a good art play', he noted, 'receiving a column's notice in the morning papers, being distinctly in point of artistic feeling & exhibition of human nature no higher than a third rate novel. Consider what a poor novel ''Mrs Tanqueray'' wd make—I mean, how little originality it wd possess—that sort of thing having been done scores of years ago in fiction'.[13]

The dramatizing of novels, he wrote to Mrs Patrick Campbell (7 March 1897), was 'questionable art'. The end of the century, which brought a greater prosperity to the theatre, caused him to harbour second thoughts (briefly) about which genre was more lucrative. As he wrote to Mrs Henniker (22 December 1904), 'It is true, as you say, that all the money nowadays goes to the dramatists & not to the novelists (except Hall Caine & Miss Corelli). Barrie, I am told, is wealthy to oppression, & money still insists on rolling in to him'.[14]

But he never changed his mind about the greater originality of a novelist's art. To J.M. Bulloch, a dramatic critic at *The Sphere,* he wrote (on 3 March 1907) that *Jude the Obscure* had employed a situation very similar to the one in John Sutro's *John Glayde's Honour.*[15] Sutro had been praised for the *novelty* of his incident, whereas Hardy, writing *Jude* some twelve years earlier, had been so abused for writing that he never again attempted a novel. As a second example, Hardy cited the similarities between Horace Annesley Vachell's *Her Son* and his own 'The Marchioness of Stonehenge', written some sixteen years earlier, 'I could give you a dozen other instances', Hardy continued. 'How is it that dramatists are always praised for imitating what novelists are condemned for inventing? (I do not mean that they are necessarily conscious imitations.)' Wary (as always) that his own works might not transfer successfully to the stage, he resisted, for years at a stretch, the temptation to adapt his own novels and short stories, partly because everything connected with the stage seemed to him to be 'so shifty & uncertain', and—for an equally weighty reason—because 'most novels become mere melodramas in adaptation'.[16]

His most explicit formulation of a long-cherished disdain for theatrical vulgarization may be located in a letter written on 1 January 1909, to William Archer. Hardy urged Archer, a friend of long standing, to write an article on the unfair & disproportionate difference of standard applied to works of the theatre & those of us poor scribblers—I mean imaginative writers—who depend upon the press for making our ideas known. A situation, for instance, which is a stale thing in a novel or dramatic poem, is hailed as one of dazzling originality when, after some years, it has been imitated from that novel or poem & appears behind the footlights. Surely a re-adjustment of terms is wanted here, so that the two arts might be reduced to a common measure.[17]

None of these strictures should be interpreted as meaning that Hardy failed to sympathize with the problems of theatrical people who were working with plays unconnected with his own work. He saw novelists and playwrights as professionals engaged in a common enterprise, attempting to satisfy a large and often fickle public, operating on limited financial resources and threatened by external forces of criticism and censorship. Hardy's views on the philistinism of most reviewers are well known (they were often couched in vituperative language): but his contributions to the fight against censorship of other writers are perhaps not as well known as they should be. His voice was raised—on several occasions—on behalf of workers in the theatre. As one instance, his conviction that both novelists and playwrights had been progressing 'in the direction of a real grasp of life' during the early 1890s turned into a *cri du coeur* when he wrote to Henry William Massingham, editor of the *Nation* (1 July 1907):

The English and American press set itself with a will to stamp out the torch, on the grounds of morality (some of the examples were bizarre enough unquestionably) & the result was that English fiction was paralyzed into feeble imitations of Dumas *père* &c., resulting in what we now see—the field being left almost entirely to women at the present time.[18]

He willingly joined seventy playwrights ('dramatic authors') when James Barrie sent him a copy of a petition against censorship of plays (7 October 1907) and recalled, in a letter to Edward Garnett written the next day, that his poem 'A Sunday Morning Tragedy' had recently been rejected by the editor of the *Fortnightly Review* on grounds very similar to those which governed censorship of dramatic vehicles. Responding to a request from Henry Arthur Jones less than two years later (20 October 1909), he joined several playwrights in a protest 'against the retention of the Censor, & in a private capacity only';[19] he took the opportunity to praise Jones's pamphlet, 'The Censorship Muddle and a Way

Out of It'. He also wrote a letter to John Galsworthy (it was published in *The Times* on 13 August 1909), intending it to be used as one of the documents placed as evidence by a joint committee of the Lords and Commons; the members of the committee were considering the problems created by irresponsible censors and debating whether these problems prevented men of letters, who had 'other channels for communicating with the public, from writing for the stage'. When, in February 1912, the Lord Chamberlain refused to license Eden Phillpotts's new play, *The Secret Woman,* James Barrie wrote to Hardy, enclosing a copy of the disputed text (the Lord Chamberlain was insisting on alterations in the script), and asked for his signature on a petition. Hardy responded in characteristic fashion, drawing a line between expressions that might be too frank for 'a squeamish public', in which case no principle seemed to be involved, and Phillpotts might well make the challenge words 'more euphemistic'; and 'something radical in the play, which cannot be altered without spoiling it'. In the latter case, Hardy assured Barrie, he would help 'in any way in a protest, or whatever you may propose'.[20] A few days later Hardy wrote again, noting that there did seem to be a reason to object to some expressions, and the play was not an ideal vehicle for a communal protest against censorship; he hoped that Henry James, A.E. Housman, Gilbert Murray and Edmund Gosse might sign ('so that there may be some signatures equally remote with mine from practical dramatic work').[21] Since time was running out, only the signatures of James and Murray could be procured before the letter of protest appeared in *The Times* (14 February 1912). Even so, Hardy, not often a willing signatory to 'worthy causes', contributed on several occasions to the artistic welfare of writers threatened by censorship of their dramatic works, and did so despite a personal conviction that the writing of plays was not one of his own major professional interests.

Hardy's interest in theatrical news was exquisitely pitched. Hardy enjoyed going to the theatre in the company of congenial souls; sometimes simply to make of the evening a social occasion, as when he looked forward to squiring Lady Londonderry's daughters, Madeleine and Dorothy Stanley, because 'They are such dears that it is a pleasure to go with them'.[22] He was eager to learn from Sir George Douglas (in a letter written on 17 March 1900) whether his friend intended to visit Paris to see Edmond

Rostand's *L'Aiglon,* newly produced. The papers had 'gone mad' over it. 'The greatness of the conception does not show in the analysis of the piece given by the newspaper correspondents—which seem to reveal it as a series of tableaux, in the main; but I suppose the genius must lie in the verse'.[23] One night, bored while walking, he dropped in on a performance of *Coriolanus,* 'a dull play to the ordinary goer', and found himself 'impressed by the beauty of the play'.[24] We can readily assume that he read fiction more than once with an eye open to its potentialities as a dramatic vehicle (as when he wrote to Mrs Humphry Ward about her novel, *The Marriage of William Ashe,* published in 1905, that a great deal of Part Two 'might be almost bodily transferred to the stage').[25] On the occasion of a visit to the Alhambra Theatre to see a series of ballets, he was sufficiently disturbed by a conjuring performance (possibly an *entr'acte*) that used animals, that he wrote a letter of protest to the secretary of the Royal Society: 'The creatures—rabbits, pigeons, barn-fowls, ducks, &c.—may possibly be drugged or blinded to make them passive—though I cannot definitely state anything about their treatment, having witnessed the scene only from a distance'.[26] When Harry Pouncy produced in the Town Hall of Dorchester an evening's entertainment entitled 'Hours in Hardyland', the first part consisting of a lantern-slide lecture 'From Casterbridge to Kingsbere and Back', and the second part of dramatized episodes from *Far From the Madding Crowd,* Hardy wrote a long, detailed and overall cheerful letter intended to encourage Pouncy's entertainment 'if it should be carried away from Dorchester to other towns'.[27] Hardy was particularly concerned that the relationship of the lecturer to the dramatic scenes should be more clearly marked to minimize confusion of the audience in its understanding of the relationships between characters. 'Long experience has shown', wrote Hardy in a letter dated 21 October 1907, 'that knowledge of a particular book, however common, by an audience, can never be assumed'.

During the first decade of this century, thoughts of Shakespeare were frequently on his mind, perhaps because *The Dynasts* was very large scale, and the handling of large numbers of historical characters aggravated the problem of a suitable diction. If he knew what the real man or woman had said, did he have the right to change that individual's sentiment to a more complex language; to heighten an effect by creating a poetic diction? 'I decided I had not, in any essential degree', he wrote to Arthur Symons on 11 March 1908, 'the date of action not being remote enough to warrant it, for one reason. What one would give to know how Shakespeare thought on that question in writing *Henry VIII*, the date of which was nearer to his time when dramatizing the reign than Napoleon's date is to ours. It must have occurred to him'.[28] But he was not looking to Shakespeare as a model for his own playwriting; despite envy of his friends who had succeeded in the theatre, despite knowledge of the substantial earnings they took home, he finally saw that he admired Shakespeare primarily in his 'literary aspect',[29] as a 'poet, man of letters & seer of life'.[30] On such grounds he refused to subscribe to the idea of a memorial theatre, or to join a committee charged with the task of developing such a concept. 'I would, besides, hazard the guess that he, & all poets of high rank whose works have taken a stage direction, will cease altogether to be acted some day, & be simply studied'.[31] So he wrote to the journalist Robert Donald; he was willing to support the erection of a memorial to Shakespeare, but not a theatre dedicated to Shakespeare's memory.

Perhaps Hardy always preferred to think of plays as literature rather than see them butchered by inadequate actors and actresses doing their pitiful best in tawdry productions. There is nothing novel in his confession to Florence Henniker, dated 17 March 1911, that his taste for the theatre was weakening;[32] he had often denied wanting to succeed as a playwright, and he was frequently annoyed by journalists who insisted that he had been negotiating with this or that theatrical personality, or trying to get an adaptation of one of his works staged. Awareness of his own limitations led to his copying (in his *Literary Notes*) some famous remarks by Voltaire: 'The merit of this author [Shakespeare] has ruined the English drama. There are such beautiful scenes, there are passages so grand & so terrible in these monstrous farces which they call tragedies, that his pieces have always been played with great success. Time which alone gives reputation to men, renders at length their faults respectable. Most of the odd & gigantesque notions of this author have acquired, at the end of two hundred years, the right to pass for sublime. Modern authors have almost all copied them; but that which succeeded in Shakespeare is hissed in them'.[33]

Shakespeare, then, was a treacherous model for moderns, and the contemporary theatre could not hope to equal his sense of what would work on the stage.

Emblematic of Hardy's affection for the theatre is the lovely painting of a theatre audience awaiting the dimming of house-lights on the occasion of the first performance of Sir Arthur Sullivan's *Ivanhoe,* in 1891; it is reproduced in *Concerning Thomas Hardy,* edited by D.F. Barber (1968), as Illustration 26. Here, in the New English Opera House, D'Oyly Carte and Lily Langtry are shown as eager for the opera to commence. Hardy's attention is apparently focused on a programme in his hand. He seems, in this painting, to be perfectly at home in the theatre.

His interest began even before he read the Greek dramatists, when he saw and thrilled to several mumming plays in Dorchester. Chapters 4 and 5 of 'The Arrival', Book Second of *The Return of the Native* (1878), use, for dramatic effect, the remembered text of one version of 'the well-known play of "St George" '. All admirers of the novel will recall how Eustacia Vye, who holds both mummers and mumming in 'the greatest contempt', dons a disguise, becomes a mummer and recites lines that she knows well (a rehearsal for her is almost unnecessary) because she wants to see again, close up, Clement Yeobright. The play, though patchily described, is presented in bold, vivid strokes. Hardy omits several elements of the mumming tradition known to his contemporaries (e.g. the wife of Father Christmas, the fool, the daughter of the King of Egypt, and for that matter the dragon, too). Hardy tells us a good deal about the costuming, which is as traditional as the dialogue; even the ribbons that the sisters and sweethearts insist on attaching to 'gorget, gusset, basinet, cuirass, gauntlet, sleeve, all alike', are a convention. Since Hardy believed that the habit of presenting mummers' plays had largely died out even before he went to London as a young architect, this episode is perhaps self-consciously anachronistic; the most provocative elements in Hardy's description may be grounded on his conviction that the mummers entertained little affection for what they were doing. Hardy preferred the mumming manner of performance, which he thought was carried on 'with a stolidity and absence of stir which sets one wondering why a thing that is done so perfunctorily should be kept up at all', to 'a spurious reproduction'. He added, 'Like Balaam and other unwilling prophets, the agents seem moved by an inner compulsion to say and do their allotted parts whether they will or no'. Hardy approved of a 'fossilized survival' to an excited, fervent production inherent in any notion that what was being produced was a 'revival'. After the cutting-off of the Saracen's head and the acknowledged triumph of Saint George, Hardy's audience, who have been watching a faithful continuation of a long-standing tradition (not a revival), refuse to become excited. 'Nobody commented, any more than they would have commented on the fact of mushrooms coming in autumn or snow-drops in spring. They took the piece as phlegmatically as did the actors themselves. It was a phase of cheerfulness which was, as a matter of course, to be passed through every Christmas; and there was no more to be said'. This rather gloomy stillness is finally broken by the singing of a ''plaintive chant'', as the ''dead men [rise] to their feet in a silent and awful manner, like the ghosts of Napoleon's soldiers in the Midnight Review'. (Hardy here refers to other versions of the mummers' play, which introduced characters like Oliver Cromwell, Napoleon and George III).

Hardy's use of conventional elements—Eustacia, for example, must disguise herself as the Turkish Knight because women are excluded from the performances Hardy had witnessed as a boy; a somber stripping away of all comic, burlesque elements to a dignified, even grim conflict between Christian and Moslem factions; Father Christmas, with a hump on his back, entering on-stage with a swinging club, announcing that he has come 'welcome or welcome not'; and spirited sword-play—may raise a legitimate question. Can such a knowledgeable employment of well-loved elements of dramatic tradition fail to evoke *any* demonstration of enthusiasm? J.S. Udal, a Dorset folklorist, claimed that he had never witnessed a phlegmatic response to the 'spirited little performances' that he himself had witnessed in West Dorset, and added: 'Any occasional want of vivacity of self-abstraction in a performer I have put down in great measure to the unaccustomed burden of having to commit so many lines to memory'. (Indeed, Hardy makes a point of the problem inherent in learning as many as nine speeches; Charley, the lad whom Eustacia replaces in the play, had to spend three weeks at the task.)

Late in 1920 Hardy was to 'concoct' a recension of 'The Play of ''Saint George'' '. This, in turn, was to be incorporated into A.H. Tilley's dramatization of *The Return of the Native* and played by the Dorsetshire Christmas Mummers before audiences in both

Dorchester and London. On Christmas Day 1920 the Dorsetshire Christmas Mummers came to Max Gate, and in the drawing room performed Hardy's script, much to the delight of the 80-year-old playwright, his wife, brother, sister and servants. 'And friends who accompanied them', wrote Florence to Sir Sydney Cockerell, describing the scene, 'fiddled to us and sang carols outside—the real old Bockhampton carols. Then they came in, had refreshments in the dining room and we had a very delightful time with them'. (In *The Return of the Native,* Mrs Yeobright does not have enough room in the apartment to accommodate all the mummers, but places a bench for them halfway through the pantry-door. 'Here they seated themselves in a row, the door being left open: thus they were still virtually in the same apartment. Mrs Yeobright now murmured a few words to her son, who crossed the room to the pantry-door, striking his head against the mistletoe as he passed, and brought the mummers beef and bread, cake, pastry, mead and elder-wine, the waiting being done by him and his mother, that the little maid-servant might sit as guest. The mummers doffed their helmets, and began to eat and drink'.

Hardy's admiration of the acting style of the mummers must be stressed; it was an important element in his view of what good theatre required. It lay behind his quarrel with Arthur Bingham Walkley, the distinguished literary and dramatic critic of *The Times* during the first quarter of this century, who decided, while reading Part First of *The Dynasts,* that a semi-dramatic work emphasizing the inability of its major characters to act freely and to shape their own destiny, might best be produced as a puppet-show. Walkley, in brief, was saying that it was very difficult to relate this work to Hardy's earlier literary achievements, and that Hardy seemed to be working with a literary or dramatic tradition that most readers neither understood nor appreciated. Hardy, understandably, was annoyed by this reaction. (More will be said, in a later chapter that deals wholly with *The Dynasts,* about its general critical reception.) Though Hardy often enough denied the actability of his study of the Napoleonic Wars, he referred to it more than once as 'the longest English drama in existence',[34] as, for example, when he sent Frederick Macmillan 'the Third & last Part of *The Dynasts*' on 10 October 1907.

He toyed with at least half a dozen names, seeking to characterize its form. He listed 'A mental drama', 'A vision-drama', 'A closet-drama', 'An epical drama' and 'A chronicle poem of the Napc wars, under the similitude of a drama'. He admitted that he could not decide which to use; but it is striking that, in every instance that he recorded, the word 'drama' seems essential to his thought.[35]

He admired particularly the 'still manner' of the actor Horace Wigan, the Irishman who first played the role of Hawkshaw in Tom Taylor's *The Ticket of Leave Man,* and whom he went to see on several occasions. On 25 July 1874 he recorded in his notebook, 'He hardly moves at all when speaking, and the effect is excellent and more impressive than that of the gesticulating actors'.[36] Three years later he was sufficiently impressed by an article entitled 'Sarcey on the Comédie Française' in the *Saturday Review,* Vol.44 (25 August 1877), page 237, that he entitled a note to himself, 'Effects of Repetition', and recorded that M. Febvre, an actor who had starred in the same role for some two hundred nights, 'no longer knew what he was saying: it was as if he were possessed by a machine that moved & spoke without his interference'.[37]

It is not surprising, therefore, that his views on the commercial theatre became rather tart on occasions when his desire for minimalist production values was offended by what he saw on a stage. He contributed to a symposium in the *Pall Mall Gazette* (31 August 1892) a series of responses to set questions that the editor was publishing under the title 'Why I Don't Write Plays'. Hardy cited as his reasons the conviction that a novel was a better way of 'getting nearer to the heart and meaning of things' than a play; the fact that parts had to be moulded to actors rather than the other way around; the unlikelihood that managers would support 'a truly original play'; the need to arrange scenes 'to suit the exigencies of scene-building'; and, more generally, the subordination of 'the presentation of human passions' 'to the presentation of mountains, cities, clothes, furniture, plate, jewels, and other real and sham-real appurtenances'. For the *Weekly Comedy* (30 November 1889), he argued that the 'regulation stage-presentation of life' impressed a middle-aged spectator thus: 'First act—it may be so; second act—it surely is not so; third—it cannot be so; fourth—ridiculous to make it so; fifth—it will do for the children'. Moreover, if one could only 'weed away the intolerable masses of scenery and costume', one might popularize the theatre among intelligent adults ('a good many hundred people'), who would be willing to come from considerable distances to see a play performed in the following manner:—The ordinary pit boarded over to make a stage, so that the theatre would approach in arrangement the form of an old Roman amphitheatre, the scenery being simply a painted canvas hung in place of the present curtain, the actors performing in front of it, and disappearing behind it when they go off the stage; a horizontal canvas for sky or ceiling; a few moveable articles of furniture, or trees in boxes, as the case may be indoors or out; the present stage being the green room. The costumes to be suggestive of the time and situation, and not exclusively suggestive of what they cost.

The last long composition of Hardy's career was cast in a more conventional dramatic form than *The Dynasts*. Hardy began *The Famous Tragedy of the Queen of Cornwall* in 1916, after a visit to Tintagel which stirred up memories—they had never been forgotten—of the Lyonnesse where, in 1870, he had met his 'dearest Emmie'. For some reason inspiration faltered, and he set the romance aside; but after seven years he returned to it, completing a rough draft in April 1923. Publication by Macmillan, and production by the Hardy Players, followed a half-year later, and Hardy was to revise the play and enlarge the number of scenes on the basis of rehearsal experiences.

Hardy had called Emma 'an Iseult of my own' and he told Sir Sydney Cockerell that she 'of course' had been 'mixed in the vision of the other'.[38] Autobiographical elements underlie this play like a granitic substratum. Hardy was recalling the scenery of Cornwall that he had already written about at length in *A Pair of Blue Eyes* (1873) and in a large number of lyrics. He wrote to Alfred Noyes (17 November 1923) that his play had been '53 years in contemplation'. The problem of a divided love—Tristram caught between the yearning of Iseult of the White Hands and the claim of Queen Iseult—may have been, during a crucial year, the question that tormented a younger Hardy whose engagement to Tryphena Sparks had not ended before he met and fell in love with Emma Lavinia Gifford. And the understandable bitterness of the Queen—one of Hardy's original contributions to the Tristram story—has suggested to more than one critic the strains in Hardy's marriage relationship during the last two decades of Emma's life.

Hardy freely adapted the varying versions of the legend by Malory, Bédier and Wagner to his own purpose, citing as his precedent the Greek dramatists, 'notably Euripides', and the play, no less than *The Dynasts,* is based upon a lifetime of readings in dramatic literature and active play-going. Merlin, who introduces the play—the role was created for T.H. Tilley of the Hardy Players—reminds the audience that the play is constructed of familiar materials: 'The tale has travelled far and wide'. The Chanters—'Shades of Dead Old Cornish Men' and 'Shades of Dead Cornish Women'— are dressed 'as in the old mumming shows', and Hardy, referring to their functions as that 'of a Greek Chorus to some extent',[39] obviously wanted them to speak monotonically, as he had specified in his preface to *The Dynasts* for 'such plays of poesy and dream': 'with dreamy conventional gestures, something in the manner traditionally maintained by the old Christmas mummers, the curiously hypnotizing impressiveness of whose automatic style—that of persons who spoke by no will of their own—may be remembered by all who ever experienced it'. The setting of the play is the Great Hall of Tintagel Castle, 'round or at the end of which the audience sits'. Hardy's distaste for accessories on a stage had led him, on more than one earlier occasion, to advocate something very similar to theatre in the round, for only if spectators could sit 'to a great extent round the actors' would they be able to see the *play* (Hardy's emphasis); the appeal would then be to their imagination rather than to their eyesight. Moreover, Hardy took great pride in the fact that in this play dramatic time coincided perfectly with real time: 'the rule for staging nowadays should be to have no scene which would not be physically possible in the time of acting'.[40] His observance of the unities was more consistent here than in the only other occasion he remembered attempting it, in *The Return of the Native.* The effect of beginning the play just before the catastrophe was to intensify the inevitability of the final knotted action, in which three of the four major characters die.

Hardy's modernization is perhaps most original in its final moments, when the Queen stabs her husband, Mark, then leaps over the cliff while 'the wind rises, distant thunder murmuring', and Iseult the Whitehanded discovers the bodies of Mark and Tristram. It may be that Hardy, attempting to avoid historical accuracy ('it would have been impossible to present them as they really were, with their barbaric manners and surroundings') at the same time that he tried to avoid turning them into 'respectable Victorians' in the manner of Tennyson, Swinburne or Arnold, gave to his characters a clotted, uneasily mixed speech that overcomplicates the task of dramatic presentation. It is not too surprising that a poet four-score and upwards should have found it necessary to intensify romantic passion by transcribing at least eight passages from his own *A Pair of Blue Eyes*.[41] But altogether, the elaborateness of the rhymes, the occasional soaring eloquence (as in the Queen's sad lyrics, vii, and Tristram's song, xi) and Hardy's continuing control of theatrical elements, are impressive for this hour's traffic on the stage. Minor work it may be, but several moments of dark beauty will stir in any audience a genuine sense of pity for the plight of Iseult the Whitehanded. It is no mean achievement to close an illustrious career with a literate, and often strikingly beautiful, recension of one of the greatest love stories of the Western world.

We come, finally, to Hardy's most direct contacts with men and women of the theatre. These may be listed under two categories: the plays that Hardy wrote (some more original than others in the degree of freedom exercised as they deviated from the texts being adapted), and the plays based on his own works, prepared by other craftsmen, and acted by players he knew in his native Dorchester. Since these categories, taken together, spanned almost half a century, well over half of Hardy's life, the notion that Hardy entertained a cool contempt for practical matters of the theatre that he never learned how to master must surely be modified.

In February 1882, Hardy travelled with Emily to Liverpool for the special purpose of seeing a dramatization of *Far From the Madding Crowd*. The man who had prepared it, J. Comyns Carr, based his version not upon the novel directly but rather upon a manuscript prepared by Hardy himself, *The Mistress of the Farm*. Why Hardy surrendered so quickly the opportunity to emblazon his own name upon a production (though, to be sure, he would have had to find interested backers) is unclear. *The Mistress of the Farm* had been written in 1879, a few years earlier, and Hardy evidently sighed in relief that something might be done with an unsuccessful manuscript as soon as he learned that Carr, a well-known dramatic critic, wanted to prepare a version of the same novel. After several months of consideration by William Hunter Kendal and John Hare, the managers of the St James's Theatre, and after a provisional favourable decision towards mounting a production had been made, the Carr–Hardy version was finally turned down. What happened next turned into one of the bleaker moments of

Hardy's literary career: Madge Kendal, wife of one of the managers and a successful actress in her own right, may well have been responsible for the decisive negative vote (this, too, is unclear); but she certainly recounted the plot to Arthur Wing Pinero, and he, working away on *The Squire,* a new play, during 1881, incorporated numerous elements of Hardy's plot—which opened in late December of that year. The more one reviews the details of this event, the more puzzling everyone's role seems in perspective. Pinero claimed he had never read or even known about Hardy's novel, while Hardy, anxious to protect the rights of a manuscript on which he had lavished no little time, claimed that he had known nothing about Pinero's interest in writing such a play, until he read a review of *The Squire.* Hardy, who detested newspaper controversies, became more and more deeply involved in an argument (e.g. his letter to W. Moy Thomas, the reviewer for the *Daily News*) that levied a strong charge of plagiarism against Pinero. He even visited a solicitor to assess the actionability of his case against Pinero; he deeply believed that what Pinero had done exceeded the boundaries of 'fair transmutation'.[42] He did not press on with a law-suit. Why? If what more than one solicitor told him was true, he should not have renounced his rights. William Black, who apparently lacked access to some essential information, took Hardy's side by rejecting Pinero's defence with the airy remark, 'We no longer live in an Age of Faith'.[43] The savagery with which the *Academy* (18 February 1882) printed parallel passages from A.B. Longstreet's *Georgia Scenes* and Hardy's *The Trumpet-Major* (Ch. 23) was designed to expose Hardy as a plagiarist who had no right to levy charges against Pinero. Carr's vigorous rewriting of *The Mistress of the Farm,* which led to the Liverpool performance already mentioned, proceeded in spite of Hardy's efforts to suggest revisions that might bring the play closer to what he conceived to be the original spirit of the story. Perhaps Carr's judgement as to the inferiority of Hardy's proposed changes was soundly based (what Hardy found so offensive in Carr's new alterations is also unclear). We know that Hardy disliked the play—despite the fact that it ran more than than one hundred performances at the Globe Theatre in London—and tried to pretend, for the rest of his life, that Carr was entirely responsible for the form and the dialogue of *Far From the Madding Crowd.* (The play was credited, on the posters and in the playbill as having been written by both men.) However, Hardy's distaste for becoming involved with quarrels about territoriality antedated this particular episode, and his distaste became intensified by the outcome, which yielded him some financial profit at the cost of considerable enbarrassment in the public prints.

At any rate, he did not try his hand again until 1893, a full decade later, when his adaptation of 'The Three Strangers', one of his *Wessex Tales,* appeared as *The Three Wayfarers* at Terry's Theatre (3–9 June). It was one of five short plays (James Barrie and A. Conan Doyle wrote two of them). If contemporary reviews may be trusted, his was by far the most dramatic. Barrie had urged Hardy to attempt the adaptation and was pleased by the result. Hardy, who attended the first performance with Lady Jeune, enjoyed Charles Charrington's performance as the hangman so much that he praised it as 'extraordinarily powerful', and wrote to him, 'You have created quite a character for yourself and quite apart from any interest of another kind I may have in the play, I should like it to be widely seen as evidence of your powers'. Although the play ran for only a week because of poor receipts, the most noteworthy aspect of this 'adventure'—unusual because so much time had elapsed since the Carr-Pinero fiasco—was the genuine enthusiasm that Hardy displayed in his collaboration with Charrington. He rewrote the ending, inserted tunes as figures 'as they used to dance them' (he did not insist on strict historical accuracy in their enactment) and even offered to explain or direct the dances.[44] In the same year, for a brief moment, he also dallied with the thought of dramatizing the events that were eventually to be recorded in a poem, 'A Sunday Morning Tragedy'. He would have called the play *Birthwort* and given it a two-act structure; but, of course, the narrative was much too sensational for the London stage of the 1890s.

A long, not easily summarized history of Hardy's dramatization of *Tess of the d'Urbervilles* may be read in Marguerite Roberts's meticulously detailed book *Tess in the Theatre* (1950), which—along with the history—generously prints two versions, one by Hardy and the second by Lorimer Stoddard. Some salient elements of this history ought to be identified here, however. As soon as *Tess* was published as a novel, Hardy became the recipient of numerous letters from actresses (Sarah Bernhardt, Mrs Patrick Campbell and Eleanor Duse, among others) and managers requesting permission to translate it into dramatic terms. In 1895 Hardy—undoubtedly convinced by his experience with *The Three Wayfarers* that writing for the stage could be undertaken successfully, even if box-office receipts had proved less than bountiful in that particular case—set aside important fractions of time to the recasting of his story for the purposes of commercial theatre. Since he saw a good deal of Mrs Campbell, who lived nearby, he may have incautiously promised her and others the starring role; subsequent embarrassment about broken promises was, as a consequence, inevitable. At any rate, Minnie Maddern Fiske appeared in New York, Hardy's text having been changed in several key scenes by Lorimer Stoddard. Hardy, though careful to protect his English copyright by allowing a performance in London to be played, refused to approve an English production, despite strong protests from Mrs Campbell that her understanding with him had been betrayed. It is likely, as Marguerite Roberts believes, that Hardy had been jogged into writing the dramatization by Olga Nethersole, who had written to him warmly about the 'great creation', and who spoke of realizing her dreams to do 'something really great' if he prepared for her a play based on his novel. It is also likely that Hardy may have had Johnston Forbes-Robertson in mind for the role of Clare; there exists a substantial correspondence between the two, and the actor seemed to have provided a useful stimulus to Hardy's efforts. Hardy completed his play by the end of the year, and apparently yielded to Forbes-Robertson's objections over the extended attention paid to 'the seduction and the coming child' in the first two acts by rewriting the first two acts of what he then called a *Tragedy in Five Acts in the Old English Manner.*

The question of why Hardy allowed Americans to do a production of *Tess,* while standing firm against an English production, is not easily answered, though we can see, on the basis of scattered remarks made to friends in conversation and in a number of letters, that Hardy was baffled by the intricacies of financial arrangements for a professional, large-scale theatrical production (he had not been directly involved in such negotiations before); he needed to devote more time to his major literary project, what was to turn into the First Part of *The Dynasts,* and copyrighting even Stoddard's revised version of his adaptation threatened to take more time than he wanted to give.[45] Moreover, dealing with strong-willed women was never one of Hardy's specialities, and Mrs Campbell was only one of the actresses to whom he had spoken fair words in response to impassioned pleadings for the chance to play Tess; withdrawing the play completely from any commercial consideration might well have proved the only convenient way of ending multiple misunderstandings about who had been promised what.

Hardy's anxiety to avoid a direct confrontation was not reduced by Mrs Campbell's visit to Max Gate in early January 1896, when she arrived on horseback and conveniently fell off her horse at the entrance, thus signifying how naturally high histrionics came to her. But Hardy had also apparently talked to Elizabeth Robins as if he believed that she could do splendidly what she wanted to do with great passion, that is to say, act the role of Tess; in addition, there must have been some tacit encouragement of Olga Nethersole, who was cheated of the role when the American production was cast, and who felt she had some claim in the matter when she heard that Forbes-Robertson was arranging for a London production (plans that fell through).

The tangled history continued to distract Hardy, because Mrs Fiske's intention to extend her two-years' successful run of *Tess* by bringing the play to the London stage had to be dealt with. Hardy had no choice but to shut off plaintive correspondence with Olga Nethersole (he had already cruelly disappointed Elizabeth Robins), and to end Forbes-Robertson's interest in playing a role that Hardy thought him eminently suited for, by cancelling all plans for a London production. Mrs Fiske had chosen wisely in selecting Lorimer Stoddard, actor-dramatist in his early thirties, for the rush job of preparing a more dramatic version of Hardy's script; Hardy had been too novelistic in his retention of details, and Stoddard, doing all that was needed in five hectic days, certainly contributed as much as Hardy (who supplied the basic emphases of act-structure and characterization) and Mrs Fiske herself.

Stoddard's adaptation not only provided Mrs Fiske with splendid opportunities for graceful and natural movement, but inspired New York critics to use freely the adjective 'great' and to rank the play as the best serious production of 1897. Those who thought it too depressing for commercial success were proved wrong by box-office receipts. Apparently large numbers of playgoers wanted to judge for themselves. Had we world enough and time, we might assess the reasons which led Mrs Lewis Waller to produce Hugh

Arthur Kennedy's unauthorized version of *Tess of the d'Urbervilles,* knowing that Mrs Fiske held the copyright. Kennedy's script was based upon Stoddard's version, though he allowed Tess to die of exposure and grief at Stonehenge, a more sentimental version than Hardy would ever have approved.

We might wish to consider in greater depth Hardy's interest in a *Tess* opera—at least in that version which went to completion, unlike the operatic *Tess* that Charlotte Pendleton had proposed in 1900, she supplying the libretto and Elliott Schenck, an assistant of Walter Damrosch, composing the score; her project did not flourish, despite Hardy's lukewarm permission: 'I should have no objection to this being done, though I can take no responsibility in the matter'. Baron Frederic d'Erlanger, friend of Puccini and a well-known composer in his own right, used Puccini's librettist, Luigi Illica, for the musical score that opened at the San Carlo Theatre, Naples, on 10 April 1906—the very night that Mount Vesuvius erupted. The audience expected for the open performance—understandably—proved timorous; the theatre was closed (the building, officials thought, might collapse); and Hardy, hearing of the near-disaster, wrote a consolatory letter to the Baron: 'The volcano was all of a piece with Tess's catastrophic career!'[46] All was not lost, however. The critics—those courageous souls who stayed for the performance—who wrote about the original production liked it, and Puccini wrote from Milan to cheer up Baron d'Erlanger. A Covent Garden production, opening in mid-July 1908, proved a glittering occasion, with Queen Alexandra in the royal box. Hardy enjoyed the dress rehearsal and some preliminary run-throughs, and did not comment publicly on the fact that Illica had prepared his libretto from a French translation, or that the ending came at an odd juncture after the 'confession' of Tess that she had once been seduced by Alec, and immediately after the parting of Tess from Clare. In 1909 the opera was further 'Italianized', and Hardy 'scarcely recognized it as his novel'.[47] Though German and Hungarian productions followed, the funeral of Edward VII made play- and opera-going somewhat guilty experiences for many Londoners, and Hardy blamed its timing ('at the beginning of the season') for checking the opera 'at the moment when it might have caught on'. At least so he wrote to Baron d'Erlanger on 10 October 1912.[48]

But Hardy could hardly have been satisfied with a version that ended with Tess drowning herself while Angel cried out her name three times over. As Desmond Hawkins, in his review of the history of this operatic retelling of the novel, commented dryly, the final tableau 'certainly confused the critics', with the reviewer for *The Times* disliking the 'transparency of the girl drowning herself', the *Manchester Guardian* talking of 'a vision of her flinging herself from a cliff into the sea', the *Morning Post* writing about Tess 'in the midst of the mill stream' and *The Daily Telegraph* convinced that the curtain fell upon the quarrel of Tess with Angel Clare upon her wedding day.[49]

The novel *Tess of the d'Urbervilles* was widely admired for its dramatic qualities by professional men and women of the theatre, but Hardy, baffled by the intricacies of commercial production, withdrew his own adaptation from consideration for almost thirty years. Others profited with their versions; Hardy, with some ruefulness, allowed them to do so, and even encouraged those who did not impose unduly upon his energies while he was busy with other projects (*The Dynasts* coming to the fore in the 1890s). There was a brief flurry of excitement on Hardy's part when Mrs Granville-Barker, known on the stage as Lillah McCarthy, expressed warm interest—in June 1910—in playing the role of Tess. Only pressing theatrical engagements prevented her from accepting Hardy's invitation to play his 'Tessy'. Hardy even agreed to some changes, for the sake of improving theatrical effects, suggested by James Barrie, though he personally preferred that she play the tragedy 'exactly as it stands', allowing him to be the scapegoat for its imperfections.[50]

It is, as always, tempting to speculate what a successful engagement of *Tess* in 1910 might have done to Hardy's resolve to write no further fiction and to concentrate exclusively on poetry and an occasional project. Hardy's estimate of novel-writing, as is well known, was low even when he most enjoyed writing as a recognized master of the craft; given full support by the practical men and women of the theatre whom he had always admired, even envied, he might have investigated seriously the financial prospects of a career of play-writing, particularly if Lillah McCarthy's fervent cry—'I love the play entire just as it is, and would not alter a thing, but these expert dramatists are useful people and you know how wonderfully kind Mr Barrie always is'[51]—had turned into the rousing successful London run that Mrs Fiske, some fifteen years earlier, had enjoyed in New York City. But the long run of *Fanny's First Play* upset the timing of Lillah McCarthy's engagements. Granville-Barker's *The Voysey Inheritance* came next, and after that a revival of a play by Shaw . . .. Grandiose schemes, some of which Hardy certainly wished to pursue, petered out.

Hardy could always find writing enterprises and worthy causes to occupy his time. No man kept more faithfully to a writing schedule; and perhaps those long silences at table with Emma enabled Hardy to contemplate at leisure the precise shape and diction of poems he was preparing for publication. But it is pleasant to report that Hardy, for the first time, was ready, during the first decade of this century, to have fun with local theatre; to write several of his own plays for actors and actresses he could advise. He had received several assurances that they would listen to his observations with respect, and even affection; he knew that he could bask in the knowledge that many of his fellow countrymen admired him as a successful local product.

Hardy admired the public readings of Shakespeare, Sheridan and Goldsmith put on by the Dorchester Dramatic and Debating Society. When Alfred H. Evans requested (and secured) permission to use a supper scene in the house of the miller in *The Trumpet-Major* as the basis of an interlude that accompanied a lecture by A.M. Broadley on 'Napoleon's Threatened Invasion of England' (8 February 1908), Hardy was so pleased that he urged Evans to dramatize the entire novel. He enjoyed hugely the adaptation of three scenes from *The Dynasts,* acted by the same players under the title *Ye Merrie Maie Fayre,* only two months later. By November, Hardy outlined, and apparently wrote a substantial fraction of, a dramatic version of *The Trumpet-Major.* It played, to popular acclaim, in the Corn Exchange of Dorchester. The Players—by now known as the 'Hardy Players'—were emboldened to tour, first to Weymouth, and then to London (Cripplegate). Then followed a respectable series of productions, some prepared by Evans; some by A.H. Tilley, an alderman with a highly developed passion for theatrical performances; and some by Hardy himself. He resurrected, of course, *The Three Wayfarers* (November 1911) and prepared his own Wessex Scenes from *The Dynasts* as a patriotic gesture during the Great War (June 1916); he developed (as we have seen) some ideas about theatrical minimalism in an original play, *The Famous Tragedy of the Queen of Cornwall*

(November 1923); and it should not be forgotten that *The Mumming Play of St George*—which Tilley expanded by means of stage business—was basically Hardy's script (November 1923). *O Jan! O Jan! O Jan!*—a slight but curious production of song and dance, designed to accompany *The Queen of Cornwall* on its first production in Dorchester—ran some seventy-two lines and traced the progress of a lover's suit as he offers various gifts, including a silken gown (rejected) and his heart (accepted), while a three-handed reel is in progress. But, most important of all the productions staged by the Hardy Players, after lo! these many years, turned out to be Hardy's script of *Tess of the d'Urbervilles* (November 1924, only a few years before Hardy's death at the venerable age of 88).

Because it summarized many strands that we have been following, this production, more than the versions already staged in New York and London, is of peculiar interest. A letter sent by Florence recorded her husband's stipulations about any performance of the long-moribund script. With scrupulous attention to possible revenues to be derived from future performances, Hardy granted rights for only this production of 1924 and insisted that an announcement of the play had to include the information that the adaptation came from the novel of 1894–5; demanded the right to approve the choice of all actors and actresses, meaning that he could reject those he did not think suitable for given roles ('though this is not likely'); abbreviated a possible long period of publicity build-up by denying Tilley the right to insert notices and stimulate news stories until discussion of *The Queen of Cornwall* opera had died down (since that had been on the boards a full year prior to Florence's letter, the stipulation did not create hardships for Tilley's plans); and—perhaps as important as any other requirement that Hardy insisted on (all of them being, in his mind, 'merely what any author expects')—'No more dialect or local accent than is written in the play is to be introduced by the performers, each part being spoken exactly as set down'.[52] The drift of all these codicils was that Hardy, wiser by far about the free-wheeling ways of theatrical managers than he had been in the 1880s, insisted on retaining the rights of an author, even though costuming, staging and directing were left in the hands of fellow townsmen with whom he had worked for more than a decade.

Moreover, Hardy read through the play to make sure that it was suitable for a dramatic company, and though he had specified in Florence's letter that his identity as author should not be revealed in the press releases, the programme prepared for the play did print his name as the 'onlie begetter'.

Gertrude Bugler played Tess and earned the applause of an enthusiastic audience. The reviewer from *The Times* (who had come down to Dorchester for the event) admired it greatly, and James Barrie thought that the actress should take the play immediately to London. Hardy, in the *Life,* reproduces a note that he made in his diary at the time that he handed over the script to Tilley: 'He had come to the conclusion that to dramatize a novel was a mistake in art; moreover, that the play ruined the novel and the novel the play'.[53] But he could not repress his growing excitement as the pre-performance rehearsals became more polished, and he was increasingly involved with the details of how the players would move on the stage, between props and in relation to each other. He watched intently at rehearsals, but made no comment; yet at an early opportunity wrote to Norman J. Atkins, a young actor playing the role of Alec d'Urberville, suggesting recommendations for voice-inflections of some of his words, and let it be known that he thought Atkins was being too nice to Tess. Atkins wrote, after the passage of fully half a century, how it felt to be the only actor in the cast to be reprimanded by the author of both the play and the novel on which the play was based: 'I felt that, at least, Alec must have had some charm of manner to have attracted Tess, and acted that part accordingly. Mrs Hardy agreed with me and said so. I was not at all happy in this situation'.[54] Tilley had to iron out the differences between Hardy and Atkins, though whether only a few lines were involved or the entire interpretation of Alec's character had to be recast is obscure in Atkins's somewhat rueful recollection of the event.

As on previous occasions, Hardy fell in love with a young and beautiful woman. Gertrude Bugler, both married and a mother, received his attention, flowers and confidences, and roused the jealous suspicions of Florence; Hardy was exposing his wife to the gossip of the Hardy Players, and even of the community. Florence had been through it before, and perhaps the most remarkable aspect of this 'affair' was not the over-familiar pattern of Hardy's courtly behaviour to a female protegée but the advanced age of her husband.

Witnesses to the rehearsal held at Wool Manor (where Tess and Angel went on their honeymoon) were deeply impressed by Gertrude Bugler's sobbing, and none more so than the author, for whom all his novels had faded into the past, with only Tess remaining behind to remind him of his immortal literary creations. The successes of the performances in Dorchester and Weymouth were equally grand, with Colonel T.E. Lawrence, Siegfried Sassoon, E.M. Forster, Augustus John and various distinguished actors and producers in the audience on successive nights. But Hardy—who for a time had attempted to dissuade Gertrude Bugler from taking the play to London for a production to be supervised by Frederick Harrison of the Haymarket Theatre—was not, in the end, responsible for her withdrawing from the London cast. Florence pointed out to her the potentially catastrophic consequences of London newspapers learning of Hardy's infatuation for a woman less than a third his age, and Gertrude Bugler, with considerable grace (and disappointment), notified Hardy that obligations to her husband and child made inadvisable her participating in the new production. Hardy, ignorant of Florence's intervention, conceded that she was probably correct in her instincts that being a wife and mother were more important than succeeding in London.

Of the London production with Gwen Ffrangcon-Davies that followed, and that ran for more than one hundred nights, there is little to say here, because Hardy, once again diffident about his ability to master the intricacies of theatrical contracts, yielded to the brisk, no-nonsense revisions (apparently none of them major) made by Philip Ridgeway, a manager at the Barnes Theatre, who after two months managed to have the play transferred to the West End's Garrick Theatre. Hardy by this time was too frail to make the trip to London, but one of the more memorable events of his final years took place on 6 December 1925, when the London cast came to Max Gate for a special performance of *Tess*, in the drawing-room. One of the company recalled the occasion, in a note that Hardy complacently reproduced in his *Life:*

It had seemed that as if it would be a paralysingly difficult thing to do, to get the atmosphere at all within a few feet of the author himself and without any of the usual theatrical illusion, but speaking for myself, after the first few seconds it was perfectly easy, and Miss Ffrangcon-Davies's beautiful voice and exquisite playing of the Stonehenge scene in the shadows thrown by the firelight was a thing that I shall never forget. It was beautiful. Mr Hardy insisted on talking to us until the last minute. He talked of Tess as if she was someone real whom he had known and liked tremendously.[55]

Hardy had doubtless approved the selection of Miss Ffrangcon-Davies, just as he had been asked for approval of Ion Swinley, Ridgeway's choice for the part of Angel Clare. She had amassed impressive credits by 1924 in various singing and dramatic roles (Shakespeare, Barrie, Ibsen, Shaw); but she needed some assistance in interpreting the role of Tess, and this Hardy supplied, to the extent requested, as generously (but with fewer unhappy repercussions on Florence's mental state) as he had with Gertrude Bugler. Perhaps, as James Agate wrote gloomily, Miss Ffrangcon-Davies lacked sufficient physical presence, and her personality did not rouse an audience to the same degree of enthusiasm that Mrs Fiske in New York or Gertrude Bugler in Dorchester had been able to do. At any rate, Hardy had nothing to do with the revival of his version of the *Tess* script, with Christine Silver at the King's Theatre, Hammersmith, which enjoyed a moderate success beginning in March 1926. Nor could he have foreseen the chilliness to be given by London audiences to Gertrude Bugler's long-delayed appearance as Tess in 1929, a full eighteen months after his death. She seemed too much the country girl, too innocent of the stratagems of acting, to exhibit the heightened colour demanded by playgoers interested more in the appearance of a Tess than in the genuineness of a Dorset girl who, by some mischance, walked the boards of the Duke of York's Theatre.

I have chronicled a history of events in Hardy's life that suggests the existence of a deep, even passionate interest in theatre. Hardy was not a gifted playwright; his talents lay elsewhere; and he consistently mistimed, mishandled or misinterpreted opportunities to do more with the scripts that he undertook to prepare. But he loved the great plays of Greek dramatists and of Shakespeare, and his thinking was affected deeply by their humanistic teachings. He was a connoisseur of acting. One would give a good deal to see him as he was in the few performances that he actually gave, because he had high ideals, doubtless measuring everything he saw and did against the performances of Charles Kean and J.B. Buckstone. He was a devoted playgoer for years, and the highlight of many London trips was a visit to the theatre; he enjoyed greatly the company of women, and he often formed part of a glittering social company. As he aged, he became increasingly disenchanted with plays that all too predictably sacrificed the art of dialogue for tinselly effects, and yearned for the innocence and sincerity of mumming plays that he had seen while still a child and that he believed (inaccurately) were no longer performed in England. On the basis of these nostalgic memories, he developed a theory of the kind of play that would respect the intelligence of adults, and wrote *The Queen of Cornwall*, in large part, to demonstrate the viability of his theory. In all the possibilities for a name for the new genre that *The Dynasts* created, the word 'drama' remains a constant; his longest, most ambitious and (still) most consistently underestimated poem was written as a play. And if his relations to the Hardy Players of Dorchester finally dwindled into weariness (he wished to see no more plays based on his stories after late November 1924), we should not minimize the warmth of the affection shown by Hardy towards a group of dedicated amateurs, and reciprocated by them, or the extent of his encouragement for their idealistic efforts to win him new audiences. He loved almost *everything* that moved across a stage.

3

Literary Friendships

We are all indebted to Richard L. Purdy and Michael Millgate for their meticulous editing of the *Collected Letters of Thomas Hardy*. It is a model of scholarship, and in a great tradition of edited manuscript material; its value to scholars and critics in the decades ahead can only be guessed at, but it has already clarified a number of obscure points, and the annotations shed light on a surprisingly large number of late Victorian figures and events.

Yet, in the Introduction to Volume I, Purdy and Millgate record a surprisingly harsh judgement: 'Few, indeed, of Hardy's friendships stood the long test of time'. That judgement was based largely on whatever correspondence between Hardy and other men and women still survives, that is on the letters that the editors have managed to assemble in several years of dedicated detective work. But not all the letters—important or unimportant—have survived. Friendships are not best measured in terms of the spoor left by correspondence. Hardy's letters are, for the most part, terse, concerned with business and dry. Moreover, as William James once wrote, most men's friendships are too inarticulate.

The tests for any definition of friendship are well known; indeed, self-evident. They include frequency of contact, length of duration, sympathy and harmoniousness of outlook and our own commonsense view of what makes one human being a friend of another. Hugo von Hofmannsthal once noted that we have fewer friends than we imagine, but more than we know. It may be that Hardy would not have bothered to react indignantly to the charge that his friendships crumbled as he aged, or to the implication that he allowed them to do so. But it is curious that Hardy's contemporaries, many of whom detested what they conceived to be his 'pessimism', and some of whom resented his success, never claimed that a hallmark of his personal life was the repudiation or neglect of friendships. Indeed, the accusation, despite the fact that it is made in the same post-war years that have seen the publication of revisionist Hardy materials, does not stand up under examination.

I will here deal with an aspect of Hardy's life that has not been treated at length before, although elements in it will be familiar to readers who have been following recent developments in Hardy scholarship. This chapter reviews Hardy's relationships with six writers whom he admired and whose friendships he cultivated and, perhaps equally as important, *kept*. It will go beyond the usual commonplaces about a tentative beginning and a successful, even complacent, career during which one commercial success followed another. Hardy's career is much like that of Dickens and Thackeray in this regard: he struggled for recognition, his peers finally accepted him, he enjoyed decades of success, and in his final years he dispensed wisdom to younger writers knocking at the door.

Nevertheless, even though Hardy's career falls into this pattern, his case, for more than one reason, is rather special. First, he grew to manhood in a relatively isolated and remote market town, and made a correspondingly delayed entrance on the literary scene. He had just turned 28 when he submitted his first novel to a publisher (it was swiftly rejected). His first *published* novel appeared three years later. He was over thirty by then. Hardy knew a great deal about literature and the standards whereby literature might be judged, of course, long before he took up his serio-comic relationship with William Tinsley; but much of what he knew he acquired from a steady diet of reading rather than from a series of personal encounters with literary types: novelists, poets, critics and reviewers, as well as publishers.

We should not underestimate the singular advantages of this delayed blooming to Hardy's professional development as a writer. Away from the turmoil of London, he found ample opportunity to develop a style that, in important measure, was unaffected by transient fashions. He could think more clearly about the kinds of subject-matter that were worth treating; not until the very end of his third decade did he have to worry about Mudie's and W. H. Smith, and the question first posed in Thomas Morton's comedy, *Speed the Plough* (1798), 'What will Mrs Grundy say?' He benefited from the unhurried pace of Dorset life, from the delay in becoming involved with the getting and spending that, as Wordsworth wrote, 'lay waste our powers'.

My allusion to Dorset's 'unhurried pace' would not have been regarded as derogatory by Hardy, who began his obituary of the Reverend William Barnes, B.D., for the *Athenaeum* of 16 October 1886, with a nostalgic appreciation of 'the remoteness, even from contemporary provincial civilization, of the pastoral recesses in which his earlier years were passed—places with whose now obsolete customs and beliefs his mind was naturally imbued'. Indeed, the Reverend William Barnes was the first genuine philologist, poet and writer encountered by Thomas Hardy, and it is worth a moment to evaluate the meaning of the fact that Hardy wrote only one book review for publication in his entire life, a review of Barnes's *Poems of Rural Life in the Dorset Dialect*. What made Barnes so admirable in his eyes? Barnes's moral integrity, for one thing; his majesty of presence; his readings of his own works in the townhalls of the shire; his sense of humour, which made 'droll' performances of such pieces as 'The Shy Man', 'A Bit o' Sly Coorten' and 'Dick and I'. Since much of Hardy's writing is autobiographical at unexpected moments, it is not fanciful to read into the following quotation an explanation of why Hardy, a lionized literary figure by the 1880s, chose finally, as the building-site for Max Gate, a location no more than four miles from his own birthplace:

> To those who knew Mr Barnes in his prime it may have been a matter for conjecture why a man of his energies should not at some point or other of his career have branched off from the quiet byways of his early manhood into the turmoils of the outer world, particularly as his tastes at that time were somewhat general, and the direction of his labours was dictated in the main by his opportunities. The explanation seems to be that the poetic side of his nature, though not always dominant, was but faintly ruled by the practical at any time, that his place-attachment was strong almost to a fault, and that his cosmopolitan interests, though lively, were always subordinate to those local hobbies and solicitudes whence came alike his special powers and his limitations.

One concern, in discussing these personal relationships, must always be what Hardy gained from them. It is clear that Barnes was personally attractive to Hardy, who speaks of his own 'warm affection' for the Dorset figure who lived to the age of 86. It is also clear that Barnes's pioneer research in establishing the antecedents of the Dorset dialect, in dignifying it as 'a distinct branch of Teutonic speech, regular in declension and conjugation, and richer in many classes of words than any other tongue known to him', served Hardy as a justification for his liberal use of native expressions in his early novels, for the Christmas Eve scene in the tranter's house which so impressed John Morley when he read the manuscript of *The Poor Man and the Lady* for Macmillan, and comparable scenes in both *Desperate Remedies* and *Under the Greenwood Tree*. The reviewers who noted resemblances between Hardy's style and that of George Eliot, and who stressed Hardy's reference to 'A Rural Painting of the Dutch School' on the title-page of *Under the Greenwood Tree*, had ample justification for doing so. Hardy praised Barnes for giving us 'whole poems of still life, unaffected and realistic as a Dutch picture'.

Hardy had strong views on the use of dialect in novels and wrote vigorous letters to both the *Athenaeum* and *The Spectator* to protest the attempt of anonymous reviewers to circumscribe the author's privilege of reproducing, as faithfully as possible, the native dialect of his speakers. From Barnes, undoubtedly more than from any of his lettered contemporaries, Hardy borrowed a view of the inherent dignity and value of a dialect that had been 'worsted in the struggle for existence' by standard English. But Hardy, more than Barnes, recognized the limitations that literal transcription placed on the potential size of his audience. He did not want to insist unduly upon the grotesque element, and thus to divert attention away from human nature and the meaning of a speaker. He resented being told that he had created a series of 'linguistic puzzles' when he had, in fact, freely translated dialect-English into readable English (as George Eliot had done) and when he had retained only those words which had no synonym among those in general use. He regretted having to compromise but recognized the necessity for doing so. By the late 1870s he had diverged sufficiently from Barnes's practice to admit that he had no right to 'encumber the page with obsolete pronunciations of the purely English words, and with mispronunciations of those derived from Latin and Greek.'[1].

The young men with whom Hardy associated as he grew to manhood, and with whom he served his apprenticeship in John Hicks's offices in South Street, Dorchester, achieved success in their respective professions. But only one of them was, or sought to be, a professional author. The next writer with whom he associated, and for whom he always cherished a very high regard, was a man eight years older than himself, of greater promise than achievement for the entire course of his tragically abbreviated life. Horace Moule, who was to die in 1873, exerted a powerful, and largely beneficial, influence upon the fateful moments when Thomas Hardy wavered between alternative careers: he dissuaded Hardy, on the first occasion, from abandoning architecture in favour of classical studies, and on the second from renouncing novel-writing after the hostile *Spectator* review of *Desperate Remedies*. The advice Horace Moule gave to Hardy—on matters ranging from the theological implications of Darwin and of 'the Seven against Christ' who wrote *Essays and Reviews* (1860), and of Newman's *Apologia* (1865), to the proper use of 'if' with the subjunctive—was earnest in a becoming Victorian fashion; moreover, his counsel was much appreciated. Moule was sensitive to—and sensible about—the qualities of serious literature. He reviewed *Under the Greenwood Tree* for *The Spectator*, and was probably responsible for the highly favourable critique of *Desperate Remedies* in the *Saturday Review* that sought to redress the balance for the scathing earlier review in *The Spectator* that had come so close to ending Hardy's career as a novelist. Hardy read whatever his friend wrote in periodicals; Horace Moule's reviews and leaders helped to shape Hardy's sense of the importance of subject-matter, an importance which transcended even that of 'writing well'. Hardy's interest in contemporary world affairs—a matter still under estimated by some biographers—was manifested by his close attention to the articles written by Horace Moule on the Franco-Prussian War. A note in the *Life* refers to Horace as 'a scholar and critic of perfect taste'. In 1922 Hardy wrote to the *London Mercury* that a poem 'Ave Caesar', by Horace Moule, deserved to be printed 'in any new edition of the *Oxford Book of English Verse*'.

Time has not been kind to the literary accomplishments of Horace Moule. His journalistic essays, commenting as they did on passing commercial and historical events, have not retained a readership. 'Ave Caesar' is a graceful treatment, in six stanzas, of Gérôme's painting of the interior of the Coliseum, as exhibited at the International Exhibition of 1862; but it is not memorable, and not finely enough wrought to deserve Hardy's high tribute. What

Hardy admired in Moule's writings, therefore, may be open to varying interpretations. Like Moule, Hardy believed that William Barnes, 'behind his word-screen', had much in common with the great poets of ages past. Like Moule, he believed in the eternality of the magnificence of Greek dramatists, philosophers and poets, and in later years was to christen *The Dynasts*, after protracted reflection on possible alternative titles, an 'epic-drama'. From Moule he acquired an interest in both Auguste Comte—a copy of Comte's *A General View of Positivism* (1965), co-signed by Hardy and Moule, is today in the Purdy collection—and John Henry Newman. Hardy's interest in Newman remained a rather equivocal one, consisting—in Lennart Björk's words—of 'aesthetic approval and ideological rejection'.[2] Leslie Stephen, pleased with the literary quality of *Under the Greenwood Tree* but baffled by the fact that it had been published anonymously, turned to Moule for information on the author's identity. The result of his learning Hardy's name led directly to his extending an invitation to Hardy to submit a novel-manuscript to the *Cornhill Magazine* for serialization; and that, in turn, led to the writing of *Far from the Madding Crowd* and to Hardy's decision that he could, after all, exchange the life of an architect for that of a full-time, professional novelist. The service rendered by Moule to Hardy at this point in his career was crucial.

Still another example of a long-lasting literary friendship: Hardy, musing about his relationship with George Meredith on the occasion of the centenary of Meredith's birth—in an essay solicited by *Nineteenth Century and After* that was to be published (February 1928) after his own death—made much of the difficulties that Meredith's works, and in particular *Modern Love*, had encountered with the reviewers; but it is fair to say that Meredith was indeed the first nationally recognized creative writer Hardy encountered as he began the writing of his own fiction. Hardy's introduction to Meredith was, all things considered, not auspicious. John Morley had turned down *The Poor Man and the Lady* as deficient in form and composition, and Alexander Macmillan, passing on the views of his reader, had added his own observation, that Hardy's depiction of Londoners, and especially the upper classes, was 'wholly dark—not a ray of light visible to relieve the darkness, and therefore exaggerated and untrue in their result'.[3] Perhaps Macmillan's avuncular judgement had been, to some extent, provoked by Hardy's brash letter of transmittal, in which yeasty generalizations about the reading tastes of the upper classes of society and the importance of 'the passion of love' in a modern novel were passed on for the benefit of all publishers and readers who might deal with the manuscript. In March 1869 Macmillan, at any rate, turned Hardy over to Chapman and Hall, whose reader was George Meredith. Called in for an interview with the gentleman who had read his manuscript, Hardy, entering a back office, did not learn Meredith's name until after the interview had been concluded; but he immediately sensed that Meredith was 'an unusual sort of man', and he listened with respect to a lecture about which, much later, in the fateful year of 1895, in fact, he was to say he had never heard 'so much good criticism packed into so little space'.

Hardy has described in two places the content of that interview, but both accounts agree on the paternal tone which Meredith, then forty-one years of age, adopted towards Hardy, who had just turned twenty-nine. (Hardy was always to think of Meredith as an Ancient; he began his commemorative essay for *Nineteenth Century and After* with the observation that Meredith had lived for four years as a juvenile contemporary of Sir Walter Scott, 'for six years as a contemporary of Lamb and Coleridge, for fifteen years of Southey, and for twenty-two years of Wordsworth, and . . . *The Ordeal of Richard Feverel* was finished before Darwin settled the question of the Origin of Species'.[4] Meredith advised Hardy not to nail his colours to the mast 'just yet'. Certainly not in a first book, 'if he wished to do anything practical in literature; for if he printed so pronounced a thing he would be attacked on all sides by the conventional reviewers, and his future injured . . . the tendency of the writing being socialistic, not to say revolutionary'.[5] Meredith's lecture—delivered in a sonorous voice—was not resented. Hardy, who had been close to a contract with Chapman & Hall (at one point they had even offered to print the book if he would put up £20 of his own money), took away the manuscript and thought about Meredith's advice. Though he tried at least twice more to market *The Poor Man and the Lady*, he finally accepted Meredith's judgement, and used small sections of the novel for later fictions.

The years passed; the two men did not meet again for at least a decade. Hardy, like many others in Meredith's expanding audience, appreciated the older man's style as ' ''chaos illuminated by flashes of lightning'', full of epigrams of thought and beauty';[6] but he did not follow the direction which Meredith, of necessity, and as a protective mechanism, had marked out for himself. Hardy never again neglected the common reader by elliptically, and even obscurely, stating his opinions, and his own plots were never excessively or deliberately opaque. He preferred to be understood, and it is one of the ironies of his work in the 1880s and 1890s that his plain speaking led to facile assumptions that his characters spoke directly for himself. Hardy always admired Meredith's perception of the close relationship between comedy and tragedy. He cited Meredith's *The Comic Spirit* as proof of Ruskin's remark, 'Comedy is Tragedy if you only look deep enough'. He believed that he was, to some extent, writing (in *Desperate Remedies*) the kind of new fiction that Meredith would have approved of, but he also wanted the manuscript to be judged on its own merits. In later years Hardy was to think back regretfully on his failure to cultivate Meredith as a guide to his own artistic development ('it was a mistake'). Meeting Meredith at intermittent intervals, Hardy grew very fond of the older man's dignity and cherished his friendship; more than once he recorded his impression of what he had written as something that would or would not have pleased George Meredith; and at a time when appreciation of *The Dynasts* was still mixed, he was cheered to receive from Meredith a generous tribute to its ambitious scale. Following Meredith's death, he was invited to succeed his mentor as president of the Society of Authors; after momentary hesitation—he knew that he lived too far from London to take as active a part in its affairs as he thought necessary for the good health of the Society—he accepted the honour.

Meredith, as he wrote to J. B. Priestley (8 August 1927), was 'in the direct succession of Congreve and the artificial comedians of the Restoration,' and there is no doubt that Hardy held reservation about the hardness of the 'brilliancy' of Meredith's style. He even noted (14 May 1915) that Henry James—who had 'no grain of poetry, or humour, or spontaneity in his productions'—remained readable even when Meredith's poetry palled on him. This is even more surprising when one remembers the generally negative tenor of Hardy's remarks on James, who wrote a kind of fiction, and who concentrated on the kind of minutiae that were, by and large, alien to Hardy's concept of story-telling. Moreover, Hardy had reason to dislike James as a person; he was fully aware of the exchange of letters between Robert Louis Stevenson and Henry James, in which James, commenting on the recent publication of *Tess of the d'Urbervilles*, sighed patronizingly, 'Oh yes, dear Louis: [it] is vile.' But Hardy's affection for Meredith was directed more towards his human sympathies, his benevolence towards younger writers, his cheerfulness, enthusiasm and warmth of manner, than towards his writings. Once Hardy declared that if it had not been for Meredith's encouragement he 'would probably not have adopted the literary career', but the occasion was a convivial evening at the Omar Khayyam Club, and some hyperbole is forgivable on such occasions.[7] The medallion-portrait of Meredith that Hardy hung above the mantel in his study may still be seen in the reconstructed study of the Dorset County Museum. And, finally, it is pleasant to record that Meredith, in his twilight years, appreciated Hardy's thoughtfulness in coming to see him frequently at Box Hill, Surrey, as well as in London, and liked Hardy as a person, not merely as a protégé who had made good. Hardy's memorial line, contained in the poem 'George Meredith (1828–1909)' that he wrote at the Athenaeum immediately after seeing the poster announcement of Meredith's death, may serve as coda to this relationship: 'His note was trenchant, turning kind.'

It would be misleading to suggest that Hardy during the years of his young manhood, right up to the age of 35, had many relationships such as those he enjoyed with the Reverend William Barnes, Horace Moule and George Meredith. Moreover, Mr Barnes was always a somewhat remote figure, being a full forty years older than Hardy and Meredith's friendship did not truly blossom until the 1880s. The point has already been made that Hardy did not belong to a literary school and did not rely on personal guidance from writers or editors to find his way (they gave him wildly contradictory advice anyway; at the beginning, John Morley, Alexander Macmillan and George Meredith had different prescriptions for commercial success, and Hardy was understandably confused as to how he should proceed). In the early 1920s, when Robert Graves, his wife and T. E. Lawrence visited Max Gate, Hardy declared that at a very early stage in his career he had found it useless to pay attention to professional critics. '[Hardy] talked of early literary influences, and said that he had none at all, for he did not come of literary stock.'[8] And even if Hardy corrected himself by recalling his fellow apprentice in John

Hicks's office who loaned him books, his overall denial of literary influence—if we understand that influence to have been exerted by personal social contact—is confirmed by the record.

In his middle years, when he lived in or commuted frequently to London and joined a number of clubs such as the Savile (in 1878), the Athenaeum (in 1891) and the Rabelais (the founding of which was intended to serve as 'a declaration for virility in literature'), Hardy associated with a great many writers, as well as actors, painters and scientists. The list of such names is long and impressive: Browning, Tennyson and Arnold, James Russell Lowell, Kipling, Gerard Manley Hopkins, Mrs Humphry Ward, Lionel Johnson, George Gissing, William Dean Howells, Max Beerbohm, H. G. Wells, Harley Granville-Barker, Walter de la Mare, John Galsworthy, Sydney Cockerell, Arnold Bennett, George Bernard Shaw, 'Anthony Hope', Hugh Walpole, J. M. Barrie and John Masefield. About many of these relationships little can be learned, regrettably, partly because of the two massive bonfires at Max Gate, the first in 1919, when Hardy personally fed a mass of letters and miscellaneous papers to the flames, and the second in January 1928, shortly after Hardy's death, when Bertie Norman Stephens, the Max Gate gardener, helped Florence Emily Hardy set a fire that consumed 'baskets full of . . . letters and private papers . . . after all the papers had been destroyed, she raked the ashes to be sure that not a single scrap or word remained'.[9] We know from what remains behind—from the 5,041 letters to and from Hardy surviving at the Dorset County Museum, and the numerous other letters that Richard Purdy and Michael Millgate are editing—that the extent and quality of these personal relationships are not easily measurable.

Even so, the middle period of Hardy's life is separable, so far as literary friendships go, from a final period, in which Hardy, the patriarch who had survived most of his Victorian acquaintances, seemed increasingly to represent to younger writers the best of an era that had permanently passed, and in which the mere fact of his longevity became fully as marvellous as his literary creations. There are three writers with whom he associated in more than casual manner, and to whom he spoke about matters of deep concern to his own philosophy: Algernon Charles Swinburne, Sir Leslie Stephen and Edmund Gosse.

We need fuller information about Hardy's childhood, a more

definite record of the relationship to Tryphena, and some means of reconciling our impression of Hardy the recluse with the abundant evidence that he enjoyed dining out, particularly in the company of the wealthy and the noble. But what most needs to be learned about Hardy's life may lie in the period of five years spent in London—from 1862 to 1867—when Hardy played at being the man about town, entered into the wider world that he had only read about, and first entertained the thought of becoming an author. We have very little correspondence from that period. Perhaps the needed data are permanently beyond recall. At any rate, one thing that we do know is that Swinburne's *Atalanta in Calydon* and the first volume of *Poems and Ballads* came out in 1865 and 1866 respectively, evoked angry critical responses, but found at least one admirer who never recanted his high praise: Thomas Hardy. The Dorset architect, at the time in the employ of Arthur Blomfield, walked many mornings from his lodgings near Hyde Park to the draughting office with a copy of *Poems and Ballads* sticking out of his pocket. At some risk to his person he said, many years later, that he was almost knocked down by pedestrians and vehicles—he read Swinburne while walking along the Strand.

A list of Hardy's uses of quotations and tags from Swinburne's writings is impressive. Hardy turned to Swinburne's poetry as inspiration, and for directly transcribed lines, in *Tess, Jude, The Queen of Cornwall* and a number of poems about Lyonnesse. He appropriated Swinburne's phrase 'the coil of things' in *The Triumph of Time* and adapted it to his own purposes in both *The Return of the Native* and *The Dynasts*; he even quoted it directly when sending Swinburne a copy of *The Woodlanders* as a token of homage (May 1887).[10] Though he never became as angry as Swinburne at the God who had condemned man to a hopeless struggle with his destiny, and hence must not be characterized as determined to confront belligerently the commonplaces of Victorian religion, Hardy seems to have undergone a religious crisis during his London years, when he was reading Mill and Huxley in addition to Swinburne. The agnostic resolution of that crisis resembled in several significant respects the anguished arguments of Swinburne's 'Anactoria', 'Dolores', *Atalanta in Calydon* and the 'Hymn to Proserpine'. And Hardy, years later, was to discover he had even more in common with Swinburne than a shared dismay at the workings of an inscrutable Providence. He, like Swinburne, was roughly treated by the panjandrums of Victorian criticism.

Hardy and Swinburne met shortly after 1887, corresponded frequently (Hardy sent him presentation copies of all his newest publications) and liked each other's company. Swinburne, in fact, had been much on Hardy's mind for many years before they met. Hardy delighted in knowing that Swinburne visited No. 8 Adelphi Terrace, or had dined in the same restaurant as he, or enjoyed swimming as much as he did, long before they met to exchange opinions on the shockingly low condition of English reviewing; they two were (so Hardy liked to think) the two most vilified authors of the Victorian Age. On the occasion of a visit in June 1904, Swinburne quoted, with amusement, a paragraph in a Scottish newspaper: 'Swinburne planteth, Hardy watereth, and Satan giveth the increase.' Swinburne may have preferred pastorals like the 'English paradise' depicted in *Under the Greenwood Tree* to Hardy's later more contemporary and realistic novels; but he admitted Hardy's right to a bent for tragedy and, as he wrote to Hardy after the publication of *Jude*, thought that Hardy had written the best tragedy in fiction since the death of Balzac. Hardy generously ascribed to Swinburne full credit for any 'faint claim to imaginative feeling' that *The Well-Beloved* might possess 'in its better parts', and yielded the palm to Swinburne for having translated, with grace and precision, a Sappho fragment that he himself had been trying to imitate. He quoted Swinburne's phrase, 'Thee, too, the years shall cover' as 'the finest *drama* of Death and Oblivion, so to speak, in our tongue'.[11]

Hardy's appreciation of Swinburne was not wholly uncritical, despite these exchanges of pretty compliments. Nevertheless, Swinburne was very close to his own age, being only three years older; they shared interests in classical poetry and Shakespeare and the Romantics; they enjoyed literary anecdotes and the pleasures of reminiscence. 'I was so late in getting my poetical barge under way, and he was so early with his flotilla', Hardy wrote in a letter two days after Swinburne's death; but the main burden of his meditation was that Burns and Shelley, like Swinburne, had suffered from the slings and arrows of contemporary reviews, and perhaps (Hardy's tone was somewhat dry) 'we are getting on in our appreciativeness of poets. . . . Swinburne has been tolerated—at any rate since he has not written anything to speak of'.[12] Prevented by rheumatism from attending Swinburne's funeral, Hardy visited the graveside at Bonchurch, on the Isle of Wight, a year later, in March 1910, and shortly thereafter wrote 'A Singer Asleep', commemorating his 'admiration and affection' for a fellow poet, one who had outlived 'the brabble and the roar' occasioned by the publication of *Poems and Ballads*, and whose poetry had proved him to be a 'disciple true and warm' of Sappho,

> the music-mother
> Of all the tribe that feel in melodies.

The second writer-friend of this middle period, Sir Leslie Stephen, has been receiving a great deal of attention during the past few years, partly because of his relationship with Virginia Woolf (the troubled father – daughter relationship is at the heart of more than one of her books), partly because of his Herculean efforts in directing and writing much of the contents of the *Dictionary of National Biography*. He is an important presence in Hardy's life, and not merely because his appreciation of *Under the Greenwood Tree* led him to invite Hardy to write for the *Cornhill Magazine* (both *Far from the Madding Crowd* and *The Hand of Ethelberta* appeared in that publication). Stephen asked Helen Paterson to provide illustrations for *Far from the Madding Crowd*, and Hardy's twinge of regret at her subsequent marriage to William Allingham was surely a direct outcome of the introduction of the aspiring novelist to the 'skilful illustrator' that Stephen provided in 1874. Speaking of his own marriage to Emma, which took place at the same time as Helen Paterson's, Hardy wrote that 'those two almost simultaneous weddings would have been one but for a stupid blunder of God Almighty'. (An odd observation: what is one to make of it?) Stephen was to reject *The Trumpet-Major* on the curious grounds that the introduction of George III into the fiction was bound to be a mistake: 'I think that a historical character in a novel is almost always a nuisance'.[13] Stephen's dismay at Hardy's historical romance was related to his belief that *The Hand of Ethelberta* was inferior to *Far from the Madding Crowd*, and to his unease at the evidence that Hardy's literary progress was creating problems for both himself and for the readers of the *Cornhill*. Hardy, summarizing his friend's long life in *Later Years*, was to say that Stephen's philosophy influenced 'his own for many years, indeed, more than that of any other contemporary'. If for the moment we postpone a review of the religious discussions between

Hardy and Stephen, we can see that Hardy benefited from the coolly pragmatic advice—relating to the concoction of commercially acceptable fiction—that Stephen provided over a period of many years. 'Though I do not want a murder in every number'—he wrote to Hardy at the very beginning of their relationship—'it is necessary to catch the attention of readers by some distinct and well-arranged plot'. When *Far from the Madding Crowd* approached the scene of Fanny Robin's seduction, Stephen, somewhat apologetic because of an 'excessive prudery' of which he was 'ashamed', urged Hardy to be 'gingerly' in his treatment. Stephen had already received complaints from 'three respectable ladies and subscribers' about an 'improper passage' in an instalment recently published, and he did not wish to incur additional displeasure. Though Hardy restored to the book what he had omitted, at Stephen's request, from the serialized version, and cited—in a conversation with Stephen—as support of his own judgement an approving comment in *The Times* on 'the very passage that had offended', the fact remains that Stephen gave Hardy more lucid, usable advice than any other editor in his entire career. In the words of Richard Purdy, 'No other novel of Hardy's had the benefit of such constant and discriminating criticism as Stephen's, though Hardy confessed at the time to no higher aim than "to be considered a good hand at a serial" '.[14]

Stephen, roughly Moule's age, swiftly became Moule's replacement, as adviser and confidant. The relationship soon developed into something more than a series of strictures on what an aspiring young novelist could and should do in order to gain wide acceptance, as in his perceptive warning, based upon a reading of the opening pages of *Return of the Native*, that Eustacia, Wildeve and Thomasin might develop into something too 'dangerous' for a family magazine. Within a year and a half after their first meeting, Stephen was to ask Hardy to call on him in his rooms, to witness his signature to a deed that renounced Holy Orders. Hardy's description of the scene—recorded in F. W. Maitland's *Life and Letters of Leslie Stephen* (1906)—continues: Stephen

said grimly that he was really a reverend gentleman still, little as he might look it, and that he thought it was as well to cut himself adrift of a calling for which, to say the least, he had always been utterly unfit. The deed was executed with due formality. Our conversation then turned upon theologies decayed and defunct, the origin of things, the constitution of matter, the unreality of time and kindred subjects. He told me that he had 'wasted' much time on systems of religion and metaphysics, and that the new theory of vortex rings had 'a staggering fascination' for him.[15]

This personal friendship deepened as Hardy perceived that Stephen was completely sincere in his repeated depreciation of the importance of critics, particularly to Hardy, who wrote in 'a perfectly fresh and original vein.' ('We [critics] are generally a poor lot, horribly afraid of not being in the fashion, and disposed to give ourselves airs on very small grounds', Stephen had written to him on 16 May 1876.) Stephen did not disturb Hardy with political issues; both men were, in one sense, 'quite outside politics'. Close to the end of Stephen's life, on 11 May 1901, Hardy quoted with approbation Stephen's remark about the impossibility of writing 'living poetry on the ancient model'. What Stephen had written ('The gods and heroes are too dead . . .'), Hardy recast in his famous passage for the Preface to *The Dynasts*, Part First, about the impossibility of relying on 'the importation of Divine personages from any antique Mythology as ready-made sources of channels in Causation, even in verse,' and one can guess that Hardy, though he did not choose to join the Rationalist Press Association to which Stephen belonged, subscribed to many of the same rationalist premises that Stephen did.

The fullest treatment of the similarities and differences between Thomas Hardy and Leslie Stephen may be found in Evelyn Hardy's biography of Thomas Hardy (1954); it contains an interesting treatment of the years of regular visitation, friendship and respect that lay behind Hardy's melancholy sigh, contained in a letter to Edward Clodd written on 22 March 1904, that Leslie Stephen, like George Meredith, was 'gone too'. If Stephen, unlike Hardy, responded with exhilaration to the discovery that his Christianity was giving way to an agnostic condition, perhaps Hardy marvelled at Stephen's willingness to do combat with a recalcitrant universe. Yet ultimately Hardy and Stephen agreed most closely on an issue that may seem strange to surivors of the declining years of this century: the importance of the *moral* quality of an artist's life. Stephen measured the worth of a book by the worth of the man whom it revealed to him. Hardy wanted the artist who guided him to have seen 'further into life than he himself has seen', and again and again he insisted on 'the author's idiosyncratic mode of regard'. Stephen, as we have seen, was crucial to Hardy's developing career as a novelist; but Stephen's views on religion and philosophy impressed Hardy as containing the good sense that his own convictions required if they were to be discussed at all.

Edmund Gosse had the melancholy privilege of serving as one of the pall-bearers at Hardy's burial in the Abbey, along with Sir James Barrie, John Galsworthy, A. E. Housman, Rudyard Kipling, George Bernard Shaw and the prime minister, Stanley Baldwin. He was by far the closest friend of all of these, and talked freely about books and literary matters with Hardy for almost fifty years, even at a time when Emma's conversation actively discouraged most visitors from exploring Hardy's current interests, which Emma regarded as speculatively dangerous. Carl Weber, who hoped that correspondence between Gosse and Hardy, privately owned in America, might some day be published, commented wistfully in 1968 that these letters would likely turn out to be 'most interesting and most rewarding, for Hardy wrote to Gosse with a freedom and an uninhibitedness that do not characterize his other letters'.[16]

Yet Gosse's reviews of Hardy's work, despite their graceful style and generally sympathetic tone, must occasionally have seemed more than a little obtuse to Hardy, who was perhaps preternaturally sensitive to adverse comment. There was the classic formulation of Gosse in *Cosmopolis: An International Review* of January 1896, on the occasion of the appearance of *Jude the Obscure* in book form: 'What has Providence done to Mr Hardy that he should rise up in the arable land of Wessex and shake his fist at his Creator?' Hardy, Gosse claimed, had arranged his new plot with too rigid a mind; the characters were studies in pathology (Gosse claimed that the neuropath had taken away the poet's pen); and anyhow, Hardy had made a mistake in leaving South Wessex for North. 'We wish', Gosse complained, 'he would go back to Egdon Heath and listen to the singing in the heather.' Hardy must have smarted at Gosse's argument that the heads of houses to whom Jude wrote his 'crudely pathetic letters' were not obligated to offer immediately a fellowship to Jude (Hardy seemed to imply that they were so obligated). Later—after the publication of the twelve 'Satires of Circumstance' in the *Fortnightly Review* of April 1911—Gosse was to contradict directly Hardy's effort to disassociate himself from the point of view expressed in the Satires. 'The wells of human hope have been poisoned for him', wrote Gosse, 'by some condition of which we know nothing.' The point is not that Gosse knew in rich detail what had poisoned those wells, and the reasons why Hardy's marriage to Emma ultimately failed as a human relationship; but rather that Gosse made it more difficult to sustain Hardy's claim that his poetry was dramatic and personative.[17] Though Hardy did not get into open debate with Gosse about these critical opinions, which he could hardly have welcomed, he did take advantage of at least one opportunity to record, privately, his own view. In his *Notebook* on 1 April 1924, he approved the way in which *The Times* had endorsed John Middleton Murry's attack on 'that ludicrous blackguard George Moore's book called *Conversations in Ebury Street*', in which, as Hardy noted, he had been 'libelled wholesale'. (He had not yet seen the book.) Hardy added, '(N.B. Mr G. M.'s disciples, to whom these things are related, are E. Gosse, John Freeman, Tonks, Granville Barker, W. de la Mare, and Cunninghame Graham, etc)'.[18] The notation seethes with an astonishing passion; Hardy believed that he had been ill-used, at one time or another, by all these individuals.

Nevertheless, it would be misleading to suggest that Gosse was able to see merit only in the *Greenwood Tree* phase of Hardy's career. At a time when Hardy was smarting from a near-unanimous collection of patronizing, haughty and ill-considered reviews of *The Dynasts*, Part First, Gosse urged him not to be discouraged. After the appearance of Part Second, he exhorted Hardy to 'Slacken not in winding this glorious poem up to a noble and thrilling conclusion'. Hardy willingly accepted the tribute of Gosse's enthusiasm for the volumes of poetry he was periodically bringing out in the new century. Moreover, he was drawn to Gosse because of the interest they shared in painting (on one notable occasion, after Hardy had introduced Gosse to William Barnes, the latter showed Gosse and Hardy his collection of engravings and paintings), his knowledge of other Victorian celebrities in whom Hardy was interested (e.g. Walter Pater, Oliver Wendell Holmes and William Dean Howells), and his willingness to listen to Hardy's working-out of structural problems in his novels of the 1880s and 1890s. It was to Gosse that Hardy wrote his tart comment on Robert Browning: 'How could smug Christian optimism worthy of a dissenting grocer find a place inside a man who was so vast a seer & feeler when on neutral ground?' (3 March 1889).[19] He admired Gosse's study of Gray, whose poems Hardy admired. The two men, meeting through their membership in the Savile Club in the early 1880s, corresponded with each other, and visited each other's homes, for fully half a century. Indeed, Gosse was the first of Hardy's London friends to make the long trip to Dorset to see him. After being knighted, Sir Edmund wrote to name him the 'Dearest and most admired of friends', and after a visit to Max Gate in June 1927, he wrote to another friend in genuine awe: 'He is a wonder, if you like! At 87½ without a deficiency of sight, hearing, mind or conversation. Very tiny and fragile, but full of spirit and a gaiety not quite consistent in the most pessimistic of poets. He and I collogued merrily of past generations, like two antediluvian animals sporting in the primeval slime.'[20] Casting their memories back on that occasion, they might well have remembered their mutual interest in Dorset dialect, and how Hardy explained curious terms in his own writings, and even the inscription that Hardy had written for his presentation copy of *Wessex Poems*: 'Vrom his wold acquaïntance'.[21]

Swinburne, Stephen and Gosse were men of letters, fluent, prolific and intelligent craftsmen who supplied Hardy with the stimulation of free exchanges of opinion on topics that lay close to Hardy's heart. But it must be understood that they were more than successful men of letters; they were living proof that Hardy, even as his bitterness over being misunderstood by critics and reviewers mounted, derived continuing satisfaction from knowing that Swinburne had been reviled and had still won through; Stephen had religious problems remarkably similar to his own, and had managed to establish a satisfactory, though delicate, equilibrium; and Gosse, despite reservations about Hardy's 'pessimism', believed in him as a poet of talent at a time when such faith was most welcome.

No biographer has yet assessed the number of requests for advice, made by younger poets, and the straightforward, unsentimental and occasionally searing judgements on modern literature that Hardy rendered both in conversation and in print. Hardy did not care much for the flashy cynicism which came into favour after the Great War, though he well understood the root causes of that despair. He disapproved of plotless fictions, commercial claptrap, obscure poetry and philistine readers, and his low opinion of criticism as a way of making a living fell (if possible) even lower. Yet Hardy was respected all the more for his integrity by those whose judgement he had some reason to value, namely the younger poets who were making, however slowly, reputations in the second and third decades of the century. This review of Hardy's literary friendships may well conclude with a consideration of that 'charming volume of holograph poems, beautifully bound', from forty-three 'fellow poets', as a gift arranged for the occasion of his eightieth birthday, 2 June 1919, and put into Hardy's hands by Siegried Sassoon. Hardy wrote in the *Life* that he thanked every contributor with a personal letter, 'though it took him a long while', and added, with quiet pleasure, 'It was almost his first awakening to the consciousness that an opinion had silently grown up as it were in the night, that he was no mean power in the contemporary world of poetry.'[22]

Sassoon gave three grounds for offering a testimony of 'esteem and affection' at this time:

> We would thank you for the pleasure and increasing delight that your art has given us.
> In picturing the manners of the folk and the loved scenery of their homes, you have planted and peopled many a countryside with enduring memories, revealing and enhancing its native charm in novels that will feed our national strength and kindle the hearts of Englishmen for generations to come.
> We would also thank you for the passionate poetry with which you have crowned your long labours.

The correspondence relating to the poets' tribute is now at the Huntington Library in San Marino, California. Those who were invited responded eagerly to the opportunity to make known to Hardy their admiration of his talents. John Middleton Murry, for example, turned out to be 'one of the most whole-hearted admirers' of Hardy that Sassoon had ever met; in fact, as Sassoon added in a letter to Sydney Cockerell, Murry 'admires practically no other living writer'. Robert Bridges, the poet laureate, was 'charmed with the idea', and urged that his contribution be written 'in some beautiful script'. Maurice Baring accepted, 'of course with pleasure'. Laurence Binyon wrote, 'I shall be proud to contribute to the anthology in honour of Thomas Hardy.' Gordon Bottomley, filled with 'reverence and admiration for Mr Hardy', praised the 'notable scheme', which he thought 'as gratifying as anything that can happen to any man in this life'. W. H. Davies thought it 'a very good idea'. John Drinkwater was 'very glad' that the tribute to Thomas Hardy was being paid. Edmund Gosse supplied one of his poems that Hardy had quoted in *The Woodlanders*. Maurice Hewlett decided not to send along a poem on death, thinking that 'perhaps it was *too* much to the point. I know that some men of Hardy's age get rather jumpy about the Hereafter, though I don't feel that I shall when it comes to the point. Anyhow I wouldn't risk it.' A. E. Housman was 'happy' to take part in the tribute. Walter de la Mare, filled with 'love & devotion to T. H.', was pleased by the coincidence of the invitation coming so soon after his own speculation 'how happy a thing it might be to show in some way how deeply & fully he is delighted in & admired by men of his own craft'. T. Sturge Moore was so 'honoured' that he promised to do his best 'not to spoil the page entrusted' to him if only Sassoon would forward it. Gilbert Murray exclaimed, 'What a nice idea!' Alfred Noyes spoke of the 'real pleasure' the invitation had given him. Arthur Symons wrote that 'Hardy's genius as well as the man himself has always seemed to me in certain senses unique'. Among the two dozen other poets who gladly consented to write special poems for the tribute were G. K. Chesterton, Robert Graves, Rudyard Kipling, D. H. Lawrence, John Masefield, Charlotte Mew, 'A. E.', Edith Sitwell, James Stephens and William Butler Yeats.

It is highly likely that knowledge of the esteem in which he was held by these poets tempered the severity of his remarks on the condition of modern poetry in the important 'Apology' that he composed for *Late Lyrics and Earlier*, published three years later, in 1922. At any rate, Hardy seemed to be blaming the unsettled conditions of the post-war age rather than the poets themselves for what he called 'the precarious prospects of English verse at the present day'. As Florence Hardy wrote to Sydney Cockerell (12 October 1919), the 'Tribute'—about which she had been forewarned—had made a great impression: Hardy was 'enormously pleased and gratified'. At that moment of his life—and, indeed, at many others—Thomas Hardy might look back on the magnificent career that he had made for himself and wonder if the principal fruit of his endeavours might have been, in measure equal to that of his literary productions, the forming of warm personal friendships with many of the most distinguished writers of his time.

4

Kipling and Haggard

Literary influence is a devilishly hard thing to prove. Despite the popularity of such studies, the linkage between the act of reading a book and the subsequent act of writing a book under the direct influence of that first book is seldom direct or clear. Many writers do not like to admit that their handiwork traces back to another writer's earlier inspiration. They argue, with some justification, that the number of themes and situations available to creative writers is limited, and that all writers borrow from one another. 'Analogues' is a more useful word than 'sources'; a book may resemble another book, but its existence does not depend on the prior existence of any single work of the creative imagination; *und so weiter*. There is no obligation that a novel be the descendant of an earlier novel; it may be based in large part on newspaper accounts of a murder trial, as in Theodore Dreiser's *An American Tragedy*; or personal experience in migrant-labourer camps, as in John Steinbeck's *The Grapes of Wrath*; or in a medical school, as in Somerset Maugham's *Of Human Bondage*; or in the memories of a tormented and unhappy childhood, as in Joyce's *A Portrait of the Artist as a Young Man*. The memory of a writer, moreover, may be unreliable. He may deny that the influence exists, as T. S. Eliot did when critics pointed to Browningesque elements in his poetry, or as D. H. Lawrence did when readers reacted uneasily to the Freudian elements in the plotting of *Sons and Lovers*. An author may not be the best judge of how his memories of a reading experience have moved the direction of his pen; he may not recall the way in which the supposed influence operated, or whether any specific influence operated more powerfully than did all the other possibilities. Ihab H. Hassan, discussing the problems of influence in literary history, argues that influencing forces may include (in addition to a specific author or a specific work) 'climate, mores or locale of a people'; historical events such as the Armada and the American Civil War; 'some particular style or literary convention'; 'a particular theory or idea'; a specific thinker; and a literary movement. In addition, the influence may be exerted upon such broad entities as the age at large, the cultural tradition or a literary movement.[1] 'Literary influence' may very well become, in these terms, too broad and generalized to be useful to literary scholars. But let us suppose that the writer is honest about his borrowings, and even, as Hardy did, maintains a meticulous record of his readings, underlines notable passages in the book he is perusing, goes to the bother of transcribing passages (some quite lengthy) for the sake of later use and takes pride in the variety and quality of his sources. Is the task made any easier? Are we, in fact, able to assert with greater positiveness that we understand the workings of the creative mind?

The answer, regrettably, must be no, for this kind of evidence is almost entirely quantitative. Many scholars interested in Hardy have had occasion to consult the table of Hardy's quotations from English literature, compiled by Carl Weber, printed in his biography of 1940 and only slightly revised in the later edition of 1962. 'This is not a list of Hardy's readings', Weber wrote, 'but merely a tabulation of those English authors whom he alludes to or quotes. They are arranged, approximately, in chronological order'.[2] Bede is the first author; Edmund Gosse the last. Weber listed sixty-seven authors in all, but since the names include only those authors whom Hardy explicitly identified, it is incomplete; the number of borrowings from Wordsworth is not an accurate reflection of the extent of Hardy's indebtedness. But Weber's list barely scratches the surface. It does not do justice to Hardy's deep, intimate knowledge of the Bible; it implies that Hardy found little or nothing in Anglo-Saxon medieval literature to his taste and knew only the works of Shakespeare and the *The Maid's Tragedy*, by Beaumont and Fletcher, of all Elizabethan dramas; that he refused to acknowledge the importance of Edmund Burke's concept of the Sublime; and that he read no novels after the last one written by Sir Walter Scott. To supplement this list, and to understand better the ways in which Hardy's mind snatched up 'trifles', we need to consult Frank Pinion's much longer list of literary quotations and allusions in *A Hardy Companion*, which is sensibly arranged in four categories: writers whose work is slight, and those with whom Hardy's acquaintance seems limited or general rather than close (a representative rather than exhaustive list); those he knew more intimately; those authors he knew unusually well; and lastly, Shakespeare and the Bible. We must look into Lennart A. Björk's *The Literary Notes of Thomas Hardy, Volume I,* and Richard H. Taylor's careful edition of *The Personal Notebooks of Thomas Hardy,* which has a number of literary memoranda. *The Collected Letters,* edited by R. L. Purdy and Michael Millgate, offers further evidence of Hardy's readings.

At any rate, thorough knowledge of the contents of the vast literature assimilated by that notorious autodidact Thomas Hardy is probably not enough. I am suggesting that even the most careful influence studies are based primarily on circumstantial evidence; the author who presumably is being influenced by someone whose work he has read is not necessarily the best witness to the nature or extent of that influence; and conclusions that seek to measure Hardy's obligations to a given text must be couched in the language of possibility rather than of certainty. Above all, I find the notion that Hardy may have been afflicted by an anxiety of influence (to use the currently fashionable phrase formulated by Harold Bloom)[3] does not agree with my sense of what Hardy read books for. His novels were not based upon the novels of others in any simple or reductive sense. He was not reacting against the dread influence of his literary progenitors.

Although he sought to become a good hand with a serial, the major sources of his inspiration were not literary. His stories were about the soil of Wessex, men and women he had known, and a cultural milieu inevitably changing under the hammer-blows of progress and industrial modernization. In a crucial sense—and it may be the sense which has endeared him to generations of readers, and enlarged his appeal to those who do not speak English—he seems to write from direct experience. The welcome irony is that this most bookish of men, who never heard a shot fired in anger, whose outer life was barren of event or excitement, and who lived to a venerable age without visiting a second continent or indeed without travelling widely within Europe, does not seem dependent on written texts for his plots, his characters, his point of view or his language.

If biographers and critics without number call our attention to the artfulness with which Hardy studied the novels of Wilkie Collins and Harrison Ainsworth; the resemblances between the inn-fire in *Desperate Remedies* and a similar event in Miss Braddon's novel *Lady Audley's Secret*; the tricks and coincidences of Hardy's fiction that, for want of a better term, have long been designated as 'Gothic', summoning up associations with an entire school of writers of fiction; the plot-echoes of Shakespeare, Shelley and George Eliot, among others—they still do not convince us that Hardy was indebted to his literary predecessors for anything essential. Strip from his novels all that is overtly a reminiscence of how someone else said it first (and Hardy, it must be remembered, is generous in his attributions of credit), and we have removed only a small fraction of his text. The true Hardy will survive any such test.

Hardy's literary friendships with William Barnes, Horace Moule, Meredith, Swinburne, Leslie Stephen and Edmund Gosse extended over a considerable period of time, as we have seen. Hardy's capacity for making and keeping friendships has been underestimated by recent biographers (Purdy and Millgate are not alone in their view that Hardy lived friendless for much of his life). Some historians of the Dorset scene have argued that Hardy retreated to his study as a consequence of hostile reviews, and from the 1890s on, for a full four decades, lived an eremitic existence. According to this view, first Emma, and Florence, protected him from unwelcome visitors, and he willingly collaborated with their efforts to keep him incommunicado.

The case is overstated but has flourished because of the existence of some elements of truth in the characterization. This chapter, however, deals with Hardy's relationship to two of his famous contemporaries, and I will begin with a consideration of Rudyard Kipling, who won, in 1907, the Nobel Prize for Literature, the first time it was awarded to an Englishman. When Kipling came back to England (after a rather leisurely trip from India via Japan and the United States in 1889), he was a very obscure journalist indeed, with no reputation among English writers or readers for the 'seven years' hard' he had put in on the *Civil and Military Gazette* of Lahore, and the *Pioneer* of Allahabad. He met Thomas Hardy, however, shortly after he came to London. He was seeking his fortune as a young writer, and found it; his success was phenomenal. There probably was nothing to compare with it during the entire century save the celebrated case of Lord Byron, who published the first and second cantos of *Childe Harold's Pilgrimage* in 1812 and 'awoke one morning' to find himself famous. Although Hardy nowhere bothers to transcribe a quotation from Kipling's works—by the end of 1890 quotations of Kipling were becoming familiar and even shopworn—Hardy recognized the clear stamp of personality in Kipling's work. He had no choice, for he rapidly became entangled in one of the numerous controversies about copyright that so embittered relationships between publishers and authors in the final decade of the century.

Kipling, in 1889, offered to write for Harper & Brothers of New York, but was summarily dismissed in a letter 'one line and seven words long'. The following year the firm helped itself to one of his stories, reprinted in book form a number of his best stories, gave them a title that Kipling had never sanctioned,[4] and sent him a payment of ten pounds as a honorarium—which he angrily returned. *Harper's Monthly* ran a patronizing review by William Dean Howells about Mr Kipling's 'jaunty hat-cocked-on-one-side, wink-tipping sketches', and Kipling, writing to William Ernest Henley, exploded:

> When the man was writing that, his blasted owners were stealing my work. . . . It isn't the critics' fault that he lives, as every man must live, under the laws of his own life and environment, when he calls my stuff lacking in appreciation of the subtler values. The thing that makes it like a Gilbert – Sullivan opera is the raw, rank theft that runs through the 'business' of his firm. When a burglar sits down on the front door steps to quarrel with the pattern of the silver-ware that he hath stolen he may be an authority on silver but he is first of all a thief and secondly he lacks a sense of humour.[5]

For Kipling it was no laughing matter; and when Harper & Brothers protested in the *Athenaeum* that it was following the custom of the trade in proffering a ten-pound cheque for payment of English material not covered by any international copyright agreement, Kipling called the firm pirates 'like Paul Jones'. To the defence of Harper & Brothers, somewhat unexpectedly, came Thomas Hardy, co-signing a letter with Sir Walter Besant and William Black, and arguing that the firm had always treated them in a 'just and liberal fashion, showing itself willing and desirous to do what is possible for the foreign author'. It was hardly a 'servile apologia', though it has been characterized as such by Lord

Birkenhead in his biography of Kipling; Hardy had enjoyed his relationship with the firm; in addition, as he wrote to James R. Osgood on 8 November 1890, he believed that the whole matter turned upon a question of fact, and not upon any general question:

> namely whether certain arrangements were or were not made between the parties; & it occurred to me that the solution would be found to lie in a slip of the memory on one or the other side. I think most people have viewed it in that light—as a purely personal matter, which had no wide bearing on the international publishing question.

The letter to Osgood was obviously never intended for publication, but the *Athenaeum* letter, printed in the issue of 22 November 1890, was patronizing in a way that Hardy himself might have found offensive had its strictures been addressed to him over a similar 'slip of the memory on one or the other side'. Unethical publishers existed in the United States (as if Kipling needed to be told!), and Kipling, Hardy implied, would be well advised to ally himself with an ethical firm such as Harper & Brothers to avoid the lamentable practice of having his fiction reprinted without proper permission or adequate payment. Kipling—so Hardy, Besant and Black agreed in telling him—was tactically misjudging the nature of his opponent; moreover, he had breached the barriers of decorum and good taste.

It is difficult, at this remove of almost a century, to understand why Hardy felt that the best way to testify to the fairness of Harper & Brothers' dealings with authors was to add his signature to a letter prepared by somebody else, which had a distinct bullying tone and which was aimed at silencing an author who had been obviously mistreated, who already understood that he had no recourse through law, and who was prepared to let the particular issue die for want of a remedy. Kipling's revenge was the writing and publishing of 'The Rhyme of the Three Captains', in which he denounced, with unrestrained fury, the three authors who had signed their names to the *Athenaeum* letter. Hardy was described as 'Lord of the Wessex coast and all the lands thereby', but Kipling's interest lay less in individual characterization than in lamenting his own fate: he had sailed from a heathen coast 'to be robbed in a Christian port' by a 'lime-washed Yankee brig'. When he asked for his own again, the Yankee 'swore' it did not belong to him. Kipling went on:

And the Captains Three called courteously from deck to scuttle-butt:
'Good Sir, we ha' dealt with that merchantman or ever your teeth were
    cut.
'Your words be words of a lawless race, and the Law it standeth thus:
'He comes of a race that have never a Law, and he never has boarded
    us.
'We ha' sold him canvas and rope and spar—we know that his price
    is fair,
'And we know that he weeps for the lack of a Law as he rides off
    Finisterre.
'And since he is damned for a gallows-thief by you and better than
    you,
'We hold it meet that the English fleet should know that we hold him
    true.'

Kipling might threaten to carry his word across the seven seas, and
tell

'How a man may be robbed in Christian port while Three Great Captains
    there
Shall dip their flag to a slaver's rag—to show that his trade is
    fair!'

But Harper & Brothers did not recall the offending book with its
pirated contents. Kipling learned through bitter experience that his
quarrel lay with the sorry state of the copyright agreements
between England and the United States rather than with individual
authors who sincerely believed that they were advocating the
cultivation of good feelings between honest folk. 'The Rhyme of the
Three Captains' attracted wide notice as satire, but, having made
his point, Kipling asked his friend Henry James to write an
introduction for a rival edition of the pirated short stories. These,
under the title *Mine Own People*, was printed by an American
publisher, J. W. Lovell & Co. in 1891.

Kipling soon made friends with the writers who had offended
him. Andrew Lang had taken him to the Savile Club shortly after
his arrival in London, and there he was proposed for membership.
His candidacy was supported by both Walter Besant and Thomas
Hardy, among more than a dozen others. Kipling tells us, in his
incomplete memoir *Something of Myself*, that he dined 'with no
less than Hardy and Walter Besant' on his introduction.

Kipling returned to the United States in 1892 and lived among his wife's relatives in Brattleboro, Vermont, for approximately five years, publishing some of his finest works—*Many Inventions, The Jungle Book* and *The Second Jungle Book* and *The Seven Seas*. In addition, he wrote that splendid novel about fishermen on the Grand Banks, *Captains Courageous*. If literary productivity were all, this must be accounted one of the richest periods in his life. But it all ended in disaster, with violent quarrels between Kipling and his brother-in-law, an embarrassing law-suit, ridicule heaped on Kipling by a vindictive press, and flight to England. Late in the summer of 1897 a seriously upset Kipling determined that his temporary residence at the Elms in Rottingdean, near Brighton, had to be changed for something better, and he came to Dorchester, to Max Gate, and to an old friend, Mr Hardy. The two of them bicycled about the neighbourhood. Kipling thought it might be nice to buy a house near Weymouth. C. E. Carrington, Kipling's official biographer, describes thus a marvellous moment during the adventurous search:

> Thomas Hardy carried him off to inspect a lonely house occupied by an elderly lady. While Kipling examined the premises high and low, Hardy was left making conversation in the parlour. 'I think you would like to know, Madam, that the gentleman I have brought to your house is no other than Mr Rudyard Kipling.' The remark fell flat; she had never heard of Rudyard Kipling. A few minutes later, Rudyard found himself alone with the lady and, not knowing what had passed, made the complementary remark, 'My sponsor is Thomas Hardy himself.' It was no use, she had never heard of Thomas Hardy; and the two celebrities admitted their insignificance to one another on the way home.
> (*Rudyard Kipling,* p.269)

I cannot resist wondering how the relationship of these two men—two of the recognized masters of English imaginative literature towards the end of the century—might have developed if Kipling had settled down in Dorset; if, for example, his offer meeting the asked-for price of a home at Rodwell, 'commanding a full view of Portland Roads', had been accepted. It was not to be, and Kipling moved to his new home, Bateman's, in Sussex. On 16 January 1928, Rudyard Kipling, along with other eminent writers, acted as a pall-bearer, accompanying Hardy's ashes to their ceremonial interment in Poets' Corner. Almost eight years later, on 23 January 1936, Kipling was laid to rest, next to the cremated ashes of Hardy, in the first such funeral service held in Poets' Corner since that of

Hardy. Two of the pall-bearers were repeating their melancholy duty: the prime minister, Mr Stanley Baldwin (who was, of course, first cousin to Kipling), and the master of Magdalene College, Cambridge, Mr A. B. Ramsay. But it is true, as Carrington points out, that Kipling's guard of honour was not made up primarily of men of letters, by poets or dramatists, but rather by men who had won distinction in the army and navy. In the manner of their interment, as in the pattern of their lives, Kipling and Hardy were strikingly different.

This kind of information tells us a great deal more about Hardy than we might expect. Hardy, a full quarter-century older than Kipling, was a well-established celebrity by the time the younger man swam across his line of vision. His note in the *Life* records the bemused reaction of a man who had nothing to fear from competition and who suddenly remembers that younger writers are still striving to impress their elders: 'He talked about the East', Hardy wrote, 'and he well said that the East is the world, both in numbers and in experiences. It has passed through our present bustling stages, and has become quiescent. He told curious details of Indian life.' Hardy became interested in Kipling as a man, a visitor who had seen the East. But he never felt threatened by Kipling's achievements. Neither borrowed themes, plots or languages from the other. Hardy was only the third person to receive the gold medal of the Royal Society of Literature, the first two recipients being Sir Walter Scott and George Meredith; Kipling was the fourth and received the medal during Hardy's lifetime (in 1926). When Percy Lubbock's edition of the letters of Henry James appeared in 1920, Hardy reacted angrily to James's sneers at himself, Swinburne, Meredith and Kipling.[6] Yet, very close to the end of his life, on 31 October 1927, Hardy quoted Dryden to one of Kipling's friends, Captain Victor Cazalet; and the line—'Kipling had given to party what was meant for mankind'—impressed his visitor sufficiently that he asked Hardy to repeat it.[7] Such a characterization of Kipling suggests the extent of Hardy's distaste for polemics carried over into the world of fiction, for an overstated position and for the possibility that Kipling had cheapened his talents by pursuing causes.

What did Kipling think of Hardy? We might guess that even the brash Kipling of 1890, with his way yet to make in the world, would appreciate genuine literary achievement by a fellow artist and would be appropriately respectful in the presence of Hardy. The *Life* records one conversation at the Savile in which Kipling, somewhat self-deprecatingly, recounts an anecdote about his years in India as a journalist; it is the sort of story that Kipling, on his best behaviour, might be expected to tell to confirm good feelings between a younger man of bustle and drive, and an older man of slower movements and more decorous taste. But perhaps the clearest statement of Kipling's true opinion may be found—as Angus Wilson has suggested, in *The Strange Ride of Rudyard Kipling: His Life and Works* (1977)—in the short story, 'A Conference of the Powers', written immediately after Kipling's first meeting with Hardy, and published in May 1890 in both the *Pioneer Mail* and *Harper's Weekly*. It is not much of a story—a sketch, really—about four soldiers but recently returned to London after a long spell of dangerous service in Burma, and their reminiscences about how it was. They are under 25 years of age, a fact which impresses the elderly, famous writer, Mr Eustace Cleever, who has come to see one of them. Mr Cleever is the author of *As It Was in the Beginning*, a book that has mightily impressed The Infant, and for that matter all the others, who have read it. 'I was brought up in the country you wrote about', The Infant tells Cleever; 'All my people live there; and I read the book in camp on the Hlinedatalone, and I knew every stick and stone, and the dialect too; and by Jove! it was just like being at home and hearing the country-people talk.' The praise is sincere, and the narrator notes that Cleever is susceptible to it: 'Mr Cleever has tasted as much praise, public and private, as one man may safely swallow; but it seemed to me that the outspoken admiration in The Infant's eyes and the little stir in the little company came home to him very nearly indeed.' 'Appreciation and reverence': thus do they regard Cleever, 'a golden talker', sitting 'in the midst of hero-worship devoid of all taint of self-interest'. The soldiers want to know about 'the birth of his book and whether it was hard to write, and how his notions came to him'. Kipling describes Cleever as a man who responds with ingratiating simplicity, and who gradually shifts from an 'elaborate choice of words' 'to freely-mouthed "ows" and "ois", and for him at least, 'unfettered colloquialisms'. Cleever has difficulty in following the crisp, curt speech of the soldiers:

> He could create men and women, and send them to the uttermost ends of the earth, to help delight and comfort; he knew every mood of the fields, and could interpret them to the cities, and he knew the hearts of many in cities and the

country, but he had hardly, in forty years, come into contact with the thing which is called a Subaltern of the Line.

In brief, Cleever is so bound in his own kind of society that the outer world doesn't trouble him a great deal. Moreover, he is out of touch with the major concerns of these defenders of Empire. 'To me', said Cleever softly, 'the whole idea of warfare seems so foreign and unnatural, so essentially vulgar, if I may say so, that I can hardly appreciate your sensations'. He knows little or nothing about the army; he is a 'home-staying Englishman'. (A world of meaning is packed within that phrase for readers of Kipling.) His ignorance goes far beyond the native words which these youngsters employ whenever English fails them. He is fascinated by what Hardy, in his autobiography, had called 'curious details' of human existence in the East. He is alert, open-minded, appreciative of enthusiasm, condescending in an attractive and likeable way to these young men who have seen and experienced so much, genuinely interested about their concerns: 'dead men, and war, and power, and responsibility'. He warns them that they won't have any sensations left at 30 if they go on as they have done. When the boys tell him that they plan to dine out somewhere and go on to the Empire afterwards, he angles for an invitation to accompany them because he wants to hear more tales. 'I don't think I've been to the Empire in my life', he says, 'but—what *is* my life after all? Let us go.' The evening proves a complete success, according to the narrator:

> At midnight they returned, announcing that they were 'highly respectable gondoliers', and that oysters and stout were what they chiefly needed. The eminent novelist was still with them, and I think he was calling them by their shorter names. I am certain that he said he had been moving in worlds not realised, and that they had shown him the Empire in a new light.

What—asks the narrator of Eustace Cleever, 'decorator and colourman in words'—did he think of things generally? Cleever replies with a quotation, running to the effect 'that though singing was a remarkably fine performance, I was to be quite sure that few lips would be moved to song if they could find a sufficiency of Kissing'. By this the narrator understands that Cleever 'was blaspheming his own Art, and would be sorry for it in the morning'.

All of which amounts to an opinion, as W. Arthur Young, one of Kipling's admirers, put it, that these 'accounts of things done in far-away Burma' have made Cleever realize 'that his own life and outlook was, after all, narrow and small.'[8] And perhaps, on Kipling's part, such an interpretation of Hardy's innermost thoughts was no more than wishful guessing, based upon Hardy's politeness in listening to his stories of a remote and exotic India, or on a number of Hardy's judiciously phrased comments of wonderment and admiration of a young man's exploits. But what impresses me most about the quick, masterful sketching of Eustace Cleever's character—and I do not doubt for a moment that it was based upon Kipling's concept of Hardy, who was 50 to his 25 when first they met—is that, subtly but unmistakably, Kipling was patronizing Hardy as a man who had not travelled extensively enough, seen enough of the wide world or understood what running the world's largest Empire involved. One would give a lot to find in writing, somewhere, Hardy's reaction to 'A Conference of the Powers'; but perhaps he never read it. Both men believed, I think, for the nearly four decades that they knew each other, that they had early taken an accurate measure of each other.

As for Hardy's relations to Henry Rider Haggard, the other Victorian luminary I want to discuss, it seems clear that the Savile Club, to which Kipling, Haggard and Hardy belonged, was the logical place for meetings and conversations about literary matters; the Savile had an extraordinary membership list of editors, publishers, authors, science-oriented intellectuals concerned in a major way with literary matters. There is no reason to doubt Haggard's account, printed in his autobiography (*The Days of My Life*, 1926), of a memorable moment in Thomas Hardy's life:

> One day . . . I was in the little writing-room of the Savile Club, that on the first floor with fern-cases in the window where one may smoke. . . . Presently Thomas Hardy entered and took up one of the leading weekly papers in which was a long review of his last novel. He read it, then came to me—there were no others in the room—and pointed out a certain passage.
> 'There's a nice thing to say about a man!' he exclaimed. 'Well, I'll never write another novel.'
> And he never did.[9]

It is possible that the review in question was Mrs Margaret Oliphant's notorious and rather lengthy article, 'The Anti-

Marriage League', which appeared in *Blackwood's Magazine*, January 1896. Hardy's anger against this review was well known at the time. But Hardy and Haggard were on closer terms than this account of an emotional outburst in a writing-room—an outburst that might have been directed at any member of the Club who was present at the time—implies. For Hardy was very conscious, throughout the 1880s and 1890s, that he and Haggard were rivals in sales. So far as popularity was concerned, one quantitative measure was a number of times an author's name appeared on the library lists; in 1893 Haggard was forty-third, Hardy forty-sixth. Hardy's realism was often contrasted with Haggard's romanticism. *Allan Quatermain*, published in 1877, was available in 2,000 copies to subscribers to Mudie's services; James Barrie lamented that, at the same time, Mudie's did not have a single copy of *A Pair of Blue Eyes*. Andrew Lang's jubilant praise of *King Solomon's Mines*, in *The Saturday Review* of 10 October 1885, led to the cementing of one of the important literary and personal friendships of the late Victorian age, that between Lang and Haggard, and when it came time for Lang to review *Tess of the d'Urbervilles*, in *The New Review*, February 1892, he suggested that Hardy might be too good for many readers, 'or good in the wrong way', while other novelists such as Haggard omitted the 'ingredients of the blackest misery' that Hardy so delighted in recording, and were far more agreeable as reading companions.[10]

Two authors with more dissimilar concepts of an audience worth writing for might be difficult to imagine. Since they have long been assumed to inhabit separate worlds—Haggard's daughter, Lilias Rider Haggard, does not mention Thomas Hardy at all in her biography of her father, *The Cloak That I Left* (1951)—it is worth remembering how much travelling Haggard did. At the age of 19 he went out to South Africa to serve as a secretary to the Governor of Natal; later, he became a master and registrar of the High Court of the Transvaal. He was present during some of the most exciting months of the Boer War. He investigated, at the request of the Colonial Office, Salvation Army settlements in the United States; between 1912 and 1917 he served as a member of the Dominions Royal Commission; as a representative of the Royal Colonial Institute, and the Empire Settlement Committee, he helped work out details of the post-war adjustment of veterans to civilian life; he circled the globe several times. Haggard tried his hand at analytical, historical and 'modern' novels; but he was primarily the romantic novelist that Andrew Lang thought and said he was, and his posthumous fame depends upon *King Solomon's Mines, She,* and *Allan Quatermain,* novels that Hardy could not, and would not, have written in a month of Sundays.

It is not my purpose to review the special characteristics of one of Haggard's romantic novels, or to show how and why the truism of the 1890s, that Haggard and Hardy appealed to different kinds of readers, was essentially true. When we look closer at the strands which connect the two men, however, we discover that Hardy and Haggard shared several interests. This is far more than a matter of exchanging gift copies of new publications, a courtesy which both men practised with a large number of fellow-authors. And it is more than the (only superficially conventional) expressions of sympathy at a death in the family, as when Hardy wrote to Haggard about his son's death at the age of 10; 'Please give my kind regards to Mrs Haggard, & tell her how deeply our sympathy was with you both in your bereavement. Though, to be candid, I think the death of a child is never really to be regretted, when one reflects on what he has escaped'.[11] It is also more than the pleasure of acknowledging an occasional gift of game, such as pheasants, or the casualness of a shared vantage-point at an historic moment, such as the time when Haggard and Hardy sat together on a balcony of the Athenaeum, watching the hearse carrying Edward VII's body pass by (1910).[12]

It is well known that Hardy early took a strong dislike to blood sports and wrote letters to *The Times,* agitated on behalf of various societies and made his feelings clear in several novels and poems. Frank Pinion has assembled a compendium of references to various works by Hardy on this subject, and entitled it 'Cruelty to Animals'.[13] The number of these references may suggest why Hardy found so interesting Haggard's decision, in July 1904, to forswear blood sports. Haggard was a good shot, and only an extraordinary event could have changed his mind about the pleasure of the hunt. Bob, his black retriever, was killed by a train on a railway bridge spanning the marshes near his home; carried along for a distance; and finally thrown off the track into the water, where he sank beneath the reeds. That same night Haggard, without knowing of the death, woke from a vivid, horrifying dream about Bob. He saw the retriever dying in some brushwood by the water, and heard it calling to him as it suffocated. He told his wife about his nightmare; the next morning he told the story again to his family. Later that day he was informed of the circumstances surrounding Bob's death. The phenomenon, understandably, aroused a great deal of interest in *The Times*, and later in the *Journal of the Society of Psychical Research* (October 1904). Haggard, like Hardy, came to believe in the 'intimate, ghostly connection between all members of the animal world', and in the possibility that animals, including man, are 'all of them different manifestations of some central informing life, although inhabiting the Universe in such various shapes'. Haggard, like Hardy, was aware of the dangers of generalizing from a particular instance, 'however striking and well supported by evidence'. Nevertheless, 'from that day forward' Haggard only brought down pheasants, in his imagination, 'with an umbrella or a walking-stick'.

Hardy admired Haggard's *The Mahatma and the Hare*, a story based upon still another dream, and a parable which, as Haggard wrote in his autobiography, 'amounts to an attack upon our habit of killing other creatures for amusement'. The little book was never very popular, but its double tale—told by a slain hare travelling towards the gates of heaven, and by the hunter who has killed him, to a mahatma who listens with understanding and sympathy—evoked a predictable response from Hardy. 'I am, as you may know, entirely on the side of the hare', Hardy wrote to Haggard in 1911. 'I feel certain that you are too, in spite of your reserve; and that delights me. There is not the least doubt that blood sport will have to go. To teach boys to like it, in the 20th Century, is monstrous.'

These are linkages, occult sympathies, if you will; or the shock of recognition that artists experience when they perceive they are not alone in a darkling world. Hardy, too, had a strange tale to recount about his own dog, Wessex, the wire-hair terrier who earned for himself a reputation of some notoriety among visitors to Max Gate. Wessex befriended few; but one man he liked was Mr William Watkins, secretary to the Society of Dorset Men in London. On the evening of 18 April 1925 the dog greeted Mr Watkins 'with vociferous barks', signifying pleasure at seeing him; then, abruptly and unexpectedly, changed to 'a piteous whine' and 'a sharp cry of distress'. Nobody understood the cause for the unhappiness of Wessex—not, that is, until the next morning when Mr Watkins's son phoned Hardy to inform him that his father 'had died quite suddenly about an hour after his return to the hotel from Max Gate. As a rule the dog barked furiously when he heard the telephone ring, but on this occasion he remained silent, his nose between his paws.'

But the major evidence of how often the views of Haggard and Hardy coincided need not be inferred from the frequency with which they dined together, not only at the Savile but at the home of Edmund Gosse, 29 Delamere Terrace, next to the Paddington Canal; or from the occasional remark of critical appreciation of a new story. (For example, Hardy said of *The Mahatma and the Hare*, 'I hope very many people will read the book, and be as much moved by it as I was and am.')[14] I do not even regard as important testimony Haggard's own admission that one of the most dramatic scenes in *Allan Quatermain* may have been plagiarized from a scene in one of Hardy's novels. 'It has been pointed out to me', wrote Haggard as he confessed what few of his readers could have guessed, 'that there exists a similarity between the scene of Umslopogaas frightening Alphonse with his axe and a scene in *Far from the Madding Crowd*. I regret this coincidence, and believe that the talented author of that work will not be inclined to accuse me of literary immorality on that account.' In *Allan Quatermain* a Zulu chieftain whirls his axe around the body of a terrified French cook in Central Africa, and finally chops off one of the curling mustachios of his victim. The scene recalls Sergeant Troy's demonstration of his skill with a broadsword to the bedazzled Bathsheba Everdene, and its conclusion, when Troy cuts off a lock of Bathsheba's hair. The differences between the two episodes are more important than the similarities, as H. F. Ellis has pointed out in his amusing essay 'The Niceties of Plagiarism' in *The Atlantic Monthly*, January 1959. A broadsword is not an axe. The veranda of a mission house on the Tana River in Africa is strikingly unlike a saucer-shaped pit near Weatherbury. In Hardy's scene, Sergeant Troy spits a caterpillar that has settled on the front of Bathsheba's bodice, and says, 'I merely gave point to your bosom where the caterpillar was, and instead of running you through checked the extension a thousandth of an inch short of your surface'. Finally, Bathsheba may have enjoyed the experience (if she had analysed her reaction). Anyhow, the Sergeant kissed her after the sword-play. Alphonse, the French cook, did not receive a kiss from Umslopogaas, and undoubtedly, after part of his mustachio went the way of all flesh, did not want one.

What, then, could Haggard have meant by drawing attention to resemblances between his narrative and that of Thomas Hardy? I think that he was being playful; that his respect for Hardy was such that he relished the thought of readers seeing similarities between his art and Hardy's fictional technique; and that he was on such good terms with his fellow-clubman that he was sure, in advance, Hardy would not mind a cheery confesssion of 'literary immorality'. There is no evidence that Hardy did mind.

Most important, Haggard and Hardy shared interests in the land, in farming and in the changes that were reshaping the world of their childhood. For Haggard, despite his popularity as a romancer, was very serious about his second career; worked hard at it; wrote several important books on the subject; and exchanged views and news about research in progress with Thomas Hardy.

Hardy's one extended essay on agricultural conditions, 'The Dorsetshire Labourer', appeared in *Longman's Magazine* in July 1883. It is a singularly straightforward, disarmingly biased defence of the countryman Hodge, language and all, as an individual. Hardy's reaction against the abstraction of the field labourer was, in part, anger at the meddling of city-folk who assumed all too readily that they understood the conditions of life in the country. He saw that the patronizing clap-trap of do-gooders, irrevelant though it might be to the colour and verve of labourer's lives in Dorset, distracted attention from the real issues of rural existence. The country poor now wore drearier clothes because of changing fashions; hiring-fairs had become a different kind of ritual; the annual removal on Lady Day now multiplied the risks of increasing contact with 'stories of the wide world'; and the increasingly nomadic labourer had a decreasingly 'intimate and kindly relation with the land he tills'. Hardy saw much to deplore, little to praise, as he chronicled the decline of older traditions, though he recognized the advantages for individual Hodges in their increased independence from masters often arbitrary and unjust. Agricultural unrest—perhaps best symbolized for Hardy in the career of Joseph Arch—and depopulation were destroying the world of his childhood. The essay may serve as a memorial to the agricultural conditions of Hardy's first two decades, the 1840s and 1850s, rather than as a faithful record of the decade in which the article was published, the 1880s. Hardy characteristically stopped short before considering the full implications of 'the houseless and landless poor, and the vast topic of the Rights of Man', which, as he rightly said, ran 'beyond the scope of a merely descriptive article'. But deep feelings had been tapped, and nostalgia over the loss of older traditions never lay very far from anger that so much of what had come in as new was tinselly, inferior and altogether less human. Nor can 'The Dorsetshire Labourer', one of Hardy's finest essays, be fairly characterized as 'merely descriptive'. Many of its readers have heard the sound of a trumpet in Hardy's sentence, 'The cause of morality cannot be served by compelling a population hitherto evenly distributed over the country to concentrate in a few towns, with the inevitable results of overcrowding and want of regular employment.'

This kind of language Haggard understood; he spoke it himself in such pioneering studies as *A Farmer's Year* (1899), *A Gardener's Year* (1905), *The Poor and the Land* (1905), *Regeneration* (1910), *Rural Denmark and Its Lessons* (1913) and *Rural England* (2 volumes, first published in 1902, and reprinted in a cheaper edition in 1906). A superb scholarly review of the major elements in Haggard's agrarian philosophy may be found in the chapter 'Agricultural Reformer' in Morton N. Cohen's biography, *Rider Haggard: His Life and Work* (1968); it identifies, as Haggard did, the reasons for concern. England had experienced a remarkable run of good luck between 1850 and 1871, when her farmers were prosperous, unthreatened by foreign imports, and two million in number (as compared to five and a half million in commerce and industry). Both farm wages and rents were high. But this affluence did not last, partly because the opening of the American West meant that grain and other crops could be shipped to England at prices undercutting those of English farmers; and partly because England reacted slowly to the news that foreign governments were imposing tariffs on agricultural products. Wet and soggy seasons ruined farmers, as did rinderpest, liver-rot and foot-and-mouth disease. Financial depression inevitably affected farm prices. In the second half of the nineteenth century the farm population was cut by two-thirds, despite the rising population. The government did little to protect its farmers. Crops fell out of favour almost entirely as English farmers turned to meat-growing. Between 1885 (only two years after the publication of Hardy's essay on the Dorsetshire labourer) and 1914, the numbers of arable acres decreased by three million. The financial value of English agriculture kept going down, down, down. Not until the Great War did the government move vigorously to help the farmer; even the Development Bill of 1909 had not been enough to stop the near-disastrous slide that was doing so much to ruin the health of English farming.

Haggard understood—with the imaginative liveliness that he brought to his fictions—the nature of the problem, but he did not limit himself to hand-wringing or to a melancholy satisfaction that after his death would come the deluge. His proposals for reform came out at least a quarter of a century before the public, and the Parliament that could implement them as legislation, were ready to act on them. Haggard, for a large part of his later years, believed that he had failed in his mission.

Yet one constant source of support that he much appreciated was Thomas Hardy, who, after all, had entertained him at Max Gate when he was conducting his research for *Rural England*. Hardy had already written about the collapse of English agriculture in *Far from the Madding Crowd, The Return of the Native, The Mayor of Casterbridge, The Woodlanders* and *Tess of the d'Urbervilles*; in effect, he had dramatized the facts of the social chronicle that Haggard was compiling, and he believed, as Haggard did, that England had suffered a mortal wound in allowing the yeoman tradition to weaken. Douglas Brown has shown how Haggard and Hardy, using different literary media, reached the same conclusions.[15] When Haggard writes, 'Free Trade has filled the towns and emptied our countryside; it has gorged the banks but left our rickyards bare', the resonances are Hardyan. Haggard requested permission to quote from 'The Dorsetshire Labourer' at some length in his chapter on Dorsetshire in *Rural England*. He also quoted a long letter that Hardy wrote to him about the past and present conditions of agricultural workers. This letter, reproduced in slightly different form in the *Life*,[16] deliberately avoided attempting to prophesy about the future; but Hardy believed that remedies existed and were 'easily applicable'.

Hardy and Haggard, therefore, were as one in their perception that village tradition—Hardy's phrase is, 'continuity of environment in their lives'—was being evaded, if it had not already disappeared: 'a vast mass of unwritten folk-lore, local chronical, local topography, and nomenclature—is absolutely sinking, has nearly sunk, into total oblivion'. Farmers had moved to town primarily because of insecurity of tenure and not because of sheer choice, despite the inevitable percentage of 'young, adventurous and ambitious spirits among them which is found in all societies'. And the accelerating disappearance of life-hold leases meant that young men found that less and less held them to the villages of their birth. It is likely that Hardy entertained reservations about Haggard's proposed remedies, with their heavy reliance on government planning; but it is significant that Hardy's letter to Haggard, of March 1902, contains a passage that Hardy finally decided to excise. I quote it because it is not well known, and indeed is not printed as one of the omitted passages in the *Life* typescripts of the *Personal Notebooks*. Hardy was talking about the swiftness with which 'the names, stories, and relics of one place' were being forgotten 'under the incoming facts of the next', and he went on to say that this could easily be documented. If one asked one of the workfolk 'the names of surrounding hills, streams; the character and circumstances of people buried in particular graves; at what spots parish parsonages lie interred, questions on local fairies, ghosts, herbs, etc., they can give no answer'. Hardy seemed reluctant to talk about responses of workfolk (the older name for 'labourers', which Hardy insisted was 'an imported word'); he wrote 'child', and his thought raced ahead. Ask a child 'about Napoleon's attempted invasion, or even Monmouth's rebellion, the child will give for an answer whatever he or she may have learnt about Monmouth or Napoleon at school, but I can remember the time when to a question on the subject you got a traditional answer that the rebellion ended at such a corner'. Hardy's first instinct, to talk about remarks made by country children, was the artist's; his second, to record the remarks made by Dorsetshire workfolk, was a more sober response to the inquiry of Haggard in his role as social historian. Yet nothing is more sure than that Haggard, in introducing the letter to the text of *Rural England*, was fully justified in speaking of Mr Thomas Hardy as his friend, 'who, as all the world knows, has made lifelong observations of this and kindred matters connected with the land'.[17]

The long and intimate relationship between Rudyard Kipling and H. Rider Haggard may be better known as a friendship[18] than that between Hardy and Kipling, or that between Hardy and Haggard. Kipling cheerfully admitted that 'a chance sentence' in Haggard's *Nada the Lily* started him off on the track that ended in his writing 'a lot of wolf stories', that is to say, the *Jungle Books*;

Haggard dedicated *The Way of the Spirit* to Kipling; Kipling could work as well when Haggard was sitting in the room as though he were alone, 'whereas generally the presence of another person while he was writing would drive him almost mad'; Haggard regularly submitted his manuscripts to Kipling for criticism; *et cetera*. But enough has been said to indicate that the ties among the three men, creative writers of the highest power, whose books were as widely read in late Victorian England as few writers had been before or have been since, were close, continuing and reciprocally beneficial. But it was never a question of influence in a literary sense; Hardy did not borrow from Haggard, nor Kipling from Hardy, nor, even in the case of the *Jungle Books*, Kipling from Haggard in any specific way. Each writer was unique, individual, *sui generis*: a world unto himself. Hardy did not need to take from his friends the inspiration necessary to complete a story or to sketch a character. What Hardy needed from writers like Kipling and Haggard—and they from him—was a sense that they were mutually engaged on an enterprise of high seriousness, and that their writings—their fictions, their poems, their essays—contributed to the happiness and improvement of the cultural tastes of a great reading public.

5

The Dynasts

The Dynasts is an extraordinary 'poem' in several aspects. It took more time to prepare for, and to write, than any other work in Hardy's career. It was undoubtedly his most ambitious undertaking. Its thirty separate rhyme-schemes illustrate his command of prosody on a very generous scale. It contains the most explicit statement of his philosophical views about man's relationship to the universe. At the time of its appearance, in the first decade of this century, it was immediately recognised as the greatest imaginative treatment by an English author of the Napoleonic Wars, and no poem, play or novel has since superseded it. During two world wars, both conducted as if the dividing-line between civilian and military targets had been obliterated by high explosives, Hardy's characterizations of Pitt, Nelson, Wellington and ordinary Englishmen served as inspiration for a very large number of readers.

Hardy felt some chagrin at the puzzled reviews that greeted the publication of Part First as a separate volume (1904), and he regretted that he had not waited until the work was complete. (Part Second was completed in 1905 and published the following year; Part Third, completed in 1907, appeared in print in 1908.) The reviewers of Part First carped at its 'hard Pyrrhonism', its 'quasi-dramatic form', and its occasionally crabbed and unpoetical language. *The Dynasts*, as they saw immediately, did not resemble anything that Hardy had written earlier.

Unless a reader returns to the original reviews, he will experience some difficulty in understanding why Hardy was so bitter towards critics. Numerous reception studies long ago made their point about Hardy's sensitivity to adverse criticism. However, a lesser-known moment in Hardy's career, specifically the first few months of 1904,

108

almost led to an abandoning of the major literary project of his life, the writing of *The Dynasts*.

The problem (as Hardy himself was later to define it) lay in the fact that *The Dynasts* was published serially, with Part First being released on 13 January 1904, before the Second and Third Parts were ready for the printer (indeed, before they were written). Hence, reviewers were unable to judge the epic-drama as a completed whole, and were compelled to judge it as something unprecedented in Hardy's career, as indeed it was, and in relation to other poems that were competing for attention—for example, William Vaughan Moody's ''The Fire-Bringer'', part of a trilogy that paid due homage to recognizable traditions of epic poetry, as *The Dynasts* defiantly did not.

There was, of course, no secret to the fact that Hardy was engaged in writing two additional sections of his poem, and many critics acknowledged that a final judgement at this early stage might be inappropriate. Yet this did not deter them from delivering some very severe blows. Arthur Bingham Walkley, writing for *The Times Literary Supplement* (29 January and 12 February), took the comments made by various Spirits on the puppet-like behaviour of Pitt, Nelson and Napoleon so literally that he urged performance of *The Dynasts* as a puppet-show, and said that he was 'dying to see the show' himself. Hardy, somewhat startled by Walkley's 'humorous' recommendation of a 'quaint and unexpected channel of real performances by means of fantoccini, Chinese shadows, and other startling apparatus', responded with two letters (5 and 19 February) that attempted to expand on the comments dealing with literary structure and philosophy in the Preface to *The Dynasts*. But it was a losing battle. Walkley reprinted his reviews in *Drama and Life* (1907), and a discouraged Hardy never reprinted his letters. Indeed, he did not attempt to answer the other reviews of Part First.

As if being told by Walkley that 'this is not the book we desired or expected' were not enough, Hardy was to hear from *The Academy* (23 January) that his great conception had been inadequately worked out because he did not have a 'lifelong intimacy with the poet's craft': 'As a whole, the dialogue is the prose of the novelist cut into lengths. Nay, it is a fact that Mr Hardy is vastly more poetic as a novelist using his accustomed vehicle of prose. We can only say, with a sigh, that we would give many such dramas for one *Return of the Native*.' A. MacDonnell, writing for *The Bookman* (February) on 'Mr Hardy's Experiment', tried to be pleasant, but sounded only patronizing:

> Indeed, in the end our doubt is not as to the advisability of Mr Hardy's plan, but whether he had any plan at all, whether *The Dynasts* is anything save a collection of vivid excerpts from a careful and interesting note-book. We English hate the discipline of form; and in every transition age, when canons of art are disturbed, we riot in the licence of the formless.

The Spectator (20 February) deplored the execution of Hardy's conception and feared that

> Mr Hardy's reach must be held to exceed his grasp. . . . The cardinal error seems to us to lie in the philosophy, which is too cold, bloodless, and formal to be adequate to the needs of human life. . . . [The Spirits] conduct their espionage in the spirit of a very young man who has just begun to dabble in metaphysics, and is imperfectly acquainted with the terminology.

The reviewer for *The Nation* (25 February) called *The Dynasts* 'uncouth and forbidding', and argued that Hardy's lack of control prevented the work from 'quite conforming to any conceivable or valid aesthetic standard. It is likely, if completed, to remain one of those pieces of imaginative incunabula which, marking as they do the thought of a moody age, are made in time the basis of better work by better workmen.'

The *Monthly Review* (March) quarrelled with the philosophy of Part First on three grounds: first, that Hardy used Immanent Will in a highly personal way, not as Kant defined it; second, that he introduced the concept of Chance, thus blurring the reader's sense of what is meant by 'the Central Will' ('if the sense of will is an illusion it is an absolutely perfect one'); and third, that Hardy left out all references to personal religion among the characters, such as Nelson's famous prayer to God before the Battle of Trafalgar, because they might 'embarrass the author's theory'.

And what did Hardy make of Josephine Preston Peabody's essay on 'The Hardihood of Mr Hardy' in *The Critic* (May), with its grumblings about how 'dry and unbeautiful' the work was, and her statement that the speeches of the Spirits were

> a poor and unconvincing substitute for the golden-earthy background that unifies—and glorifies—*Tess*. . . . These choral abstractions . . . are unbeautiful merely, and they are sometimes unpronounceable. . . . We have the right to

demand more from all this verse. Why will not Mr Hardy write Poetry when he writes poetry? He can do it in prose.

Harsh judgements were also printed in *The Athenaeum, Literary World, Dial* and *The Atlantic Monthly*, but these excerpts may be enough to demonstrate that the reception of Part First—taken review by review or *en masse*—could do nothing but discourage Hardy from getting on with the job of completing Part Second and Part Third. Moreover, they very nearly ended the project. Writing to Edmund Gosse (17 January), Hardy despaired of finishing the work, and he brooded for a full two months before deciding to buckle down. We must be grateful that he once more refused to listen to the critics who ungenerously attempted to circumscribe his genius, and who denied his poetical gifts. As if to show once and for all that he was a professional in poetry no less than in prose, he went back to the text of Part First and carefully revised some of the language that had been censured; for example, dropping 'an untactical torpid despondency' (objected to by three critics), smoothing out some rough lines, breaking up others to prove that he had not written in the rhythms of Gilbert's nonsense songs. These corrections were incorporated into a second, revised impression printed in the spring of 1904. Later corrections were made for both the Wessex and the Mellstock Editions. (They are listed in the New Wessex Edition, published by Macmillan in 1978.)

Hardy believed the considerations of form were distracting readers from an appreciation of what, in fact, he had accomplished, and the degree to which he had achieved his multiple intentions; and Hardy early formed the notion—unchangeable to his dying day—that adverse reactions to *The Dynasts* had developed from a dislike of his 'argument' with its reliance on the idea of Immanent Will, and of its fundamental principle, Predestination.

Like any author, he treasured the praise of those who liked it. Max Beerbohm, Edmund Gosse, Ford Madox Ford, Siegfried Sassoon, Walter de la Mare and A. M. Broadley, among others, told him of their admiration. Years later Hardy confided to Ellen Glasgow that he considered it 'his greatest work (he may have said 'best')'.[1] *The Dynasts*, more than any other single work, earned Hardy his Order of Merit. At the time of conferral of the honorary degree of Doctor of Letters at Oxford in 1920, a special and flattering mention of *The Dynasts* was part of the ceremony. St John Ervine, sending him, in 1921, an address that had been signed by 106 younger writers, concluded:

> From your first book to your last you have written in the 'high style, as when that men to kinges write', and you have crowned a great prose with a noble poetry.
> We thank you, Sir, for all that you have written . . . but most of all, perhaps, for *The Dynasts*.[2]

A masterwork, *The Dynasts* is perhaps the greatest long poem in English published during this century (the claim has been made more than once). Yet, oddly enough, many lovers of Hardy have not read it, and many books about Hardy dismiss it in a footnote or a desultory paragraph. Some critics are still bemused by 'its experimental mixture of epic and drama, prose and poetry, narrative, theatrical, and even cinematic technique';[3] by the attraction that it exerts on 'writers interested only in philosophy';[4] and by the somewhat patronizing judgement, 'As a whole it is flawed . . . the ambition and the form were not quite manageable'.[5]

These views, current more than half a century after publication of *The Dynasts*, should warn us that Hardy's epic-drama does not clearly resemble his earlier and more readily understandable productions. Hardy's determination to write a new kind of fiction grew from a number of reasons, not all clearly sorted out in the memoirs that he dictated to Florence Emily Hardy many years later. Moreover, the doctrine of the Immanent Will has never been congenial to all readers, and Hardy, in *The Dynasts*, made his concept of Its nature inescapable, something not to be rushed over. And it is understandable that he did not, perhaps could not, achieve complete success in handling a full decade of European history in three parts, nineteen acts and 131 scenes.[6] Still, the degree of success that Hardy achieved is astonishing, and will be best appreciated if we take a closer look at what he thought he was up to. That, in turn, requires our looking at some biographical considerations.

Hardy's renunciation of the novel after the publication of *Jude the Obscure* (1895) is usually attributed to the hostility of the reviews. Jeannette Gilder's two notorious attacks in the *New York World* (Hardy's mind 'seems to run to pigs—animal and human'; when she finished the story, she opened the windows 'and let in the fresh air';

Hardy's realism was 'disgusting') appeared almost simultaneously with a review entitled 'Jude the Obscene' in the *Pall Mall Gazette*, a denunciation of Hardy's 'morbid animality' in the *New York Critic*, a sneer at the 'prevailing gloom' of the novel in *The Daily Telegraph* and a slating in the *Manchester Guardian*, which accused Hardy of having insulted 'marriage, religion and all the obligations and relations of life which most people hold sacred'. Other angry notices, all assuming that realism had its limits and that Hardy had overstepped them, sternly notified Hardy that still another effort to depict the 'night-cart' side of nature would not be tolerated.

Hardy's reaction—'A man must be a fool to deliberately stand up to be shot at'—followed immediately. He did not relish being described, by Mrs Oliphant, as a member of 'The Anti-Marriage League', one who seemed to suggest that hanging a child was the best way to remove the principal obstruction to the abolition of marriage. He had always been sensitive to unfriendly reviews (and had ample reason to be); but not even the reception of *Tess* had prepared him for what seemed to be an orchestrated outcry.

In addition, he knew well the hostility of his wife to the dangerous direction that his career as a novelist was following.[7] More novels along the lines of *Jude* might well destroy his marriage for all the world to see.

Yet these facts do not justify the speculation that Hardy, in 1895, thought he had accomplished all he wanted to in the world of prose fiction, and that *Jude* had been sent to press as a self-conscious final statement. Even riskier is the claim that Hardy had no more stories to tell that warranted novelistic treatment; that his blaming the reviewers proved a convenient method of ending a long dry spell of failed creativity. The point is important for two reasons: first, Hardy never admitted, either in the mid-1890s or later, that such a spell existed, and such speculation cannot be confirmed by anything that Hardy himself wrote or said; second, Hardy had always regarded the novel as a form of literature inferior to poetry, and the decision to renounce novel-writing was an inevitable event once Hardy had assured himself of financial independence.

Hardy's resolve to turn away from novels meant that he could devote time to a vast, still awkwardly defined project about the Napoleonic Wars that he had been considering, on and off, for more than two decades *before* he started on *Jude*. After all, he had grown up among adults who remembered and reminisced about alarums when it seemed that Boney's troops might invade Dorset; about the Peninsular Campaign, and foot-slogging across the Continent. He had read with fascination several numbers of *A History of the Wars,* a periodical that he discovered in a cupboard at home. His grandfather, a volunteer, had subscribed to it; as Hardy wrote in the *Life,* 'The torn pages of these contemporary numbers with their melodramatic prints of serried ranks, crossed bayonets, huge knapsacks, and dead bodies, were the first to set him on the train of ideas that led to *The Trumpet-Major* and *The Dynasts*'. He read, and often quoted, Carlyle's *The History of the French Revolution.* From the age of 15, when he first began to study the French language, his studies led him to Thiers, and to Hugo's view that the Bourbons were dynasts no less subject than Napoleon to the workings of destiny. By 1868 Hardy was toying with the notion of a narrative poem on the battle of the Nile; he completed an outline, now lost, of the poem. (What would Hardy have made of Napoleon's first direct confrontation with Nelson?) Within two years he paid the first of several visits to Chelsea Hospital, conducting interviews that tested the vividness of veterans' memories of Waterloo. The reading in primary and secondary sources that he conducted during 1878 and 1879 for *The Trumpet-Major* included C.H. Gifford's two-volume *History of the Wars Occasioned by the French Revolution, 1792–1816,* a work that he would return to some two decades later.

'Let Europe be the stage', Hardy wrote on 13 March 1874, 'and have scenes continually shifting'. Perhaps, as Hardy thought when he discovered his note after more than a quarter-century, it was then that he first thought of 'a conception of *The Dynasts*'. His puzzlement indicated that he had forgotten the exact moment of genesis. Far more likely, indeed, that there was no one moment; that the associations and leisure readings of a lifetime were preparing him for a major dramatization of the most significant European wars of the century; and that his visit of 1874 (with Emma) to locales in France associated with Napoleon, and again in 1876, to Waterloo, provided him with the continuing inspiration he needed. By June 1875 he was considering the possibility of '"A Ballad of the Hundred Days"', another ballad on Moscow, and a series of ballads about earlier campaigns, 'forming altogether an Iliad of Europe from 1789 to 1815'.[8] These interlinked ballads would have constituted 'an epic on the war with Napoleon'. In

June 1877 Hardy recorded his intention of creating 'a grand drama, based on the wars with Napoleon, or some one campaign (but not as Shakespeare's historical dramas)'. He was uncertain whether to call it 'Napoleon' or 'Josephine', or some other person's name. Josephine as heroine would have feminized his subject-matter in ways that are difficult to imagine today, and Hardy still had not made up his mind about the span of years he intended to cover; but his jotting of 1877 was indicative of a growing interest in the *form* of his new work. By November 1880, when he called it a 'Great Modern Drama', his use of the word 'modern' signified the resonances of the theme to Englishmen three-quarters of a century after Trafalgar. On 27 March 1881, he conceived of Napoleon as 'a sort of Achilles' who would serve as the protagonist of 'a Homeric Ballad', yet a few days later he returned to the thought that drama was more suitable as a genre: 'Mode for historical Drama. Action mostly automatic; reflex movement, etc. Not the result of what is called *motive,* though always ostensibly so, even to the actors' own consciousness. Apply an enlargement of these theories to, say, ''The Hundred Days!''''9 Here, for the first time, Hardy was relating the Napoleonic era to a 'philosophic scheme or framework', something larger in import, 'enclosing the historic scenes'.

During the 1880s, in brief, *The Dynasts* became a lingering, obsessive concern to which he could not devote as much time as he would have liked. In 1886 he was reading systematically in the British Museum Library 'and elsewhere', preparing himself for what he was later to call 'the question of *The Dynasts*'. In the spring of 1887 he visited the roof of Milan Cathedral, and there probably imagined the scene in *The Dynasts* which uses the Cathedral as a means of character revelation. In November he worked on another outline scheme: Napoleon would be 'haunted by an Evil Genius or Familiar, whose existence he has to confess to his wives'. Perhaps unsurprisingly, this concept proved deficient; and similarly to be abandoned was the scheme of Napoleon's use of necromancy to 'see the thoughts of opposing generals'. Yet, within a month, he knew that Coleridge's rule ('a long poem should not attempt to be poetical all through') would guide him as he concentrated the 'ornaments of dictions' in particular passages of the epic he was yet to write.

Most biographers and critics underestimate the length of the gestation-period. By 1895 Hardy had clearly identified the historical period he wished to treat (1805–15), regarded Napoleon as his major figure, thought of this unwritten work as differing in scope from, and presenting a greater challenge than, anything he had written before, and intended to present a recension of his opinions on the nature and significance of the Immanent Will. Moreover, he planned to cast it in the form of a drama or of an epic; possibly, he had begun to speculate, as a hybridized genre. An illuminating note was recorded on 21 September 1889: 'For carrying out that idea of Napoleon, the Empress, Pitt, Fox, etc., I feel continually that I require a larger canvas. . . . A spectral tone must be adopted . . . . Royal ghosts . . . . Title: 'A Drama of Kings'. It is true that the striking similarity of this projected title to that of Robert Buchanan's closet drama (1871) has caught the eye of scholars;[10] but Buchanan's fustian, historical digressions and failure to consider adequately the English role in defeating Napoleon could have presented Hardy with only the feeblest type of inspiration for this own *magnum opus.* Moreover, Hardy needed a tighter time-frame than Buchanan had used (two of the three parts of Buchanan's play dealt with 1870–1), and he soon dropped plans to review the stormy events of the French Revolution as a luxury of chronology that he could not afford. Then followed a note dated 1891, when Hardy was completing *Tess:* 'A Bird's-Eye View of Europe at the beginning of the Nineteenth Century . . . . It may be called "A Drama of the Times of the First Napoleon"'. The 'Napoleon drama' was to obsess him for the next fifteen years.

At one level, then, Hardy was writing about a French general whose character and actions had affected the lives of millions. If he focused on the time-period between the day when Napoleon put the crown of Lombardy on his own head in the Cathedral of Milan and the day when he was 'stung by spectral questionings' in the wood of Bossu after the battle of Waterloo, he had ready-made a reasonably well-shaped drama of the meteor-like fall of a dynast. For almost any other writer of his generation, that would have been enough of a creative problem.

But *The Dynasts,* as the Fore Scene informs us, takes place partly in the Overworld, where choral observers named Spirits talk continually about the Immanent Will and Its designs. Hardy's epic-drama is (among other things) an eloquent, detailed and, by and large, consistent statement about the relationship of human beings to the forces that shape the universe. The Preface maintains with prudent modesty that the doctrines of the Spirits are 'but tentative', and should be taken 'as contrivances of the fancy merely'. Hardy argues that these doctrines might, at best, secure, 'in the words of Coleridge, "that willing suspension of disbelief for the moment which constitutes poetic faith"'

Nevertheless, Hardy knew, even better than most of his critics, how radically his epic-drama differed from previous literary models. Since the gods of the old dispensation were no longer believed in, the 'celestial machinery' of the *Iliad,* the *Eddas,* and *Paradise Lost* was irrelevant to a modern poet. God was no longer creditable as an 'anthropomorphic conception'. Napoleon's defeat, if it were ever to become important to the modern world, must be rendered in the language of an artist, certainly not that of a biographer or historian. He would invent—as he put it—a 'modern expression of a modern outlook'.

The notion that a participant in battle does not perceive the larger outlines of strategy had been dramatized by Stendhal; the doctrine that war moves at its own lumbering, inevitable pace, unaffected by anything Napoleon did, or could do, had been argued by Tolstoy (a writer whom Hardy greatly admired, though Hardy had not as yet read his *War and Peace*). Still, the 'supernatural spectators of the terrestrial action' had a great deal more to say about the follies of mankind at war, and much of it was bound to disturb those readers and reviewers who had already been upset by authorial comments made in *Tess* and *Jude.* The Immanent Will had already been discussed seriously, and at length, by Eduard von Hartmann (*Philosophy of the Unconscious,* translated into English in 1884) and Arthur Schopenhauer (*The World as Will and Idea,* read by Hardy in its 1890 translation), but Hardy knew even as Part First moved through the press that his treatment would stir up British philistines. If we keep in mind that Hardy's renunciation of the novel as an art-form was not meant to be taken as a renunciation of literature itself or of his personal religious views, and the fact that Hardy had formulated most of the overall plan for *The Dynasts* well before the turn of the century, the famous note of 17 October 1896, may be seen as doubly artful:

Poetry. Perhaps I can express more fully in verse ideas and emotions which run counter to the inert crystallized opinion—hard as a rock—which the vast body of men have vested interests in supporting. To cry out in a passionate poem that (for instance) the Supreme Mover or Movers, the Prime Force or Forces, must be either limited in power, unknowing, or cruel—which is obvious enough, and has been for centuries—will cause them merely a shake of the head; but to put it in argumentative prose will make them sneer, or foam, and set all the literary contortionists jumping upon me, a harmless agnostic, as if I were a clamorous atheist, which in their crass illiteracy they seem to think is the same thing. . . . If Galileo had said in verse that the world moved, the Inquisition might have let him alone.[11]

Hardy's opinion—that the Immanent Will is indifferent to man's aspirations—is lucidly argued by the Spirits (and *The Dynasts* is 'a passionate poem', as we shall see). The Immanent Will does not speak directly for Itself; it is 'viewless' and 'voiceless'; most of what we learn about it comes from the speeches of the Spirits. It works unconsciously. We may cherish only the faintest hope that some day, after the passing of aeons, It may become self-aware, and thus help to improve the lot of the human race. At the present time, It controls the human race. Whether history is to be regarded as terrestrial tragedy (according to the Spirit of the Pities) or comedy (Spirit Ironic), 'these flesh-hinged mannikins' do not operate independently, and cannot. They move as one organism. Wars have long been ordained:

> Ere systemed suns were globed and lit
> The slaughters of the race were writ
> (Part I, Act II, Scene v)

Thus Napoleon's schemes for the continuation of dynastic power are foredoomed, and at the end of the epic-drama the dynasts who succeed him have no clearer sense of their own limitations, of their vulnerability to 'the Immanent Unrecking'. Men do not learn from one generation to the next. After Waterloo, when—presumably—the forces of humanity have defeated the discredited, exhausted army of the emperor, the Spirit of the Years can say, in melancholy tones no less intense because its message has been prefigured:

> So hath the Urging Immanence used to-day
> Its inadvertent might to field this fray;
> And Europe's wormy dynasties rerobe
> Themselves in their old gilt, to dazzle anew the globe!
> (III, VII, viii)

The Spirits are as much subject to the will as 'the frail ones' who 'gyrate like animalcula/In tepid pools'. Hardy differentiates them, nevertheless. Most important is the Spirit of the Years, to whom the deterministic shape of this grim decade is clear from the very beginning. Years rationalizes whenever he speaks:

> The Will has woven with an absent heed
> Since life first was; and ever will so weave.
> [Fore Scene]

Years sees no point in moaning about 'the World-Soul's way'. He insists that the Semichoruses of the Pities pay attention again to 'the ordered potencies,/Nerves, sinews, trajects, eddies, ducts' of the Will (I, VI, iii)—as if by grim repetition the refractory student will learn his lesson.

More attractive for many readers is the Spirit of the Pities, who came into the world late, during the Tertiary Age of human beings, and hence must defer to the older Years. Remembering Christianity from 'its early, loving kindly days', before it became ceremonial and institutionalized, Pities recognizes the illogicality of emotion:

> I feel, Sire, as I must! This tale of Will
> And Life's impulsion by Incognizance
> I cannot take.
> (I, I, vi)

Unable to accept the grimness of Year's teaching, Pities cannot delay the passing of men 'to dark corruption, at the best' (II, IV, viii), and cannot change its inevitability. The importance of this Figure lies in the advocacy of compassion; the suggestion, however faint, that men may choose between alternatives.

The names of the other Spirits are suggestive: Ironic, Sinister, Rumours, Recording Angels. Shade of the Earth must be thought of as feminine, even Shelleyan: she regards herself as the 'ineffectual Shade' of the earth, and looks forward to a time when those 'who love the true, the excellent' will inherit her bounties. She is on the side of Pities, who, after all the campaigns have ended, speaks last.

Hardy refracted through the speeches of his Spirits the significance of a grand cavalcade of events that no mere human participant could appreciate. He solved the problem of perspective by viewing Europe as the Spirits might, from an awesome height above the earth. For some readers, this has always been Hardy's most original contribution, the angles of vision that relate 'the mindless minions' wheeling 'in mechanised enchantment' to huger vistas, to the curvature of the earth itself. The Fore Scene begins with one such spectacle, as the nether sky opens to disclose Europe: 'a prone and emaciated figure, the Alps shaping like a backbone, and the branching mountain-chains like ribs, the peninsular plateau of Spain forming a head. Broad and lengthy lowlands stretch from the north of France across Russia like a grey-green garment hemmed by the Ural mountains and the glistening Arctic ocean'. Hardy moves closer: 'The point of view then sinks downwards through space, and draws near to the surface of the perturbed countries, where the peoples, distressed by events which they did not cause, are seen writhing, crawling, heaving, and vibrating in their various cities and nationalities'. At times Hardy imagines himself 'on high over the Straits of Dover, and stretching from city to city' ('The Route between London and Paris', II, I, ii), or above the open sea between the English coasts and the Spanish Peninsula ('Four groups of moth-like transport and war ships are discovered silently skimming this wide liquid plain', II, II, v), or over the spacious field later to be commemorated by the name of the village Borodino (III, I, v), or so high that Leipzig may be seen as 'somewhat in the shape of the letter D, the straight part of which is the river Pleisse' (III, III, ii). Some of Hardy's finest descriptive writing may be found in these openings to scenes of momentous import, of sanguinary excess, whether at Cape Trafalgar or Torrès Védras or Vimiero, and as representative as any, and as splendidly imagined, is the field of Waterloo itself, to which an impatient reader may be referred (III, VII, i).

This mode of seeing may be termed Burkean. Hardy found ample warrant for it in a book he knew well, *A Philosophical Enquiry into the Origin of Our Ideas of the Sublime and Beautiful* (first published in 1757, enlarged in 1759). There he found defined several causes of the Sublime, among them vastness, also called 'greatness of dimension'. Burke mused that looking down from a precipice was probably more striking 'than . . . looking up at an object of equal height' (II, vii), and Hardy took the thought as a guide to the writing of dozens of descriptions throughout the poem.

In addition to his desire to impose order upon a jumble of childhood impressions, to confer significance upon history by the devising of a philosophical and theological argument, and to exploit a novel way of treating European vistas (one that still defies the technical resources of the cinema), Hardy had still another reason for wanting to write *The Dynasts.* In his preface he admitted that completing *The Trumpet-Major* and seeing it into print had brought him only to 'the fringe of a vast international tragedy', and he had been unable to do more artistically with its 'events'. 'But', he added, 'the slight regard paid to English influence and action throughout the struggle by so many Continental writers who had dealt with Napoléon's career, seemed always to leave room for a new handling of the theme which should re-embody the features of this influence in their true proportion; and accordingly'. What Hardy was saying, in brief, was that the Napoleonic Wars had failed to attract writers willing to give proper credit to the younger Pitt, Nelson, Wellington and the thousands of English soldiers and sailors who had fought, and finally defeated, the French emperor. The failure of imaginative writers—of Romantic and Victorian poets and novelists—to exploit the riches of these materials has puzzled not only Hardy but also historians and literary critics. William R. Rutland, for example, has dismissed as relatively minor efforts the celebrated Waterloo passage in the third canto of Byron's *Childe Harold,* and the 'Odes in Contribution to the Song of French History' written by Meredith (less than a thousand lines survive). When Tennyson memorialized the Great Duke, he predicted that in some later age ('Far on in summers that we shall not see') another poet would celebrate Wellington's triumph over Napoleon; he did not attempt the task himself. Rutland went on to say, in a judgement that has not been challenged,

> *The Dynasts* is to-day the greatest imaginative representation of the Napoleonic epoch in the literature of Western Europe. As far as English is concerned, it is likely to remain without successors, as it was without forerunners. No major English poet before Hardy had cared to dedicate himself to that theme; and after Hardy none will either dare or desire to sing again the lay he sang once for all.[12]

At this point we come to the baffling problem for which no critic has yet proposed a satisfactory solution: the discrepancy between Hardy's grim, unrelenting vision of a helpless humanity, 'atoms', entangled by the weavings of an unthinking Will, and the heroism of a few individuals (most English, though Hardy admired Marshal Ney, and always depicted him favourably). *The Dynasts,* without descending to the level of crude caricature of 'Boney' save in a few Wessex scenes, and without flinching from the unflattering record of English war-profiteering, cowardice and a strong desire to act as if Napoleon were an ephemeral phenomenon, is essentially a patriotic work. It is true that the first long movement of *The Dynasts* describes Trafalgar, a naval battle that pitted Villeneuve of the *Bucentaure* against Nelson of the *Victory* (I, v), with Napoleon only a name; that Napoleon is not directly involved as a character in any of the scenes depicting Spanish battlefields (II, II–IV, and VI), and that Wellington is not in direct confrontation with Napoleon during the Russian campaign (III, I–II). But England is throughout and everywhere the Nemesis of the French emperor's dynastic schemes. It is certainly more real to him than the Immanent Will, the workings of which he only faintly apprehends. For Napoleon, the English are 'licentious', like all 'canting peoples' (III, II, ii), insolent, able and willing to stir up dissension on the Continent, using their wealth to frustrate him, a nation skilled in a 'tough, enisled, self-centered, kindless craft'. If Nelson had not blocked him at sea and, at the cost of his own life, crippled his great armada, Napoleon would have invaded England. If England had not heartened and supported the guerilla forces on the Iberian Peninsula, he could have secured a minimal army there while he turned his attention to Russia. He blamed England for turning the Tsar's head from his resolve to destroy that nation, a pledge made at Tilsit and the River Niemen (II, I, vii). The English resolutely refused to recognize the government of Joseph, King of Spain. Later, if he succeeded in his Russian invasion, he would march on to the Ganges, and then

> Once ripped by a French sword, the scaffolding
> Of English merchant-mastership in Ind
> Will fall a wreck
>
> (III, I, i)

All that he did in Russia (Napoleon told himself) was done to revenge himself upon England.

Hardy's emphasis on Napoleon's monomaniacal hatred of his enemy across the Channel distorts the historical record, for

England was not Napoleon's primary concern for long periods of time. But these iterations do redress the balance for generations of neglect by previous historians, and do give the English their due for the first time in imaginative literature. Moreover, Hardy's heroes are astonishingly godlike. When the candle-snuffers do their duty (I, I, iii), Pitt rises to speak, and 'During the momentary pause . . . the House assumes an attentive stillness, in which can be heard the rustling of the trees without, a horn from an early coach, and the voice of the watch crying the hour'. To Pitt a 'strange fatality' now 'haunts the times' wherein the lot of Englishmen is cast, but he is determined to face the perils created by Napoleon. The king may reject his counsel (Pitt wants to form a coalition government with Fox and Lord Grenville), but he will not despair. After Nelson's astonishing victory—England is not to be threatened at sea for the remainder of the century—he proffers a toast at the Guildhall:

> . . . no man saved England, let me say:
> England has saved herself, by her exertions:
> She will, I trust, save Europe by her example!
>
> (I, V, v)

Years calls this speech 'his last large words'; but dying, Pitt is to call, 'My country! How I leave my country! . . .' (I, VI, viii) and we are reminded of Nelson's valedictory, after the great sailor has ordered Beatty to 'Go to the others who lie bleeding there', and Hardy to kiss him. (Hardy framed and kept the portrait of Sir Thomas Masterman Hardy, his kinsman and Nelson's flag-captain, framed opposite a portrait of himself in the drawing-room of Max Gate.) 'I'm satisfied', Nelson murmurs. 'Thank God, I have done my duty!'

Wellington is less quotable, and Hardy indicated, by printing his name in italics among the list of characters at the beginning of Part Second, that he would remain mute throughout the Peninsular Campaign. But Wellington is no less devoted to king and country than Pitt or Nelson: he speaks often of 'poor devils' and 'brave men'; he never loses faith in the ultimate victory; and every speech at Waterloo—during the most perilous and undecided moments of that see-saw engagement—is a rallying-cry:

> At Talavera, Salamanca, boys
> And at Vitoria, we saw smoke together;

And though the day seems wearing doubtfully,
Beaten we must not be!

(III, VII, vii)

The royal blood of courage runs freely among the common people, in the scenes of Wessex ('Rainbarrows' Beacon, Egdon Heath, I, II, v; and Durnover Green, Casterbridge, III, VI, vi), the streets of London, the reception-room of the Marchioness of Salisbury's ('At last, then, England will take her place in the forefront of this moral struggle, and in pure disinterestedness fight with all her strength for the European deliverance. God defend the right!'—II, II, iii), in a Viennese café in the Stephans-Platz, at the Ford of Santa Marta, Salamanca, on the plain of Vitoria, and at the famous ball in the now-legendary ballroom of the Duke and Duchess of Richmond's, Brussels, the night before Waterloo.

These men and women regarded Napoleon as someone to take seriously. He is, of course, the most important character in the epic-drama. Hardy's characterization of the nineteenth-century Alexander depended heavily on 'oral tradition, accessible scenery, and existing relics', as well as 'the abundant pages of the historian, the biographer, and the journalist, English and Foreign', as he wrote in the Preface. The historians were by far the most useful. Among the most important were Sir Archibald Alison's *History of Europe* (ten volumes, useful as background for III, I); William Hazlitt's *Life of Napoleon Bonaparte* (four volumes); Adolphe Thiers' *Histoire du Consulat et de l'Empire* (twenty volumes, and perhaps Hardy's most important single source, available to the poet in both the Paris edition of 1857 and the D. Forbes Campbell translation); W.F.P. Napier's *The History of the War in the Peninsula* (six volumes); and le Comte de Ségur, William Beatty and the Baron Claude-François de Meneval.[13] If occasionally the inconsistencies of Hardy's characterization puzzle us, if the Napoleon who acts as master of his destiny seems oddly incongruous with the Napoleon who cowers before premonitions, ghostly warnings and dreams, the roots of the problem lie in the baffled studies of the emperor's life that Hardy consulted. The historians, despite the passage of more than seven decades, had not formed a consensus. The legend of Napoleon as legitimate heir of the French Revolution and as Lawgiver still seemed attractive. Part of Hardy's originality must be accounted his willingness to endorse the historian Pierre Lanfrey's harsh verdict on Napoleon's character. In his structuring of scenes that dramatize the impossible and thankless assignment to Villeneuve, the hypocritical negotiations with representatives of rival nations, the ruthless treatment of Josephine, Marie Louise and Louisa of Prussia, and the delight in war's carnage, Hardy presents us with a loveless and unlovable hero.

Nevertheless, a *hero;* and Hardy's portrait, despite its sombre coloration, is more subtle, human and credible than any other fictionalized version. Napoleon unifies the work; he is present more often, and has more to say, than any other of the 297 human beings with speaking roles. His vision of himself as emperor, and of the king of Rome as his legitimate successor, is at least as appealing as the mean and corroded ambitions of the other dynasts of Europe. If such a vision is to be bought at excessive cost, Hardy makes sure that we know how much the royal houses have earned their destruction. (Hardy reserves his pity for the soldiers who die for causes they do not understand, and for the civilians who suffer for no cause at all.) Napoleon's interest in moral and ethical questions, his sincere belief that he works 'for France', and his obvious zest in holding centre-stage, make him more than two-dimensional. As his character deteriorates, the images of his physical debilitation multiply, particularly after Borodino; yet for most of the epic-drama, as in life, he exerts a genuine, almost sexual attraction over worldly-wise men and women who share with him his conviction that he follows a personal star. The speech to Queen Louisa, delivered at a moment when he is determined to deny her Magdeburg, or what she prizes most, impresses us as a statement of what Napoleon must, in fact, have believed about himself:

> Know you, my Fair,
> That I—ay, I—in this deserve your pity.
> Some force within me, baffling mine intent,
> Harries me onward, whether I will or no.
> My star, my star is what's to blame—not I.
> It is unswerveable!
>
> (II, I, viii)

In recent years, and particularly since the Second World War, Hardy's work has been praised more generously and seen for what it is: the central event of his life, and not an aberration from a developing career as a poet of love lyrics and dramatic sketches and satires. *The Dynasts* treats issues of great magnitude, challenges the imagination and achieves something very close to sublimity in the Burkean sense. It triumphs over its faults, the mixed materials, the lengthy passages of ill-disguised prose and only partially versified transcription, the tedious repetitions of the querulous Spirits, the inconsistent treatments of heroism in a predetermined universe. These faults are inseparable from a splendour of vision unique to Hardy.

Disillusioned by the Great War and by the Treaty of Versailles, Hardy wrote, years later, that Napoleon had thrown back 'human altruism scores, perhaps hundreds of years'. If he could have foreseen the Great War, he might not have written *The Dynasts* at all, or at least might not have concluded it with a carefully worded promise of a developing self-awareness on the part of the Immanent Will. Two months before his death he brooded that 'he had done all that he meant to do, but he did not know whether it had been worth doing'. The starkness of the final views, recorded in the poignant section of the *Life* entitled 'Life's Decline', should not obscure the fact that, long before the revulsion caused by trench warfare, Hardy had recorded the strongest possible indictment of the bloodiness and impersonality of modern warfare. No reader of Hardy's descriptions of the debacle of the Satschan lake (Austerlitz), the 'ghastly climax' of Albuera, the slaughter at the bridge of the Beresina, or of what takes place during the snow-storm in the road from Smolensko into Lithuania, can mistake Hardy's moral indignation as being that of a cynical or neutral perspective. Anger at the futility of war, compassion for the defenceless and the defeated, admiration for the inspired leadership of Nelson, Pitt and Wellington, and love of country—the epic-drama surges with emotion. Thomas Hardy never spoke more directly than through the Chorus of the Years in that great lyric timed just before the fighting begins at Waterloo (III, VI, viii). One may not read it unmoved; nor, once having read the whole, remember it without affection.

As the years have passed, it has become more clear that *The Dynasts* is an authentic continuator of epic tradition. It fulfils every requirement listed by E.M.W. Tillyard in *The English Epic and Its Background* (1954): high quality and high seriousness, amplitude and variety, rigorous control and choric appropriateness.

6

Hardy's Interest in the Law

In March 1894 Thomas Hardy visited some friends in London and was particularly intrigued by some '*odd* legal experiences' recounted to him by Lord Herschell the Lord Chancellor.[1] Hardy, who underlined the word 'odd' when he recorded it, did not recount any of these anecdotes, though we would enjoy having them in his dry and wittily understated style. More disappointing still is the fact that he regarded the encounter of insufficient interest to be worthy of retention in his thinly disguised autobiography, and omitted the passage. Nor are there other entries of much concern to us, or to my chosen topic, in the assemblage of deleted paragraphs edited by Richard Taylor in *The Personal Notebooks of Thomas Hardy*. To be sure, there is an allusion to Lady Coleridge, wife of the Lord Chief Justice, who, on 29 June 1889, confided to Hardy that on occasion she had gone on circuit, and sat in court half-an-hour 'to please her husband'. If she did not do so, she added, he would say that she took no interest in his duties.[2] One would never guess from what was left out—or, for that matter, what was retained—that Hardy's labours as Justice of the Peace for the Borough of Dorchester from 1884 on, and for the County of Dorset from 1894 on, were serious, deeply-committed, and living testimony to his involvement in local affairs. We have already disagreed with the stereotyped image of Hardy as a recluse in Dorchester who paid little attention to local events because his mind turned continually to national and international developments, or to his relations with publishers, or to a truly massive correspondence with well-wishers, friends and total strangers. But that image must be modified even more drastically in the light of our knowledge of still another pattern of Hardy's life that can be constructed on the basis of available documents.

Rather curiously, however, not from biographical treatments. Hardy's interest in the law and in the problems created by the administration of human justice was an abiding one, but one would never guess it from reading the two volumes of Robert Gittings's life of Hardy—a work admirable in so many other ways—any more than from the two volumes of Florence Emily's work. The Toucan Press seems not to have identified Hardy's concern with legal problems as significant during his years at Max Gate. Apart from a first-rate piece of research on Hardy's court experiences written up by Edward C. Sampson in the *Colby Library Quarterly* of December 1977, I do not know of any investigation that renders in its true dimensions, and with full consideration of its implications, Hardy's willingness to sit in court at least thirty-eight times as a magistrate and to serve at least sixteen times on grand juries for the Assizes.

This review of some biographical materials considers Hardy's awareness of criminals and cases under adjudication, his friendships with various judges, solicitors and barristers, his fictionalizations of legal problems that demonstrate rather sophisticated knowledge of courtroom procedure, and his own experiences as a magistrate in the courts of Dorchester.

I will begin with Hardy's knowledge of real criminals and real prison-sentences. Hardy, towards the end of his life, signed (in 1923) a petition for abridging the sentence of a former director of a bank, Walter Crotch, who at the time was serving a gaol-sentence for fraud. Crotch had already spent the major part of two years of a four-year sentence behind bars. But Hardy was more moved by Crotch's illness, and by his memory of Crotch's campaign to raise £25,000 to establish a home for blinded soldiers.[3] It would be equally pleasant to report a number of cases in which Hardy, appalled by the harshness of criminal sentences, sought to temper with mercy (or at least to describe with mercy) the fate of various prisoners brought to judgment. What we find instead is a series of narratives, sketches and notations made for possible future use, in many instances without editorial comment, about men, women and young people ensnared in the toils of the law.

There is, for example, the well-known story of Martha Brown, the murderess whose execution Hardy witnessed when he was sixteen. The memory of the way in which her 'fine figure . . . showed against the sky as she hung in the misty rain, and how the tight black silk gown set off her shape as she wheeled half-round and back' was committed to paper on 20 January 1926, in a letter to Lady Hester Pinney, who had been kind enough to send him some stories relating to the incident.[4] Lady Pinney, as a district councillor and a Poor Law guardian, was able to interview old, bedridden patients at the Beaminster Infirmary, and she learned of Martha Brown's beauty, as well as of her folly in marrying a man twenty years younger than herself, who apparently had been interested only in her money. Jealous at the sight of another woman sitting on her husband's knee, she hit him on the head with a hatchet. Though she called in a neighbour and claimed that she found her husband dying at the door from kicks from her horse, 'the story was not believed'.[5] It is understandable that Hardy's memory of the hanging should have remained vivid for seven decades, but perhaps a little unexpected that he should have felt obliged to apologize to Lady Pinney for having attended the event ('my only excuse being that I was but a youth, and had to be in the town at the time for other reasons'). But a note of subdued erotic appreciation, even of prurience, in his description of Martha Brown's body rather startles us, particularly when taken in conjunction with the descriptions of the execution of another woman, Mary Channing, whose sentence for supposedly poisoning her husband in 1705 included both strangulation and burning.

The way in which Mary Channing died, as recounted by Hardy in a notebook entry dated 25 January 1919, as well as in Chapter 11 of *The Mayor of Casterbridge,* the poem 'the Mock Wife', and an article on Maumbury Ring published in *The Times* on 9 October 1908, was so horrifying that the kindly J.O. Bailey, in annotating the sources of the poem 'The Mock Wife', wrote with some dismay, 'Some shocking details are here omitted'.[6] My point is, at least partly, that *Hardy* did not omit them. Mary Channing was first strangled; the burning of her body revived her; she 'writhed and shrieked', and one of the constables, seeking to stop her cries, 'thrust a swab into her mouth, . . . & the milk from her bosoms (she had lately given birth to a child) squirted out in their faces ''and made 'em jump back''' [7] Hardy, who was transcribing these details at the age of 79, depended for his source on Charles Prideaux, at that time secretary of the Dorset Field Club, who in turn was remembering what he had been told by 'old M---, a direct descendant of one who was a witness of the execution'.[8] Hardy was fascinated by this and 'other details—(such as the smell of roast meat, etc.)', and in this account, at least, there is not the faintest indication, as Evelyn Hardy noted, of the existence of either horror or pity 'in the heart of the beholder and mediator'.[9]

But I am more interested in Hardy's re-thinking of the evidence used to convict Mary Channing; for Hardy regarded the case against her as 'not proven' (that famous Scottish formulation for equivocating one's point of view). Mary, not yet 19 when she died, had been married 'against her wish by the compulsion of her parents', and the wedding, from the first, had been marked for unhappiness. 'The present writer has examined more than once a report of her trial', Hardy wrote in 'Maumbury Ring', 'and can find no distinct evidence that the thoughtless, pleasure-loving creature committed the crime, while it contains much to suggest that she did not. Nor is any motive discoverable for such an act'.[10] As Bailey remarked, Hardy's real feeling lies buried in the phrases 'Guilty she may not be', and 'truly judged, or false', used in the somewhat fictionalized account contained in 'The Mock Wife'.[11] If Hardy really believed that justice had gone astray in this case, or (what is tantamount to the same thing) that the evidence on which the judicial decision had been based deserved re-examination because it was largely second-hand in nature and extenuating circumstances had not been taken into account, the horribleness of the details of the execution, recorded faithfully by a soon-to-be octogenarian, underscored the need for officers of the law to move more slowly and majestically before proceeding to a final disposition of a capital judgment. In other words, Hardy's feeling for Mary Channing may have been more susceptible to pity than Evelyn Hardy was willing to concede.

A respectable number of accounts of transgressions against the law turn up in Hardy's non-fictional writings, and these are often linked with the sentences meted out as appropriate punishment. For example, at the British Library, while working on his *Trumpet-Major Notebook*, Hardy recorded with some care an attempt of two soldiers of the York Hussars to desert. They stole a boat, intending to go to France, but by mistake landed at Guernsey; they were captured; and, after praying for twenty minutes in the company of two priests, they were 'shot at by a guard of 24 men; they dropped instantly, & expired without a groan. The men wheeled in sections, & marched by the bodies in slow time'.[12] This incident was to become the basis of the story 'The Melancholy Hussar of the German Legion', later collected in *Life's Little Ironies* (1894).

Hardy's probable view, that this punishment exceeded the requirements of justice, may be confirmed by examination of his remarks made on other occasions, as when he noted, after a visit to Chelsea Hospital and Ranelagh Gardens on 27 October 1878, that soldiers sentenced to 600 to 900 lashes 'if the doctor said it could be borne',[13] would have salt rubbed on their backs 'to harden' the flesh. Hardy wrote somberly, 'In those days if you only turned your eye you were punished'. He was describing a common custom in the first decade of the 1800s; the German Hussars were executed in 1801.

But if we restrict our attention, for the moment, to Hardy's interest in murders, we find a surprising number of notations on this particular transgression. It is sometimes forgotten that Hardy witnessed a second hanging in addition to that of Martha Brown.[14] It took place some two or three years later. Hardy, remembering that the duly announced carrying-out of the sentence would take place at 8 a.m., left his breakfast table at Bockhampton, walked hastily to a nearby hill, and clapped to his eye a 'big brass telescope that had been handed on in the family', just at the moment that 'the white figure dropped downwards, and the faint note of the town clock struck eight'. Hardy was appalled by both the suddenness of the event and by his feeling of being alone with the hanged man. He 'crept homeward wishing he had not been so curious'.[15]

Hardy's interest in murders may be described as an obsession. On 9 September 1882, a Dr Brine, over teacups, mentioned that 'Jack White's gibbet (near Wincanton) was standing as late as 1835—*i.e.* the oak-post with the iron arm sticking out, and a portion of the cage in which the body had formerly hung'. Hardy would doubtless have gone to see it 'if some young men had not burnt it down by piling faggots round it' on a Guy Fawkes day.[16]

Hardy carefully recorded the fact that a travelling waxwork proprietor used 'heads of murderers . . . as a wholesome lesson to evildoers'.[17] On 10 September 1888, he wrote that a T. Voss 'used to make casts of heads of executed convicts'. A 'Dan Pouncy held the heads while it was being done. Voss oiled the faces, and took them in halves, afterwards making casts from the masks. There was a groove where the rope went', and Hardy added with an historian's love of exactitude, one could see 'a little blood' in the case of one murderer, 'where the skin had been broken', though not in the case of another.[18] Hardy was fascinated when he learnt that the bodies of Lord Frederick Cavendish and of Thomas Henry Burke, the under-secretary in the Irish Government, after their murders in Phoenix Park (6 May 1882), had been placed in a room at the chief secretary's lodge. After their removal from thence, the room was not properly cleaned out. Mrs Lyttleton, Hardy's hostess, told 'some gruesome details of the discovery of a roll of bloody clothes under the sofa after the entry of the succeeding Secretary'.[19] To Hardy all this came as thrilling news; he had personally inspected the scene of the Phoenix Park murders only the day before (23 October 1893). A similar intense emotion overcame him when he learned that the splashing of a fountain outside his window at the Hotel de la Paix in Geneva was the very sound heard by the Austrian Empress just before she was murdered by the Italian anarchist Luigi Luccheni (10 September 1898). 'His accidental nearness in time and place to the spot of her doom', wrote Hardy, 'moved him much when he heard of it, since thereby hung a tale. She was a woman whose beauty, as shown in her portraits, had attracted him greatly in his youthful years, and had inspired some of his early verses, the same romantic passion having also produced the outline of a novel upon her, which he never developed'.[20] Hardy recalled, with some pride of association, that a Dorchester hangman named Davies, who presided over a number of executions in the early part of the nineteenth century, had been a friend of the Hardy family. (So he confided to Rebekah Owen.)

Hardy took more than a casual interest in the trial of Mrs Edith Thompson of Ilford and of Frederick Bywaters for the murder of Percy Thompson, Edith's husband, in 1922. The steady administration of poison over a four-month period, climaxed by a stabbing, as well as Mrs Thompson's demure and iron-controlled demeanour in the courtroom, led to the printing of sensational headlines, stories and photographs. Hardy paid special attention to the passionate letters that had passed between Mrs Thompson and Frederick Bywaters, letters introduced as evidence in the trial. Hardy had no doubt that Mrs Thompson did what the prosecution maintained she had done. She was no Mary Channing, and her death-sentence roused him to no protest (though many Englishmen and women protested in marches and parades at Holloway Prison); but it did inspire one of his most intriguing poems, 'On the Portrait of a Woman about to be Hanged', first printed in the *London Mercury* (February 1923) and collected in *Human Shows* (1925). A key element in Hardy's thinking about the case must have been the unwillingness of Percy Thompson to grant his wife a divorce, even though he knew of her adulterous relationship to Bywaters. Hardy's own strong feelings about the necessity for revising England's outdated divorce laws scandalized his wife, invaded his fictions and became a major concern from the 1890s on. His poem, however, suggests that Mrs Thompson, so 'comely and capable' in a 'gown of grace', could not do other than what her destiny necessitated. God, who had brought her into being (Hardy calls God her 'Causer'), made her 'sound in the germ', but then sent 'a worm/To madden Its handiwork'. The real question, as Hardy propounded it, was why the It who had made Mrs Thompson did not choose—on the basis of Its knowledge of what she would become—*not* to have 'assayed' her. Why, in brief, did the Causer implant in her a 'Clytaemnestra spirit'?

Like many similar rhetorical questions in Hardy's poetry, this one does not find its answer. But Hardy's view towards capital punishment for such crimes was once committed to the record, and despite his open doubting of the wisdom of some death sentences, it fairly enough reflected his life-long belief. An economist at Stanford University, securing data for a survey on opinions, wrote to Hardy early in the new century and asked whether Hardy believed in the advisability of abolishing capital punishment in highly civilized communities. Hardy's response is worth quoting in full:

> As an acting magistrate I think that Capital Punishment operates as a deterrent from deliberate crimes against life to an extent that no other form of punishment can rival. But the question of the moral right of a community to inflict that punishment is one I cannot enter into in this necessarily brief communication.[21]

The striking aspect of this opinion, I believe, is Hardy's pointing to his experience on the bench, where he met with capital offences. He was conceding that justice might err, and sometimes did; but the existence of capital punishment as a judgment on murderers possessed an intrinsic, and salutary, deterrent effect.

Of lesser crimes Hardy had much to say. Even the most casual reader may observe how vivid a fact of life—both to Dorset history and to Hardy's imagination—smuggling was. Mother Rogers, who carried slung round her hips bullocks' bladders in which she carried illegal spirits that she sold for cheap prices, was an active smuggler in the early years of the nineteenth century. Hardy's grandfather passed some of his spare time left over from superintending of church music in the storing of some eighty tubs of spirits in a dark closet in his lonely Higher Bockhampton home. 'The spirits often smelt all over the house', Hardy wrote in a memoranda book, 'being (13) proof & had to be lowered for drinking'.[22] These tubs, brought at night by men on horseback, 'slung' or in carts, were taken away the following evening by 'groups of dark long-bearded fellows'. The smugglers were so bold that they tried delivering the tubs by day, to which Hardy's grandmother objected; but they would not leave off bringing them by day until a second house was built about 100 yards off. For elaboration of this and other smuggling episodes, Hardy invented the story of 'The Distracted Preacher' (1879); he even used the real name of a customs officer from Weymouth, Will Latimer. Other anecdotes about smuggling he picked up from his landlord at Swanage, 'an invalided captain of smacks and ketches'.[23] One story turned out so strangely that Hardy wrote it down in full: smugglers were discovered, at sea, by a revenue-cutter; they pretended to fish by rigging bits of tobacco-pipe above the shank; and lo and behold, they began to haul in mackerel: 'The fish had made their deception truth'. Hardy devoted four pages to smuggling in *The Trumpet-Major Notebook,* and though these pages contain serio-comic elements, the war between smugglers and customs officers—tilting back and forth without harm to property or life and limb on a number of occasions—at other times (faithfully transcribed by Hardy from his sources) resulted in real deaths. Hardy read books about smuggling, such as Mary Kettle's *Smugglers and Foresters* (London, 1851) and a three-volume work called *The Smugglers* (Edinburgh, 1820). He became interested in the way in which the establishment of coast-guard and preventative stations finally ruined the smuggling trade. And, although Hardy does not editorialize about the claim of the crew of a small smuggling vessel, *Hope of Lymn,* that their captain 'was washed overboard the preceding night',[24] the possibility that mutiny had taken place on the high seas did not escape his notice.

For a landlubber, Hardy acquired more than a minimal amount of useful information about sailors and the sea (perhaps because he took a muted but still genuine pride in the likelihood that Admiral

Nelson's Hardy was a descendant from a common ancestor in the remote past); after all, much of the crucial Part First of *The Dynasts* takes place at sea, and involves naval personnel. The point I want to make, however, is that Hardy frequently visited law-courts in order to acquire background materials for his fiction. His last visit to the Assizes took place in October 1919, when he attended a trial of three men arrested for mutiny 'on the high seas which might have happened a hundred or two hundred years before'.[25] The threat of the mutineers to hoist the red flag (an act which differentiates them from pirates, who use a black flag with skull and crossbones) did not materialize, because a second ship, called in by wireless, came to the rescue; but Hardy, invited to the Assizes by the judge, Mr Darling, surely remembered his jottings in a comparably sinister case for the *Trumpet-Major Notebook,* largely prepared during the years 1878 and 1879.

The real issue lies not in the frequency with which Hardy recorded, in various contexts and over a period of more than six decades, cases of human behaviour that ultimately required the adjudication of law-courts, though it is readily apparent that Hardy made notes of far many more cases than he was able to use in his fictions. Rather am I struck by the difficulties inherent in ascertaining Hardy's personal opinion on sinners and sufferers. A number of generalizations, however, may reasonably be made: first, Hardy preferred to record a well-shaped tale about the workings of justice—one that had an intrinsic point—rather than a number of philosophical musings on the fallibility of justice; second, he was consistently interested in the basis of a judge's verdict; third, he believed in the overarching necessity of there being human laws and human judges, inasmuch as the understanding of why a crime had been committed did not substitute (in Hardy's mind) for the forgiving of the crime; fourth, social and political conditions in Victorian England guaranteed a hardness of spirit among a very large number of men and women of all social classes; and finally, war between nations was the ultimate crime, for the instigation of which no punishment beyond that of victory in the field had been conceived, and for the punishment of which no tribunal as yet had been devised. Hardy thought more seriously about these matters than most of his novel-writing contemporaries; and they are worth investigating a little more fully.

I am struck, for example, at how often Hardy thought about prisoners. In 1887, on a visit to Rome, he admitted that he had become 'obsessed by a vision of a chained file of prisoners plodding wearily along towards Rome, one of the most haggard of whom was to be famous through the ages as a founder of Pauline Christianity',[26] Some of his attentiveness to the rugged conditions under which prisoners moved wearily through their terms of punishment may be traced back to his father, who had told him, on many occasions, of how prisoners were treated in Dorchester. A poignant note in the *Life,* dated 9 September 1888, reads as follows:

> My father says that Dick Facey used to rivet on the fetters of criminals when they were going off by coach (Facey was journeyman for Clare the smith). He was always sent for secretly, that people might not know and congregate at the gaol entrance. They were carried away at night, a stage-coach being specially ordered. One K. of Troytown, on the London Road, a poacher, who was in a great fray at Westwood Barn near Lulworth Castle about 1825, was brought past his own door thus, on his way to transportation: he called to his wife and family; they heard his shout and ran out to bid him good-by as he sat in chains. He was never heard of again by them.[27]

Very early during the Great War Hardy was fascinated by the thousand German prisoners in and around Weymouth who had acquired enough broken English to cry, 'Shoot Kaiser!' and enough knowledge of the melody of *God Save the King* to play it on their concertinas and fiddles: 'Whether this is 'meant sarcastic', as Artemus Ward used to say, I cannot tell' Hardy wrote somewhat wryly in a letter to Edward Clodd (28 August 1914).[28] But Hardy's acquaintance with prisoners was to become more intimate than this somewhat sardonic notation anticipated. By late 1916 a prisoners' camp in Dorchester, including a hospital, held more than 5,000 men. Hardy visited sick men in both English hospitals and the German camp, and wrote about these 'sufferers' with deep-felt anguish. 'One Prussian, in much pain, died whilst I was with him—to my great relief, and his own. Men lie helpless here from wounds: in the hospital a hundred yards off other men, English, lie helpless from wounds—each scene of suffering caused by the other!'[29] Hardy understood that the use of German expressions in Dorset carried a significance that went beyond linguistic peculiarity. In his poem 'The Pity of It', published in the *Fortnightly Review* of April 1915, he claimed that the German and the English people were 'kin folk kin tongued'. As war passions had by this time risen quite high, many objected to Hardy's call for understanding of the blood-ties that war had torn asunder. Hardy responded with some asperity, that those who wrote letters to the editor protesting against his poem were 'fussy jingoes', and that 'the Germans themselves, with far more commonsense, translated the poem, approved of it, & remarked that when relations did fall out they fought more bitterly than any'.[30]

Hardy believed that England was fighting to save what was best in Germany—not to exterminate it. He sincerely held the conviction that oligarchs, munitions-makers and war-lords had begun the war; common soldiers were mere puppets by contrast and deserved every man's compassion. It was not just a matter of rhetoric for members of the English intelligentsia, Hardy sent German books to the prisoners, gave food and medicine to them, enquired several times about their welfare, and through his largeness of spirit was directly responsible for letters sent by the prisoners to their families in Germany and, soon afterwards, for an amelioration of conditions experienced by English prisoners in Germany.

This is recognizably the same Hardy who wrote, on 12 February 1879, a bleak note on the way in which Jack Ketch whipped prisoners by the Town Pump of Dorchester with lashes of knotted whipcord, so fiercely that 'the prisoners' coats were thrown over their bleeding backs before they were conducted back to prison'.[31] He took the time, on a sightseeing expedition to Paris in June 1888, to visit the Correctional Courts to listen to a number of 'trivial cases'.[32] But it may not be as widely known that Hardy took the time to write to Charles Carrington, congratulating him for his 'extraordinarily powerful' performance as a hangman in a production of *The Three Wayfarers* in June 1893,[33] a fact which suggests Hardy's capacity to see suffering from two perspectives, that of the prisoner who must pay the penalty for his crime, whatever it may be, and that of the hangman who inflicts the penalty. It explains—it does not wholly extenuate—Hardy's decision not to make a public statement at the time of the re-trial of Captain Dreyfus, when he was requested to do so by the editor of *La Vogue* and later by the *Daily Chronicle*. Hardy's ground for remaining silent was that 'English interference might do harm' to the Dreyfus case.[34] But he had no doubt about Dreyfus's innocence.

An intriguing comment was made by Hardy in a letter to Emma, dated 6 November 1900, about a visit he made to the Assizes in a non-official capacity: 'One of the sons of Dairyman Kingman, whom you knew when he was alive, was sentenced to 5 years penal servitude for nearly killing his wife. He is supposed to be wrong in his head by the family—owing to the kick of a horse in the temple', and then Hardy adds a characteristic touch, 'but the judge did not know this as he ought to have'.[35] Here we see combined two elements of Hardy's feelings: obvious sympathy with the Kingman boy, who had been sentenced too harshly in what amounted to a miscarriage of justice in Hardy's mind; and a more baffling reticence about the reasons why Hardy, who possessed special information about mitigating circumstances, did not call them to the attention of the judge.

Nevertheless, Hardy in old age was the same as the young man in London in the early 1860s who enjoyed seeing the 'Judge and Jury' mock trials at the Cider Cellars and the Coal Hole.[36] Some aspects of Hardy's attitude towards the law may depress us; it sometimes smacks of the flippancy of the remark of a young struggling lawyer, made to his friends *à propos* of a hanging at the Old Bailey which he wanted to see: 'Who knows; we may be judges some day; and it will be well to have learnt how the last sentence of the law is carried out'.[37] Hardy thought of the law as a record of investigation, a cumulative documentation, a patient accretion of small pieces of information. In the late 1880s he noticd, somewhat dispiritedly, that 'the public' at judicial proceedings appeared 'to be mostly represented by grimy gentlemen who had had previous experience of the courts from a position in the dock: that there were people sitting round an anteroom of the courts as if waiting for the doctor; that the character of the witness usually deteriorated under cross-examination; and that the magistrate's spectacles as a rule endeavoured to flash out a strictly just manner combined with as much generosity as justice would allow'.[38] Nevertheless, the last phrase, 'with as much generosity as justice would allow', resonates, and I take it to be a key to much in Hardy's thinking. He concerned himself with the problem created by institutional behaviour in a larger sense. In his notes we find information about his attitude towards those parallel creations of the nineteenth century, the lunatic asylum and the poorhouse. In May 1891 he paid a visit with his friend Dr (later Sir) T. Clifford Allbutt, then a commissioner in lunacy, to 'a large private lunatic asylum'. The cases proved so fascinating that Hardy, who had intended to stay only fifteen minutes, 'remained the greater part of the day'.[39] There he found a 'gentleman who was staying there of his own will, to expose the devices of the Commissioners'; an old man who offered snuff to everybody; a 'scholar of high literary aims' who seemed as 'sane in his conversation as any of us'; an artist whose 'great trouble was that he could not hear the birds sing', which, he told Hardy, was 'hard' on a man of his temperament; and a number of fascinating women, some who had been seduced, some who thought themselves queens (one of them, 'who was really a Plantaganet by descent, perversely insisted on being considered a Stuart'), and all of whom seemed 'prematurely dried, faded, flétries'. Hardy was so moved by the plight of one young woman, whose eyes brimmed with reproach as she enquired when the doctor would let her out, that he appealed for a re-examination of her—'which was done afterwards'. (The result of the re-examination was not specified.)

Hardy knew a lot about poorhouses; after all, some had stood in the village of his birth 'just at the corner turning down to the dairy'.[40] On the occasion of the opening of a club-room, dedicated as a war memorial in Bockhampton, Hardy reminisced about the buildings in which parish paupers lived before workhouses were built: 'In one of them lived an old man who was found one day rolling on the floor, with a lot of pence and halfpence scattered round him. They asked him what was the matter, and he said he had heard of people rolling in money, and he thought that for once in his life he would do it, to see what it was like'. But the lightness of the anecdote should not deceive us. Hardy did not think of the population of poorhouses in Dorset as being carefree; he did not yearn for a return to the past. 'There is no fuss or foolishness about ''the good old days'' in Hardy's picture of the changing world', as R.J. White rightly says in *Thomas Hardy and History*.[41] Hardy believed in the painful, creeping slowness of any changes in human nature that might make poorhouses, lunatic asylums and wars obsolete; in the words of Lennark Björk, 'Hardy did not share Comte's confidence in the Idea of Progress'.[42] The Great War permanently destroyed his belief in the gradual ennoblement of man. By 1915, when his 'very dear cousin' Frank George, second lieutenant in the 5th Dorsets, died at Gallipoli, he gloomily withdrew from all movements 'of a spiritual or even ethical nature' because his 'faith in the good there is in humankind' was so rudely shaken.[43] Björk is correct in his assessment: 'Hardy's belief in progress does not, in fact, seem to have been strong at any time . . . and his late claim to ''evolutionary meliorism'' in the ''Apology'' (1922) is but faintly supported by any public statements'.[44]

I do not have the space needed to explore Hardy's laboriously acquired knowledge of an author's rights when dealing with a publisher, and of the encyclopaedic mastery of information about royalties, reprints and copyrights that his correspondence clearly demonstrates. Hardy never wanted less remuneration for his creative labours than the law allowed. Exploited in his earlier years by relatively ungenerous publishers like William Tinsley, Hardy rapidly learnt how to play the game, and correctly evaluated his worth in the publishing marketplace; but the details of his negotiations on such matters are too tedious for this chapter. For a quick and readable review of the ways in which Hardy's understanding of legal niceties pertaining to the profession of an author surpassed that held by many of his contemporaries, one may consult John Gross's readable and quite wonderful survey, *The Rise and Fall of the Man of Letters: Aspects of English Literary Life since 1800* (London: Weidenfeld & Nicolson, 1969); and, of course, the scores of letters written by Hardy in the first five volumes of the correspondence edited by Richard L. Purdy and Michael Millgate.

Hardy's knowledge of the law served him in good stead as he came to write his fictions, and I will cite two examples drawn from the history of *Tess of the d'Urbervilles*. In 1892 the businessman and politician Walter Morrison objected that Angel Clare was 'arguably an accessory before, certainly an accessory after the fact of Tess's murder of Alec', and that he 'would have got 12 months at least, and so could not have been outside Winchester on the morning of Tess' execution'.[45] Hardy pointed out that Angel Clare could not have been an accessory, since he had not believed Tess's story. 'If guilty of culpable negligence 3 months wd have been enough—&this wd have elapsed by time of execution—the time he had waited for trial being taken into account in sentence'. To another correspondent, the humorist Jerome K. Jerome, Hardy wrote a sharp rebuke to the notion, first promulgated by Andrew Lang, that the hanging of Tess was 'rather improbable in this age of halfpenny newspapers and appeals to the British public. The black flag would never have been hoisted'.[46] He gave as his evidence to the contrary a statement, made by a home secretary, 'that he would have seen no reason for interfering with her sentence'.

Hardy's knowledge of the ways in which courts operate was used to buttress the probability of actions taken by individual characters. Judges, solicitors, barristers, their clerks, bailiffs and customs officers, turn up in the novels and short stories more frequently than the members of any other profession, including those of architecture and medicine. Here, in alphabetical form, as derived from Frank Pinion's *A Hardy Companion: A Guide to the Works of Thomas Hardy and Their Background,* is a list for reminders: Fred Beaucock of *The Woodlanders,* who informs Melbury about the new divorce law; Mr Blowbody, the magistrate, whose wife sits next to Lucetta on the occasion of the royal visit to Casterbridge; Mr Cecil, Lady Constantine's solicitor in *Two on a Tower;* Mr Chancerly, the lawyer to whom Lady Petherwin goes when she decides to change her will, after Ethelberta has refused to withdraw her published poems; Charles Downe, a young lawyer in 'Fellow Townsmen', *Wessex Tales,* whose wife is drowned when they sail beyond the cliffs; Mr Grower, the magistrate who attempts to affix responsibility for the skimmington-ride in *The Mayor of Casterbridge;* Hanner and Rawles, the solicitors in *Two on a Tower* who serve Swithin St Cleeve's paternal great-uncle, Dr Jocelyn St Cleeve; Cunningham Haze, the chief constable who on three occasions comes close to arresting Dare in *A Laodicean;* Henry Knight of *A Pair of Blue Eyes,* who in addition to being a reviewer and essayist, is of course a barrister; Will Latimer of 'The Distracted Preacher', *Wessex Tales,* the fictional recreation of a real Will Latimer, a customs officer from Weymouth; Lawyer Long of Casterbridge, in *Far From the Madding Crowd;* Mr Nyttleton, the solicitor in *Desperate Remedies* who gives Miss Aldclyffe good advice on the appointment of a steward—which she rejects; Pennyways, the bailiff at Weatherbury Upper Farm dismissed by Bathsheba Everdene for stealing barley, who re-enters the story at a critical stage when Troy uses him to re-establish himself at Weatherbury; Timothy Petrick, a clever lawyer in 'Squire Petrick's Lady', *A Group of Noble Dames,* who amasses considerable wealth (the character is based on Peter Walter of Stalbridge House); Charles Bradford Raye, a barrister in 'On the Western Circuit', *Life's Little Ironies,* who wins over the servant-girl Anna 'body and soul' at Melchester; Stubberd, the constable in *The Mayor of Casterbridge*; Mr Timms, the Southampton lawyer who, in *Desperate Remedies,* gives advice on the illegal marriage of Manston and Cythera Graye; and Lord Uplandtowers of 'Barbara of the House of Grebe', *A Group of Noble Dames,* a harsh judge, who cures his wife Barbara of her devotion to her first husband by means that Professor Pinion describes are 'as sadistic' as they are 'effective, and typical of his "cynical doggedness"'.[47]

These characters are, by and large, relatively minor. They do not have the temperaments necessary for the entertaining of large passions, with the possible exception of Henry Knight, or dominate the stage for more than a few moments in any short story or novel. But colourless though they may be, as a class they are professionally competent, and as individuals they are—almost uniformly—worthy of respect; they have earned their rights to a certain degree of complacency; and, as we know from the biographical evidence, Hardy was able to observe them from the very beginning, or at least from the year 1870, when he worked at Mr Raphael Brandon's office in Clement's Inn, very close to the Royal Courts of Justice (in fact, only a narrow lane separates the office building from the law courts). All his life Hardy liked to dine with judges and lord chancellors. On one occasion (17 December 1892) Hardy wrote that their telling stories 'old and boring to one another' but 'all new' to himself, 'delighted' him.[48] He was particularly interested in the details of the Tichbourne case, which he followed from its earliest stage to its conclusion. Although he did not view himself as politically committed, he held strong opinions on the inadequacies of some laws and on the need for reforms. There are, for instance, his strong views on the desirability of liberalizing the divorce laws of England. His preface to *Jude the Obscure* was amplified by a lengthy note, dated April 1912, which claimed that he had used the marriage laws 'in great part as the tragic machinery of the tale', and that the 'general drift [of the novel] on the domestic side' tended 'to show that, in Diderot's words, the civil law should be only the enunciation of the law of nature (a statement that requires some qualifications, by the way)'.[49] By then he had come some distance from 21 March 1897, when he refused the request of the editor of the *New York Journal* to make public his views, by means of an article for that periodical, on the subject of 'such spectacles'.[50] But even in that letter he spoke of leaving to others 'the consideration of how to right, remedy, or prevent the wrongs which some of them, undoubtedly are'; his marriage to Emma, by that time, had dwindled into something less appealing than he had anticipated in the early 1870s. Hardy, as we all know, strongly opposed vivisection, the blinding of birds, the harming of horses and other animals, and above all, the weakness of the legal machinery that permitted such transgressions against the weak and dumb fellow creatures who inhabit our planet.

I am reviewing, therefore, a pattern of beliefs that rendered almost inevitable Hardy's willingness to assume the duties of a borough magistrate in 1884. According to the *Dorset County Chronicle,* he met the qualifications on 5 April and took his oath of allegiance and a judicial oath on 23 August. An interviewer found Hardy willing to talk about his playing the role of ' Justice Silence with great assiduity, though admitting that the duties of office' kept him 'in touch with some sterner facts of existence that are apt to be lost sight of in the dream-world of books'.[51] Hardy reviewed a number of cases, not all of them involving legal offences; many dealt with the licensing of local public houses and excessive school absences by children who had been summoned to court. But he also heard cases of abusive or obscene language, theft, the selling of bad meat, drunkenness, committing a nuisance in 'Bollam's Passage', horse-theft, violation of swine-fever regulations, failure to provide a proper supply of water to a house under the Public Health Water Act, a wife-stabbing by a labourer (he was sentenced to twelve months hard labour, and she received a judicial separation), and even attempted buggery by a labourer with a mare. Hardy shifted his energies from the lower court to the higher courts when he began to sit as a grand juror for the Assizes on 1 November 1897. Although these cases included colourful human experiences that were, in general, broader in range than those Hardy had heard while sitting as a magistrate in the Petty Borough Sessions and the County Petty Sessions—'bigamy, indecent and criminal assault on young girls, theft, fraud, incest, forgery, arson, rape, attempted murder and murder'[52]—all Hardy was expected to do was cast a vote for or against indictment of the defendant in the cases presented to the grand jury. He did not decide guilt or innocence. Nor—if the regular jury decided that the defendant was guilty—did he play any part in the sentencing of a prisoner.

Even so, Hardy's concern for the way in which justice was administered went beyond his active service in the Assizes, which apparently ended in 1916. Hardy returned to the Borough Petty Sessions five more times, to adjudicate cases of food-profiteering between December 1917 and September 1919. One case required a special sitting of the children's court. 'A thirteen-year-old boy, charged with trying to steal 9d from ''the automatic lock of a public lavatory'', was given ''six strokes with the birch'''.[53]

A brief summing-up, at this point, is appropriate. Hardy began his interest in human laws and courts of justice by paying close attention to the lurid and melodramatic tales about smugglers, murderers and prisoners that were current in the Bockhampton and Dorchester of his youth; he found usable literary materials in the courts (he called them 'novel padding')[54] during his years as novelist (as, for instance, in his note of 14 July 1884, that 'Witnesses always begin their evidence in sentences containing ornamental words, evidently prepared beforehand, but when they get into the thick of it this breaks down to struggling grammar and lamentably jumbled narrative');[55] and a growing sense of 'social feeling'[56] led him to active service as justice of the peace, both for the Borough of Dorchester and for the County of Dorset.

Hardy's efforts on behalf of the law received their due meed of honour after he died on 11 January 1928. Five days later, on 16 January, the Borough Petty Sessions met, and the magistrates stood in silence as a mark of respect. They may have been paying tribute more to a fellow magistrate than to a world-renowned author. At least, I believe so, and, I imagine, Hardy would have liked to think so.

And one last note is appropriate: Florence Emily Hardy served as a borough magistrate from 1924 on, filling in for her husband, whose age and health had become precarious. She rendered noble service in that position, particularly after the Children's and Young Persons' Act of 1933 was passed. Her work in the juvenile courts, dealing with girl offenders and cases of child welfare, led her to generous interpretations of probationary rules. How deeply she would have become involved in such problems without the prior participation of her husband in Borough and County Petty Sessions, the Quarter Sessions and the Assizes, may be debated; but her labours as a magistrate for the juvenile court, and later as chairman of the Mill Street Housing Society, when she sought to improve housing conditions in the notorious area called 'Mixen Lane' in *The Mayor of Casterbridge,* are still remembered, with gratitude, by many people in Dorchester.[57]

7

Hardy and the Developing Science of Archaeology

The science of archaeology came into its own during the second half of the nineteenth century; this chapter evaluates Thomas Hardy's interest in the developing science. It may be that Hardy's concern with the pagan and Roman past of England has been treated somewhat cavalierly, even dismissed by the all-embracing term 'antiquarianism', as if Hardy's investigations of that past required no more than an intermittent focusing of attention on his part. Hardy's concern was far more than that of an antiquarian. Moreover, English archaeology was grossly amateurish in the years before General Pitt-Rivers defined what was needed if digs were to reveal the truth about man's past; Hardy knew well the General and his work. Another look at the primary documents is worth the trouble if we are to appreciate the reasons why Hardy brooded so often about the past. Indeed, we can hardly assess the full power of such a scene as that which concludes *Tess of the d'Urbervilles* unless we know what generations of Englishmen thought they knew about Stonehenge.

The following couplet concludes a Newdigate Prize-winning poem, 'Petra', written by the Reverend John William Burgon in 1845:

> Match me such marvel save in Eastern clime;
> A rose-red city—'half as old as time'.

Petra, often called 'the Treasury of the Pharaohs', is a splendid, even theatrical city founded by the Edomites and built in its present form during the fourth century BC by the Nabataeans. In the ancient world Petra was notorious for its exaction of tolls; Pliny talks about a levy of 25 per cent paid, unwillingly, by passing caravans. After the Romans conquered the Nabataeans in AD 106, the city became a necropolis, silent, deserted, yet indescribably romantic. It is impossible to approach it head-on; after turning off the Desert Highway at Ma'an, one must descend by horse through the Siq, a tunnel with sides rising sheerly to 200 feet, to behold a city rediscovered in 1812 by the Anglo-Swiss traveller J.L. Burckhardt; a city with a plaza, tombs, shops, a large theatre, all carved from rock that contains spectacular streaks of colour; and the Treasury itself, rose-red, just as the parson Burgon described it. What many of us today do not understand about Burgon's characterization of this Nabataean city was that the phrase 'half as old as time' meant more to the Victorians than it has ever meant since; it was more than a poetic image; it was a calculation of the age of Petra in terms of the widely accepted chronology of Archbishop Ussher. That seventeenth-century English divine published in 1658 an English version of his highly influential work, *The Annals of the World Deduced from the Origins of Time and Continued to the Beginning of the Emperor Vespasian's Reign and the Total Destruction and Abolition of the Temple and Commonwealth of the Jews.* 'I incline to this opinion', he wrote, 'that from the evening ushering in the first day of the Christian era, there were 4003 years, seventy days, and six temporarie howers'. In terms of this chronology, man was created on the sixth day, a Friday, and—more specifically—28 October. I do not mean to suggest in any way that Archbishop Ussher's time-scheme represented a novel zaniness. After all, the Bible had emphasized the chronology of man. Genesis has a great deal to say about the length of the lives of various characters in the Old Testament. Jerome, in all sincerity, believed that 2,242 years had elapsed between Adam and the Flood, and only 942 years between the Flood and Abraham. His translation of Eusebius into Latin led Jerome to make some corrections in his calculations: 2,242 years became 1,656; 942 years became 292. It was not a giant step for subsequent historians of the West to conclude that the world was six thousand years old. Indeed, Luther recorded his conviction that the earth was created in 4000 BC, and Kepler's 'discovery' of a four-year error in the chronology of the Christian era was, as much as any other single factor, responsible for the date of 4004 BC that the Authorized Version of the Bible, printed in 1611, printed in the margin. And

Archbishop Ussher's contemporary, Dr John Lightfoot, Master of St Catherine's College and Vice-Chancellor of the University of Cambridge, differed only slightly in his reckoning: 'Man was created by the *Trinity* about the third houre of the day, or nine of the clocke in the morning on 23 October 4004 BC'. Thus the Reverend Burgon's phrase, 'half as old as Time', means that Petra, to the best of man's knowledge, is some three thousand years old. The age of this beautiful necropolis was not being described in a metaphor for unknown millennia, but was being precisely delimited.

Now it is easy to say that Archbishop Ussher's view of the prehistoric past could not survive the tests of science, or the doctrine of uniformitarianism that became so popular in the second quarter of the nineteenth century. But the elders of the Churches of England (both Catholic and Protestant) gave ground slowly, and many a free-thinker was to discover that he was expressing an independent view of chronology prematurely. As one example, the Reverend James Douglas (1753–1819) became excited over the bones of a mammoth that had been discovered, at a depth of twelve feet, in the sand and gravel of the Medway at Chatham. These bones, he believed, were far too ancient to be accounted for by the myth of a general deluge in the Medway valley. He was never to find preferment within the Church; the Archbishop's chronology had a more powerful official status; and Douglas's work among pagan Saxon barrows, based though it was on personal and meticulous observation, proved irrelevant to this world, though wise. He retired from the priesthood a disappointed man.[1]

Thomas Hardy's readings in science were extensive, and his spiritual crisis of the mid-1860s must have been affected more by what he knew of contemporary scientific developments than by what he had read in religious literature; but, as Michael Millgate points out in his biography, 'There is little surviving evidence of Hardy's early thinking on the great contemporary issues of science and religion'.[2] Hardy left no annotations in his copy of Darwin's *On the Origin of Species,* and only scattered remarks about the writings of Fourier, Comte, Newman and Mill. Hardy may have never experienced a 'loss of faith' in the classic Victorian sense; the erosion of his religious convictions was probably a 'gradual process'.[3] Yet Hardy was quick to put to fictional use his understanding of evolutionary doctrine. There was, even as early as

148

A Pair of Blue Eyes (1873), a notable brooding passage in Chapter 22 on the passage of geological time. Henry Knight, a barrister, reviewer and essayist, found himself trapped—and very close to death—on the face of 'the Cliff without a Name'. Knight had slipped on a piece of quartz, on what had originally been 'an igneous protrusion into the enormous masses of black strata', and he, more than most men, was equipped to appreciate the irony of his situation. (Hardy described him as being ' a fair geologist', in other words, as one who had acquired some geological knowledge along with other educational necessities for a young gentleman at mid-century.) Henry Knight

> reclined hand in hand with the world in its infancy. Not a blade, not an insect, which spoke of the present, was between him and the past. The inveterate antagonism of these black precipices to all strugglers for life is in no way more forcibly suggested than by the paucity of tufts of grass, lichens, or confervae on their outermost ledges.

That Hardyan delight in being able to employ a technical term such as 'confervae' should not distract us from Hardy's primary purpose, to prepare us for a passage that all readers remember for years, long after other incidents of this particular narrative have sunk into the well of memory, the moment in which Knight suddenly became aware that there, before his eyes, 'was an imbedded fossil, standing forth in low relief from the rock'. This creature had eyes, 'dead and turned to stone', that regarded him: 'It was one of the early crustaceans called Trilobites'. Neither Hardy nor Knight had any illusions about the intelligence of zoophytes, mollusca or shellfish. These formations 'had known nothing of the dignity of man. They were grand times, but they were mean times too, and mean were their relics. He was to be with the small in his death'. The famous sentence 'Time closed up like a fan before him', introduces a splendid meditation on the generations of 'fishy beings of lower development', the 'dragon forms and clouds of flying reptiles', the 'sinister crocodilian outlines' that succeeded them, the 'huge-billed birds and swinish creatures as large as horses' next in line, the huge elephantine forms ('the mastodon, the hippopotamus, the tapir, antelopes of monstrous size, the megatherium, and the myledon'), and the prehistoric cavemen—'the beginning and all the intermediate centuries' appearing simultaneously within his bemused imagination.

There is in Hardy's fiction a portrait of an archaeologist who had really lived; it is not fully shaded, and Hardy clearly has some reservations about the way in which the archaeologist follows his calling. But first, recall that 'inclusive and intersocial' organization known as the Wessex Field and Antiquarian Club, the members of which meet in the linking fragments of *A Group of Noble Dames.* (This collection of short stories appeared in 1891, but Hardy began working on individual items as early as 1878). Hardy's wryness extends to his enumeration of 'the regulation papers on deformed butterflies, fossil ox-horns, prehistoric dung-mixens, and such like, that usually occupied the more serious attention of the members', and the 'varnished skulls, urns, penates, tesserae, costumes, coats of mail, weapons, and missals' that, as a consequence of firelight, 'animated the fossilized icthyosaurus and iguanodon' in the museum. At the end of this gathering, 'the benighted members of the Field-Club' (in my dictionary the word 'benighted' is defined as meaning 'involved in or due to moral darkness or ignorance') go their separate ways, out into the night-deserted streets; and after they depart, 'the curator locked up the rooms, and soon there was only a single pirouetting flame on the top of a single coal to make the bones of the icthyosaurus seem to leap, the stuffed birds to wink, and to draw a smile from the varnished skulls of Vespasian's soldiery'.

The prehistoric past, the long ago for which time had to be measured in geological eons, was one of three periods in which both archaeologists and Hardy were deeply interested (the other two being the barrow-building world of several millennia back and the relatively more recent world of Roman generals and soldiers). For all these periods Hardy exhibited the same kind of fascination that Sir Charles Lyell showed when travelling (in a literary note recorded by Hardy); Lyell was so excited by the view along a cutting that he would gaze out of the railway carriage as if the sides were hung with beautiful pictures.[4] In his notable poem 'In a Museum', included in *Moments of Vision,* Hardy wrote of the oldest fossil bird, the *archeopteryx macrura,* separated from Upper Jurassic Lithographic stone in Solenhafen, Bavaria, and shown in the form of a skeleton cast at the Albert Memorial Museum of Queen Street, Exeter. Hardy, who saw the bird in 1915, wrote of it with a wonder tinged by awe (the skeleton of body and tail extends fifteen inches; plumes may have added considerably to its size):

> Here's the mould of a musical bird long passed from light,
> Which over the earth before man came was winging . . .

Hardy added a characteristic comment:

> Such a dream is Time that the coo of this ancient bird
> Has perished not, but is blent, or will be blending
> Mid visionless wilds of space with the voice that I heard,
> In the full-fugued song of the universe unending.

Nothing, in Hardy's views as expressed here, truly perishes. The universe is a concatenation of all sounds, energies, wills to be; the link with Schopenhauer's *The World as Will and Idea* is plain. It hardly matters that Hardy romanticized the 'coo' of the *archeopteryx macrura* (its song was probably a croak) and compared it to a contralto voice that he had heard the previous evening, one that he still remembered because of 'its sweet singing'. The bird's immortality, like that of any human being, was assured so long as memory functioned, so long as we are able and willing to recall the past.

This brings us to Hardy's rather unflattering portrait of an archaeologist, contained in the slight but striking anecdote 'A Tryst at an Ancient Earthwork', first published in the *Detroit Post* in March 1885. Hardy here provided a comment on his experience as a member of the Dorset Natural History and Antiquarian Club, which he had joined during 1881, three years before the Dorset County Museum opened in what is today its current location. Henry J. Moule served as the curator of the Museum, and Hardy so admired him that, after his death, he paid tribute to 'a friendship of between forty and fifty years' by writing an introduction to Moule's posthumously published *Dorchester Antiquities* (1906)—a kind of assignment he usually did not much like or often accept. The story 'A Tryst at an Ancient Earthwork' refers to Mai-Dun, a hill-fort dating back to the Iron Age, and known today as Maiden Castle. It deals with two characters, the author and an archaeologist determined to demonstrate that the earthworks contained, in addition to Celtic artifacts, some relics of the Roman past. This hypothesis was to be tested by Sir Mortimer Wheeler during the 1930s; Sir Mortimer did the enormously significant work that he later wrote up in his book *Maiden Castle* (1943), which established a new system of excavation, based in part on the work of Pitt-Rivers but going far beyond it in its emphasis on broad sectioning, excavation by squares or quadrants with key separating baulks, the rigorous recording of everything, accurate and detailed survey, and full publication as soon as possible; Sir Mortimer was destined to confirm the guesses of the two characters in Hardy's story, that those who had lived near the ancient earthwork had fought against a Roman who was later to become the Emperor Vespasian.[5] In 'A Tryst at an Ancient Earthwork', Hardy was describing Edward Cunnington, the 'local Schliemann' of Dorchester (so he referred to him in a paper prepared for a meeting of the Field Club, read by Hardy himself on 13 May 1884). Cunnington—in Hardy's view—was not always careful about how he handled the relics of the past, nor did he always recognize the significance of what he had unearthed; moreover, his behaviour, at least as described in Hardy's story, was less than scrupulous; and the story, for the benefit of those who have not looked at it recently, recounts the reasons for the belief of the author, one of the 'two enthusiastic scientists' on the fictitious nocturnal adventure, that his companion has pocketed for his own use, and as a private treasure, a gilt statuette of Mercury unearthed during the night's digging. The conviction comes close to certified fact when the statuette, discovered among the archaeologist's effects after his death, is presented to the museum at Casterbridge.

Why was Cunnington presented with such disdain as an unethical archaeologist, when, after all, Hardy's imagination was so greatly stirred by the discoveries of members of this profession? Millgate characterizes Hardy's portrait as 'almost' libellous, and notes that a paper read by Hardy to the Field Club in 1884 was 'mysteriously omitted from the Club's published *Proceedings* for a full six years—possibly because of animosity toward Hardy on the part of Cunnington or one of his friends'.[6] (Hardy was describing Max Gate excavations; I shall return shortly to this paper.) Whether this be the case or not, Hardy would surely have agreed with Sir Mortimer Wheeler's sentiment about the need for being scrupulously careful at the site of any dig:

> It cannot be affirmed too often that bad scholarship in the field generally involves the fruitless and final obliteration of evidence, and bad scholarship is still all too prevalent there . . . If there be a connecting theme in the following

pages, it is this: an insistence that the archaeologist is digging up, not *things*, but *people*. Unless the bits and pieces with which he deals be alive to him, unless he have himself the common touch, he had better seek out other disciplines for his exercise . . . In a simple direct sense, archaeology is a science that must be lived, must be 'seasoned with humanity'. Dead archaeology is the driest dust that blows.[7]

Hardy saw Cunnington as a throwback to a pre-Pitt-Rivers period of British archaeology. Not only was he aware of advances in scientific knowledge about the geological age of the earth because he knew his Lyell and Chambers and Darwin, but he knew more than a little something about the behaviour of diggers— particularly in the earth-barrows that cover the face of England—as it had manifested itself over the preceding century. These diggers violated good sense no less than the sites they were excavating. Prior to Hardy's lifetime they did not draw precise contour plans; they had no concept of the need for developing three-dimensional methods; many of them did not distinguish between primary and secondary interments; most of them kept no notes and told their successors nothing about what they had done, even when the same sites were involved. A surprising number behaved like pirates; whatever they found, they expropriated; and their collections of relics were private Sutton Hoos; so far as these diggers were concerned, they owed nothing to history, to the nation or to the rights of those whose bodies and final resting-places they destroyed. Like Cunnington, they often stepped on, and ruined, the very objects they were seeking to unearth.

In the years prior to the nineteenth century the motives of these diggers were seldom scientific. Perhaps the most common reason for undertaking such work was the hope that some treasure might be unearthed, and if beadworks or Roman coins were discovered, they were hawked about, and knowledge of their provenance soon disappeared. (The Romans themselves were barrow-plunderers in Derbyshire, Somerset and the Mendips, among other locations.) There exist records of digging for pious purposes, for example by the monks of St Albans, who were looking for the relics of Christian martyrs. They found what they were after; the skeleton of some anonymous Anglo-Saxon was identified as St Amphibalus, he who converted St Alban himself, the first Christian martyr of England. Other diggers in the eighteenth century were antiquarians, looking for information about the druids, priests and bards in whom they deeply believed, and their religious tracts, posing as serious objective case studies, distracted generations of readers from interpretations based on the available evidence. (William Stukeley, the first important English field archaeologist, populated his barrows with numberless imagined archdruids, priestesses and kings while he was conducting his fieldwork between 1719 and 1743.) Another motive was closely allied to the widespread interest in sepulchral urns and graveyard imagery that marked the pre-Romantic movement of the late eighteenth century; every dig seemed to confirm a melancholy reading of the meaning of existence and of the vanity of worldly ambition, and many antiquarians enjoyed documenting their disenchantment with relics such as flints, trinkets and pots drawn from the bowels of the earth. Some diggers were after records for the number of barrows that they could cut into: the churchman-antiquary Bryan Faussett (1720–76), who worked in and around Kent, opened 106 barrows in eleven days (spread over the years 1760, 1762 and 1763, to be sure), performed prodigies of digging on 29 July 1771, when he opened thirty-one barrows, and died content with the knowledge that he had dug 777 barrows. Such a formidable total was by no means without parallel in other parts of the country. Some diggers engaged in the sport for the sake of exercise. William Cunnington (1754–1810), a Wiltshire draper and wool merchant, was an antiquary who needed recuperation in the open air because of continuous headaches; his doctor told him that he had to ride out or die; and he entered into a partnership with Sir Richard Colt Hoare (1758–1838), author of *The Ancient History of Wiltshire*, to dig into and open 465 mounds. Let us hope that Cunnington's migraines diminished as a consequence of his labours.

We have not mentioned thus far the most striking reason for the investigations of many of the diggers, who conducted their work at great financial cost (frequently beyond their means), and who, ignorant of the best way to cut into the earth, sometimes risked life and limb in inadequately buttressed trenches. They were patriots, seeking to demonstrate to their neighbours and to the world that the antiquities of the British past were worthy of attention, and in some respects rivalled the antiquities of the Mediterranean Basin. They were also aware that their first journey to Greece and Rome might well be their last; the Grand Tour, for most English tourists, was the only tour that took them to truly remote lands because of the difficulties of travel and the formidable expenses involved. What better way to investigate family history or place names or local architectural curiosities, than to begin to think seriously about the traces of mankind available for study within the immediate vicinity? Earthworks were everywhere. The great names of this free-ranging antiquarian tradition are, of course, William Camden (his *Britannia* was printed in 1586), John Leland, John Aubrey (his *Itinerarium Curiosum* was published in 1724), Edward Llwyd, William Stukeley (whom I have already mentioned) and such writers of county histories as William Dugdale (Warwickshire), Robert Plot (Staffordshire), Samuel and Daniel Lysons (Gloucestershire) and, greatest of them all in Thomas Hardy's mind, John Hutchins (Dorsetshire). Gradually inexorably, a shift in emphasis was taking place: the prehistoric past was assuming a grandeur of its own, and antiquarians were beginning to study the evidence provided by material remains of that past. In part their writings, tentative and frequently inaccurate though they were, hampered in large measure by the free-wheeling amateurism of the diggers on whom they based their generalizations, benefited from the serious studies of classical remains that were published during the eighteenth century: such works as James Stuart and Nicholas Revett's *Antiquities of Athens* (1762), Nicholas Revett's *Antiquities of Ionia* (co-authored with Richard Chandler and William Parr and printed between 1769 and 1797), and Robert Wood's *The Ruins of Palmyra* (1753) and *Ruins of Baalbec* (1757). Lord Elgin's 'marbles', now housed in the British Museum, were the most outstanding of several collections brought back to England by enthusiastic travellers; they provided inspiration to stay-at-homes who wanted to produce comparable-quality measurements and plans of earthworks and stone monuments on British soil. Excavations became larger in scale as the eighteenth century yielded to the nineteenth, and as the inadequate written records of the past were supplemented by regional and local histories, such as Charles Warne's *Celtic Tumuli of Dorset* (1866), which emphasized the importance of digs. Inevitably, these in turn led to speculations—unsettling, unorthodox speculations—about the true age of man. Putting it another way, Archbishop Ussher's chronology of 4004 BC seemed increasingly suspect during the years when prehistoric archaeology was defining itself as a discipline.

It is hard for us today to appreciate the significance of the fact that, when Hardy was a young man, evidence pointing to the true age of the human species was widely scattered, randomly arranged and in general misinterpreted. The Three-age system, which rearranged artefacts in a Stone Age, Bronze Age and Iron Age sequence, was developed first at the Danish National Museum in Copenhagen by Vedel-Simonsen and C. J. Thomsen, whose works were published in the second decade of the nineteenth century; but these pioneer efforts at systematizing a large body of seemingly disparate data were not swiftly assimilated by scientists in other lands. Scandinavia and Germany understood the implications of the work of Vedel-Simonsen and Thomsen long before the British Museum acknowledged the validity of this dating process; the Guide to the Exhibition Rooms of the British Museum, based upon the Three-age system, was not published until 1871, when Hardy had passed his thirtieth year.

Thus we come back to the critical work of Charles Lyell, whose *Principles of Geology* appeared in the early 1830s, for Lyell destroyed the widely held theory that some catastrophe—a flood, an earthquake or an ill-understood event best appreciated in terms of Ussher's calendar—was responsible for the layering of the earth's strata. It would be an over-simplification to argue that Lyell won his case immediately; decades were needed before Henry Knight, precariously suspended from the face of an escarpment, could see for what they were, close-up, the numberless slaty layers of the Cliff without a Name; before Hardy could count on the geological sophistication of average Victorian novel-readers.

It was not until William Pengelly, working at Windmill Hill Cave, Brixham, in 1858 and 1859, demonstrated a relationship between tools made by human beings and the bones of animals long vanished from the earth; these 'remains' lay beneath stalagmite sheets three to eight inches thick; and since the slow rate of deposit which creates a stalagmite had already been measured, the age of the artefacts—here, as elsewhere in digs conducted in France—put paid to the notion of Catastrophism. In brief, the crust of the earth was shown to have developed over eons of time; Darwin's *The Origin of Species*, published in the same year that Pengelly concluded his work in Devon, amassed an awesome amount of documentation for his critical thesis that the animal kingdom was much more ancient than conventional chronologies could accommodate; the climate of thought favoured a reassessment of the true age of man; and Hardy, whose literary notes abound with transcribed quotations from Darwin's writings, who considered himself a very early 'acclaimer' of *The Origin of Species*, who alluded often and approvingly to the doctrine of evolution in his short stories and novels, and who believed that his own perception of ethical implications in Darwin's work was superior to Darwin's perception, journeyed to Westminster Abbey in a final act of homage on the occasion of Darwin's interment there on 26 April 1882.

It is therefore no accident that Hardy's most interesting writings based upon archaeological insights and data begin in the 1880s, when the full implications of General Augustus Henry Lane-Fox Pitt-Rivers' work were exciting a new generation of barrow-diggers and antiquarians. The General inherited his estate through a series of fortuitous deaths, and he was allowed to change his own name, Lane-Fox, to Pitt-Rivers after the passing of the sixth Baron Rivers in 1880, and to add 'Pitt' to his children's names; but there is no question that he would have made a stir no matter what his name or title. Since he, more than any other man in the history of this developing science, helped to codify its procedures and bring order out of the chaos I have been describing at some length, a few words about his accomplishments prior to Hardy's meeting him may not be amiss. He was, for one thing, an experimental researcher, and he helped to improve the army rifle; as an educator and organizer, he originated the Hythe School of Musketry; and, applying the principles of natural evolution to his rapidly growing collection of firearms, he was able to demonstrate that improvements in particular weapons evolved over a period of time, just as they did in the other artefacts he was assembling: in the respectful words of the *Dictionary of National Biography* article written by Edward Burnett Tylor, the distinguished anthropologist-author of *Primitive Culture* (1871), 'boats, looms, dress, musical instruments, magical and religious symbols, artistic decoration, and writing', until the collections reached the dimensions of a museum. (Today the Pitt-Rivers Museum in Oxford, though twice the size of the gift made by the General, retains the general principle of evolutionary change rather than the more widely adopted classifications of geography or nationality in other museums.)

The General, fighting the diabetes and recurring bronchitis that had forced his premature retirement from the service, developed—first as a hobby and then as an obsession—a typology of prehistoric artefacts during the 1860s and 1870s. His reputation grew. Darwin acted as one of his sponsors for elevation to the Royal Society (1876), and eminent scientists paid attention to his writings. He donated his collection to Oxford in 1883. Before he died he was to receive a DCL from Oxford, and to serve as president of the Anthropological Institute. In 1880 the General took over his second cousin's estates, specifically Rushmore in Wiltshire, which lies on the Dorsetshire border, and began active excavations at Bokerley Junction and a number of other sites in Cranborne Chase. (Bokerley Junction is the junction of Bokerley Dyke and the Roman road which is clearly visible on today's Salisbury–Blandford Road.)

It is hard to exaggerate the tremendous impact of this energetic, systematic and intelligent pioneer on what had been a crankily eccentric and only fitfully productive pastime of amateurs; but, without going into detail about the General's archaeological discoveries, or the astonishing dedication he gave to his work as the first inspector of ancient monuments (a post created after the passing of the Ancient Monuments Preservation Act in 1882), we can marvel, as Tylor did, at the General's interest in educating and improving the masses. This interest led to the construction of accurate models of tombs and forts for public exhibition, the display of all kinds of specimens of ploughs, looms and pottery as well as a collection of paintings and other examples of visual arts, and to the creation of pleasure-gardens at the Larmer Tree. (The General refused to charge admission to these experiments in self-education for the public.) Thus one might take a family to the Museum at Farnham or to King John's House and the Larmer Tree Gardens at Tollard Royal, and enjoy free cooking utensils; provisions or foodstuffs were available for very modest prices; the public were invited to play at German skittles, bowl or swing, largely at the General's expense; enjoy the General's zoo animals; listen to the General's band; or even, for the price of sixpence (threepence for ladies), play a full day on an eighteen-hole golf course.[8].

Pitt-Rivers was, of course, delighted at the way in which his experiments at popular education succeeded in attracting more than ten thousand people a year to the Larmer Grounds, and he was honest with himself that entertainments, the availability of picnic sites and the handsomeness of the terrain, served as an additional, or perhaps even the primary, inducements. But it is not as a *grand seigneur* that we remember him, but rather as the collector of common things, which he believed to have more importance than particular things (because they were more prevalent); for his excavations of Roman-British villages and fortifications; for the mathematical exactness with which he insisted all trenches had to be dug; for his detailed drawings of the sequence, contents and characteristics of the strata unearthed by his teams of diggers; for the great care with which he avoided the destruction of any artefact;[9] and, as Jacquetta and Christopher Hawkes have written in *Prehistoric Britain* (p.156), the General's four-volume *Excavations in Cranborne Chase (1887–1898)* 'is in most respects a model of what such a publication should be when money is unlimited'.[10]

Hardy's acquaintance with the General grew from a number of personal conversations; from a slightly bemused contemplation of the arguments which raged around the family table at Rushmore, sometimes with scant recognition of the fact that outsiders were present (Bertrand Russell, commenting in his *Autobiography* on one visit to Rushmore, wrote that with the exception of the General, 'most of the family were more or less mad'); from a knowledge of the slightly scandalous stories that circulated about the General's behaviour (for example, the General believed in cremation, and glowered at his wife, who had expressed a desire to be buried as a whole human being, 'If I say you'll burn, woman, you'll burn!');[11] and from his delight in the Larmer Gardens. Hardy saved for three decades a clipping from the *Dorset County Chronicle* which described a typical enchanted evening in the mid-1890s:

'After nightfall the scene was one of extraordinary picturesqueness and poetry, its great features being the illumination of the grounds by thousands of Vauxhall lamps, and the dancing of hundreds of couples under these lights and the mellow radiance of the full moon. For the dancing a space was especially enclosed, the figures chosen being mostly the polka-mazurka and schottische, though some country dances were started by the house-party, and led off by the beautiful Mrs Grove, the daughter of General Pitt-Rivers, and her charming sister-in-law, Mrs Pitt. Probably at no other spot in England could such a spectacle have been witnessed at any time. One could hardly believe that one was not in a suburb of Paris, instead of a corner in old-fashioned Wiltshire, nearly ten miles from a railway-station in any direction.[12]

That note, included in the *Life*, was transcribed by Hardy after the occasion of a week's visit to the General's estate; Hardy danced on the greensward for the last time and suffered from stiffness in the knees for several days afterwards. The development of Hardy's idealized romance with Agnes Grove, the General's daughter, who became a replacement literary pupil after Florence Henniker more or less renounced that kind of relationship, need not be traced here. However, Hardy's knowledge of the General's contributions to taxonomy, typology, ethnography and prehistoric archaeology, and of his emphasis on scientific stratigraphy at any dig, was extensive. The General had 'devotedly crawled among the stones on his hands & knees inspecting rabbitholes, &c.', Hardy wrote to Mrs Henniker, and was, in Hardy's view, the proper authority for James Milne of the *Daily Chronicle*, to consult on any question concerning Stonehenge, rather than himself as author of only one scene involving that prehistoric monument, and that scene coming at the end of a very long novel.[13] But by that time—August 1899—the General was very ill indeed, and 'at loggerheads with the nurse' (a characteristic touch recorded by Agnes),[14] and unable to talk to a journalist; he died on 4 May 1900, after urging those he left behind to authorize an autopsy of his body, so that 'a competent anatomist' could record the particulars of his physical constitution for the information of his descendants, 'more particularly the form and peculiarities of the cerebral convolutions'; he added that he 'should even think it reasonable if it were practicable to preserve the skeleton for comparison with those of any of [his] progeny who might be similarly minded to have it done'.[15]

Thus General Pitt-Rivers established archaeology as a recognizably modern discipline and, as R. G. Collingwood has suggested, he was in many ways ahead of twentieth-century archaeologists as well. To what uses did Hardy put his knowledge of the developing science of archaeology? There is, as one item, the article on the Maumbury Ring excavation that Hardy wrote at the request of Moberley Bell, manager of *The Times*, who published it on 9 October 1908. That dig was conducted by Harold St George Gray, who had been trained by the General. It unearthed a series of surprises, including a prehistoric pit, some thirty feet deep, making it, in Gray's opinion, 'the deepest archaeological excavation on record in Britain'.[16] Hardy writes as an amateur scientist, in the precise language of the General:

Of irregular shape, and apparently excavated in the sold chalk subsoil, it diminished in size from a diameter of about 6 ft at the mouth to about 18 in. by

15 in. at the bottom. The picks exactly resemble those which Mr St George Gray found in the great fosse at Avebury last May. Roman deposits and specimens were found in the upper part of the pit down to the level of the chalk floor of the arena, but not below it.[17]

This dig, undertaken at the request of the Dorset Field and Antiquarian Club, was designed to ascertain 'the history and date of the ruins', and though diggers and onlookers had expected to find evidence of gladiatorial combats, of 'the Colosseum programme on a smaller scale', and did indeed find markings of a Roman amphitheatre that had adapted 'some earthworks already on the spot',[18] the real thrill came from the discovery of 'prehistoric implements, chipped flints, horns, and other remains' of the palaeolithic or neolithic age, 'and not Roman at all!'[19] This was a moment, Hardy wrote, 'when the blood of us onlookers ran cold, and we shivered a shiver that was not occasioned by our wet feet and dripping clothes'. Fascinated by the confusion of dates in the remains, Hardy did not restrict his musings to the Roman era, which at most did not exceed three centuries in this area; and indeed much of his article—after a brief mention of Sir Christopher Wren's visit to the site—dealt with the execution of Mrs Thomas Channing in the first decade of the eighteenth century, and with an anti-Catholic demonstration held at the Ring during the No-Popery riots.

Hardy often had occasion to write about the barrows which dotted the countryside. He knew that they were not unique to Britain, and as William Greenwell, whose *British Barrows* (1877) is a classic treatment of the subject, pointed out, 'they spread like a covering over the wide plains, the Steppes of Northern Asia, from the Euxine almost to the Icy Sea, where a few wandering nomads now feebly represent a population which was once large, wealthy, and powerful'.[20] Barrows similar to those of Britain may be found everywhere in India; in the United States and in Central America they sometimes reach impressive heights; and in Egypt several of these cairns—stone-barrows, if you will—are known as the pyramids, as sepulchres of the Pharaohs. In the lecture given by Miss Josephine Dool at Salisbury Museum on 9 December 1980, Hardy's literary uses of the barrows are identified as including Rainbarrows in *The Return of the Native* and Conquer Barrow near Max Gate. Miss Dool is quite correct in emphasizing the fascination that these barrows—sometimes called lows, houes and tumps in various parts of this island—exerted on Hardy's imagination. Hardy's descriptions of barrows, although sometimes adapting particular details to fictional ends, as in his presenting as one barrow the three Bronze Age round barrows of Rainbarrows, are invariably conscientious and exact in their archaeological detail. Twenty-five years later, Hardy correctly identified the number of tumuli atop Rainbarrows' Beacon, Egdon Heath, when he came to the writing of *The Dynasts,* Part I, Act II, Scene V. He had always known that there were three; after all, Rainbarrows was no more than half a mile south-east of his birthplace; but his increased emphasis on historicity in *The Dynasts* meant that he no longer saw a good artistic reason to conflate three barrows to one. Hardy drew at least two illustrations for the first edition of *Wessex Poems* (1898) in which barrows are conspicuous, one for 'The Alarm' and the second for 'Her Death and After'. 'My Cicely' describes how, on Salisbury Plain, a rider passes a number of 'bleak hill-graves of Chieftains' who lived during prehistoric times. In the opening poem of *Time's Laughingstocks*, 'The Revisitation' speaks of the bulging barrows that loom

> As before, in antique silence—immemorial funeral piles—
> Where the sleek herds trample daily the remains of flint-tipt arrows
> Mid the thyme and chamomiles.

There are cross-links between the tumuli of 'By the Barrows' that bulge as if they were bosoms 'Of Multimammia stretched supinely there', and the tumuli of Chapter 45 of *The Mayor of Casterbridge*, which resemble 'the full breasts of Diana Multimammia extended there'. Nor, in this connection, should we forget Tess's journey to Flintcomb-Ash (Ch. 42), when 'she reached the irregular chalk table-land or plateau, bosomed with semi-globular tumuli—as if Cybele the Many-breasted were supinely extended there'. And in 'Evening Shadows', a poem published the year of Hardy's death and subsequently reprinted in *Winter Words*, Hardy muses on the length of the shadow cast by Conquer Barrow, 'the neighbouring Pagan mound', upon the greensward, and comes to the conventional conclusion that the future is unknowable.

Hardy fully agreed with Charles Warne's angry charge, made in the Introduction to *Celtic Tumuli of Dorset*, that the diggers of his home county had desecrated 'time-hallowed monuments for no better purpose than the indulgence of a craving acquisitiveness and the adornment of glass cases with ill-understood relics, to be paraded for the empty admiration of those who may descend to flatter the equally vain and ignorant collector';[21] certainly Dorset excavations in the hundred years preceding the General's appearance at Rushmore had damaged archaeological sites more ruthlessly or more ignorantly than they had comparable sites in most British countries. But the opening of Conquer Barrow, only a few hundred yards east of Max Gate, had benefited from new insights and new techniques. 'The Clasped Skeletons', another poem in *Winter Words*, imagines a 'closely clasped' man and woman uncovered to view; Hardy conjectured that they might have lived 1,800 years before Christ; and he knew of such an event as recorded in Hutchins's *History of Dorset*, which describes the remains of a man and woman—not embracing each other, however—in a barrow 'about half-a-mile south of the Afflington Barn, upon the Swanage and Kingston Road'. Moreover, Hardy wrote a paper, 'Some Romano-British Relics Found at Max Gate, Dorchester', and his description of what the archaeologists found on the site of what was to become his home was couched in the language of a scientist. First, and naturally enough, he stressed the fact that he had been one of the only two persons who had seen most of the remains *in situ*, 'just as they were laid bare, and before they were lifted up from their rest of, I suppose fifteen hundred years'. Next, Hardy noted the appearance of the ground before the excavation was made: 'practically a level, bearing no immediate evidence that the natural contour of the surface has ever been disturbed more deeply than by the plough'. The details of the discovery were recorded with an almost painful precision:

On this comparatively level ground we discovered, about three feet below the surface, three human skeletons in separate and distinct graves. Each grave was, as nearly as possible, an ellipse in plan, about 4 ft long and 2½ ft wide, cut vertically into the solid chalk. The remains bore marks of careful interment. In two of the graves, and, I believe, in the third, a body lay on its right side, the knees being drawn up to the chest, and the arms extended straight downwards, so that the hands rested against the ankles. Each body was fitted with, one may almost say, perfect accuracy into the oval hole, the crown of the head touching the maiden chalk at one end and the toes of the other, the tight-fitting situation being strongly suggestive of the chicken in the egg shell. The closest examination failed to detect any enclosure for the remains, and the natural inference was that, save their possible cerements, they were deposited bare in the earth. On the head of one of these, between the top of the forehead and the crown, rested a fibula or clasp of bronze and iron, the front having apparently been gilt. That is, I believe, a somewhat unusual position for this kind of fastening, which seemed to have sustained a fillet for the hair.[22]

Hardy told William Archer that he had removed the fibula from her skull with his own hands, and that it lay in the corner cupboard.[23] Like the statuette of Mercury appropriated by the archaeologist of 'A Tryst at an Ancient Earthworks', the fibula finally found its way to the Dorset County Museum.

Hardy also describes the contents of the graves, as revealed by a most careful search, and he adds what few diggers of the eighteenth century would have bothered to record: 'There was naturally no systematic orientation in the interments—the head in one case being westward, in the other eastward, and in the third, I believe, south-west'.[24] More important is Hardy's regret that the excavations laying bare the Roman past of Dorchester had not been reintegrated to present interested viewers with 'an unmutilated whole' such as had been done, for instance, with the evidences of Pompeian life—'a whole which should represent Dorchester in particular and not merely the general character of a Roman station in this country'.[25]

Hardy's excitement over this find was contagious and helped to inspire at least one painting by Sir Lawrence Alma-Tadema.[26] And there was another find, as Hardy told Archer: 'five Roman soldiers, or colonists', had been decapitated, quite by accident, while workmen were moving earth in order to construct a drive at Max Gate'.[27] Nor should we forget to mention Hardy's Druid Stone, dug up from a depth of three feet by seven workmen at Max Gate; levers and other appliances scarcely made possible the unearthing of an object that had lain undisturbed, next to a quantity of ashes and half-charred bones, for perhaps two thousand years. 'It was a primitive problem in mechanics, and the scene was such a one as may have occurred in building the Tower of Babel', Hardy noted.[28] He loved to take visitors to see it, and many photographs were taken there; one day he found Emma behind the stone, burning his love-letters to her; and even though he conceded that Druidical associations were fanciful (*any* large stone of unknown origin might be imagined to be a Druid's altar), he asked Clive Holland, in 1898, if the latter believed in ghosts. 'If you do you ought to see such manifestations here, on a moonlight night'. After saying which, he laughed.[29] Many readers may prefer Hardy's romantic notion—as expressed in the poem 'The Shadow on the Stone'—that Emma's spirit haunted near the stone, to Henry J. Moule's more prosaic explanation, that the stone may have been set up first as a menhir, that is to say an upright rough stone or monolith, and that, in after ages, it was found a hindrance to the plough and was buried out of the way. The antiquarian Moule added, 'This might account for the relics of the burial being round it & (perhaps) under it'.[30]

Moule's interpretation might not be the one we would make if Hardy's great stone were in *our* garden. At any rate, it was not Hardy's. His attitude towards the prehistoric past was one of awe; much was unknown; much about it could never be reclaimed or fully understood; and the point about Henry Knight's face-to-face encounter with an imbedded fossil, a trilobite, on the Cliff without a Name, is that both stared at each other with mutual incomprehension; the eyes of the trilobite were 'dead and turned to stone'. Nor could Hardy imagine with much certainty the kinds of lives led by those interred in the countless barrows that populate his fiction and his poems, though his fascination with archaeology meant that he kept attempting to probe the impenetrable curtains that shrouded the millennia before the Roman invasion of Britain; kept hoping that more would be learned, or that some great find might be unearthed in Dorset, preferably by a personal friend; and who is to say, knowing something of the history of the science and of Hardy's astonishingly wide range of acquaintance, that the hope was unreasonable?

The archaeologists and the historians had joined forces to draw not only the outlines of Britain's Roman past, and had filled in many of the most needed and even piquant details. As a consequence, Hardy thought long and hard about the Roman roots of Dorchester. It is not often remembered that Hardy, when he came to the writing of *The Mayor of Casterbridge*, at first intended to write a novel about Roman Dorchester, but even though the nineteenth-century atmosphere of the novel he did write is utterly convincing, one of the most famous passages in all of Hardy—that which describes Maumbury Ring in Chapter 11, the scene in which Henchard meets Susan during the evening dusk, 'the proper hour at which a true impression of this suggestive place could be received'—is worth quoting again:

Casterbridge announced old Rome in every street, alley, and precinct. It looked Roman, bespoke the art of Rome, concealed dead men of Rome. It was impossible to dig more than a foot or two deep about the town fields and gardens without coming upon some tall soldier or other of the Empire, who had laid there in his silent unobtrusive rest for a space of fifteen hundred years.

There follows an enumeration of kinds of burials, and of artefacts discovered in barrows and other tombs, very similar to the listings (and even the language) of Hardy's address to his fellow antiquarians in 1884. Hardy's poem 'The Roman Road' speaks of 'helmed legionaries, who proudly rear/The Eagle.' He knew his Hutchins, and Hutchins continually spoke of Roman ruins; he knew his Barnes, and Barnes had written about the Roman amphitheatre of Dorchester in a letter to the *Gentleman's Magazine* in 1839; and he knew personally a number of archaeologists whose primary interests were concentrated on the hill-forts and the burial-grounds of the Roman past rather than the more remote past of the trilobites or the Celts. Hardy's poems speak often of British memories of Roman occupation, as in the poignant lines of 'Her Death and After', in *Wessex Poems*:

> One eve as I stood at my spot of thought
> In the white-stoned Garth, brooding thus her wrong,
> Her husband neared; and to shun his nod
>   By her hallowed sod
> I went from the tombs among
>
> To the cirque of the Gladiators which faced—
> That haggard mark of Imperial Rome,
> Whose Pagan echoes mock the chime
>   Of our Christian time
> From its hollows of chalk and loam.

In 'In the Old Theatre, Fiesole', written in April 1887, Hardy speaks of how easy it is to dig up Roman coins from the English soil which hides them; the sight of a child who shows him an ancient coin bearing the image of a Constantine reminds him, inevitably, of 'the power, the pride, the reach of perished Rome'. In 'After the Fair', in *Time's Laughingstocks*, Hardy, momentarily melancholy because the merry-making of the Dorchester fair has died down and left only ghosts behind, recalls

> those old Roman hosts
> Whose remains one yet sees,
> Who loved, laughed, and fought, hailed their friends, drank their
> toasts
> At their meeting-times here, just as these!

'Aquae Sulis', in *Satires of Circumstance*, is a poetic interpretation of how Sul-Minerva speaks, ghost-like, to the Christian god of the Saxon monastery that was built out over part of the hot springs of Bath during the eighth century; Hardy's thought, though wryly phrased, was a reaffirmation of the equality of all religions, and he was to express this view frequently; if anything, all credos are equally susceptible to the ravages of time. And many of Hardy's readers treasure 'The Roman Gravemounds', that witty and characteristic lament for a white cat, 'Kitsey', whom he had to bury in his garden, 'by Rome's dim relics'. The poet—Hardy himself, for the poem is very personal and autobiographical, and deals with an event occurring in November 1910—cannot help contrasting Rome's vastness 'in the world's regard', and the insignificance of his 'little white furred thing, stiff of limb'; he wishes that his cat, his 'only friend', might live, even if it means the obliteration of the record 'Of Caesar, his legions, his aims, his end!'

Finally, I return, once more, to that singular essay he wrote—in the form of a five-page rough draft—for the benefit of James Milne, the 'special correspondent' of the *Daily Chronicle* who used it as the basis of his 'interview' with Hardy, which was published in that newspaper on 24 August 1899. Before I quote Hardy it is useful to recall what viewers of Stonehenge—probably the most widely known of all prehistoric monuments in Great Britain, and the objective of thousands of pilgrimages and visits even before the advent of General Pitt-Rivers—believed about it. William Camden, in his *Britannia* (1586), thought that the stones constituting this 'huge and monstrous piece of worke' were not natural stones at all, 'but artificially made of pure sand, and by some glewie and unctuous matter knit and incorporate together'. Camden quoted the 'common saying' that *'Ambrosius Aurelianus*, or his brother *Uther* did reare them up by the art of *Merlin* that great Mathematician, in memorie of those Britaines who by the treachery of Saxones were there slaine at a parley'.[31] The notion that these trilithons were brought—magically—from an Irish mountain to the Salisbury plain did not appeal particularly to Inigo Jones, who, at the request of James III, inspected the site; Jones thought that the stones were too 'elegant in Order', too sophisticated in their stately aspect, to have been erected by the barbarians who populated England in the time of Arthur. Jones's conclusion, that the stone monument had been erected by the Romans, was vigorously denied by William Stukeley; in 1740 Stukeley's book, *Stonehenge: A Temple Restored to the British Druids*, appealed to a wide audience, and its thesis has never failed to find supporters. (To this day modern Druids—members of the British Druid Order—visit Stonehenge on 21 June, Midsummer Day, to celebrate the rays of the new season of the sun.)

Hardy did not pretend to know more than he did about the Stonehenge that he had already used, to artistic advantage, in perhaps the greatest of his novels. He confessed to 'a liking for the state of dim conjecture' in which archaeologists, no less than members of the general public, stood with regard to the history of Stonehenge. But he believed that Stonehenge had probably been erected after the barrow period of interment, and based his conjecture on the fact that one or two barrows seemed to have been interfered with as a consequence of its construction. Excavation of possibly a few days might narrow the possible dates and shed light on the purpose, of construction; but only, Hardy added swiftly, 'under the strictest supervision'.[32] Two additional matters deserve comment. First, Hardy had noticed that the south-west side of the monument was eroding most rapidly as a consequence of wet weather and frost, and he proposed the construction of a belt of plantations, a wood 'approaching no nearer than, say, ten chains to the bank of earth surrounding the stone circle', to break the force of 'disastrous winds and rains'. Also, since Hardy was responding to the threat created by the landowner's proposed sale of Stonehenge (an American purchaser was interested in the possibility of transporting the stones across the Atlantic, so that he might re-erect them in the New World), he made a strong claim for the obligation of the nation to buy Stonehenge as 'a sacred possession', to ensure forever its remaining where it was in all its 'solemnity and fascination'.

The Stonehenge interview may be taken as a characteristic statement of Hardy's abiding interest in archaeology. It serves here as a fitting conclusion to this assessment of its importance in

Hardy's life. It is a restrained plea for the need of fuller scientific investigation before positive conclusions could be drawn about why Stonehenge was built, or when. Hardy knew the pernicious consequences of careless digging; he might have been equally amused and depressed by the recently published news that an excavator, 'on lifting a fallen slab in search of dating evidence, found instead a bottle of port wine generously laid down by an earlier investigator';[33] but even though he did not read the story during his lifetime, he wanted no more of such carelessness. He knew what his neighbour, the General, had accomplished, and that, he believed, was the true direction of the future of archaeology. He wanted the nation to pay attention to its archaeological treasures; and perhaps as important as anything else, he remembered the poetic and human associations that linked past with present. 'The size of the whole structure is considerably dwarfed to the eye', he wrote for Milne's benefit,

'by the openness of the place, as with all such erections, and a strong light detracts from its impressiveness. In the brilliant noonday sunlight, in which most visitors repair thither, and surrounded by bicycles and sandwich papers, the scene is not to my mind attractive, but garish and depressing. In dull, threatening weather, however, and in the dusk of the evening its charm is indescribable. On a day of heavy cloud the sky seems almost to form a natural roof touching the pillars, and colours are revealed on the surfaces of the stones whose presence would not be suspected on a fine day. And if a gale of wind is blowing the strange musical hum emitted by Stonehenge can never be forgotten.'[34]

Indeed, when we examine Hardy's writings, we discover an interest in the developing science of archaeology—its aims, its blunderings, its true achievements and its ability to inspire some of his finest speculations on the relationship between human beings and the Immanent Will—that leads to this conclusion: Hardy would not have written as he did, would not have shaped the specific philosophy that he did, if the intellectual excitement created by increasingly serious investigators in several hard sciences—geology, astronomy, biology and archaeology, among others—during the nineteenth century had remained crudely amateurish or theologically driven, as in previous centuries. The implications of this conclusion for future interpretations of Hardy's development as a literary artist and as a commentator on his age are exciting.

Notes

Chapter 1: An Architect's Eye

1. Robert Gittings, *The Older Hardy* (London: Heinemann, 1978), p. 42.
2. James George Frazer, *The Magic Act and the Evolution of Kings* (London: Macmillan, 1911), Vol. II, p. 136.
3. Florence Emily Hardy, *The Life of Thomas Hardy 1840–1928* (London: Macmillan, 1962), p. 174.
4. Michael Millgate, *Thomas Hardy: A Biography* (Oxford: Oxford University Press, 1982), p. 259.
5. Foreword, *The Architectural Notebook of Thomas Hardy*, ed. C. J. P. Beatty (Dorchester, Dorset: Dorset Natural History and Archaeological Society, 1966), p. vii.
6. The dedication was not attached to the original printing in *Harper's Monthly Magazine*, December 1912, but seems to have been an afterthought at the time of preparation of *Satires of Circumstance*.
7. F. E. Hardy, p. 357.
8. *The Collected Letters of Thomas Hardy, Volume I, 1870–1892*, ed. Richard L. Purdy and Michael Millgate (Oxford: Clarendon Press, 1978), p. 95.
9. *Ibid.*, p. 205.
10. *Ibid.*, p. 221.
11. *Collected Letters, Volume II, 1893–1901*, ed. Richard L. Purdy and Michael Millgate (Oxford: Clarendon Press, 1980), p. 176.
12. *Ibid.*, p. 268.
13. *Collected Letters, Volume III, 1902–1908*, ed. Richard L. Purdy and Michael Millgate (Oxford: Clarendon Press, 1982), p. 50.
14. *Ibid.*
15. *Ibid.*, p. 235-6.
16. *One Rare Fair Woman: Thomas Hardy's Letters to Florence Henniker 1893–1922*, ed. Evelyn Hardy and F. B. Pinion (London: Macmillan, 1972), p. 205.
17. *Collected Letters*, Vol. III, p. 224.
18. *Ibid.*, p. 227.
19. *Ibid.*, p. 283.

20. *Ibid.,* p. 337.
21. *Collected Letters, Volume IV, 1909–1913* (Oxford: Clarendon Press, 1984), p. 18.
22. *Ibid.,* p. 56.
23. *Ibid.,* pp. 73–4.
24. *Ibid.,* p. 122.
25. *Ibid.,* p. 222.
26. 'Memories of Church Restoration', in *Thomas Hardy's Personal Writings: Prefaces, Literary Opinions, Reminiscences,* ed. Harold Orel (Lawrence, Kansas: University Press of Kansas, 1966), p. 204.
27. *Ibid.,* p. 205.
28. *Ibid.,* p. 217.
29. *Ibid.,* p. 216.
30. *Ibid.,* p. 217.
31. *Ibid.*
32. F. E. Hardy, p. 79.
33. *Collected Letters,* Vol. IV, p. 262.
34. F. E. Hardy, p. 301.
35. Joan Grundy, *Hardy and the Sister Arts* (London: Macmillan, 1979).
36. Susan Dean, *Hardy's Poetic Vision in The Dynasts* (Princeton, NJ: Princeton University Press, 1977), p. 19.
37. The concept of 'imprinting' was familiar to several other authors at the turn of the century. For example, Edith Wharton wrote, in 'Hudson River Bracketed', that 'There was no amount of psychic sensibility one could not read into the walls and furniture of an old empty home.'
38. *Personal Writings,* p. 215.

Chapter 2: Hardy's Interest in the Theatre

1. 'Candour in English Fiction', in *Thomas Hardy's Personal Writings,* ed. Harold Orel (Lawrence, Kansas: University Press of Kansas, 1966), p. 131.
2. *Thomas Hardy's Notebooks: And Some Letters from Julia Augusta Martin,* ed. Evelyn Hardy (London: Hogarth Press, 1955), p. 105.
3. Florence Emily Hardy, *The Life of Thomas Hardy 1840–1928* (London: Macmillan, 1962), p. 425.
4. Walter F. Wright, *The Shaping of The Dynasts: A Study in Thomas Hardy* (Lincoln, Nebraska: University of Nebraska Press, 1967), p. 9; William R. Rutland, *Thomas Hardy: A Study of His Writings and Their Background* (Oxford: Basil Blackwell, 1938), p. 35.
5. F. E. Hardy, p. 53.
6. *The Collected Letters of Thomas Hardy, Volume I, 1840–1892,* ed. Richard L. Purdy and Michael Millgate (Oxford: Clarendon Press, 1978), pp. 214–15.
7. *Collected Letters, Volume II, 1893–1901,* ed. Richard L. Purdy and Michael Millgate (Oxford: Clarendon Press, 1980), p. 11.
8. *Ibid.,* p. 76.

9. *Ibid.*, p. 294.
10. *Collected Letters, Volume III, 1902–1908*, ed. Richard L. Purdy and Michael Millgate (Oxford: Clarendon Press, 1982), p. 192.
11. *Collected Letters, Volume IV, 1909–1913*, ed. Richard L. Purdy and Michael Millgate (Oxford: Clarendon Press, 1984), p. 37.
12. *Collected Letters*, Vol. II, pp. 13–14.
13. *Ibid.*, p. 43.
14. *Collected Letters*, Vol. III, p. 151.
15. *Ibid.*, p. 249.
16. *Ibid.*, pp. 297–8.
17. *Collected Letters*, Vol. IV, p. 2.
18. *Collected Letters*, Vol. III, p. 258.
19. *Collected Letters*, Vol. IV, p. 53.
20. *Ibid.*, pp. 200–1.
21. *Ibid.*, pp. 202–3.
22. *Collected Letters*, Vol. II, p. 52.
23. *Ibid.*, p. 251.
24. *Ibid.*, p. 285.
25. *Collected Letters*, Vol. III, p. 163.
26. *Ibid.*, p. 213.
27. *Ibid.*, p. 281.
28. *Ibid.*, p. 305.
29. *Collected Letters*, Vol. IV, p. 310.
30. *Ibid.*, p. 313.
31. *Ibid.*
32. *Ibid.*, p. 143.
33. *The Literary Notes of Thomas Hardy*, ed. Lennart A. Björk (Göteborg, Sweden: Acta Universitas Gothoburgensis, 1974), Vol. II, p. 148.
34. *Collected Letters*, Vol. III, p. 277.
35. *Collected Letters*, Vol. IV, p. 5.
36. *Thomas Hardy's Notebooks*, p. 49.
37. *Literary Notes*, Vol. I, p. 119.
38. *Friends of a Lifetime: Letters to Sydney Carlyle Cockerell*, ed. Viola Meynell (London: Jonathan Cape, 1940), p. 284.
39. F. E. Hardy, p. 423.
40. *Ibid.*, p. 234.
41. Reginald Snell, 'A Self-Plagiarism by Thomas Hardy', *Essays in Criticism*, Vol. II (January 1952), pp. 114–17.
42. *Collected Letters*, Vol. I, p. 103.
43. Michael Millgate, *Thomas Hardy: A Biography* (Oxford: Oxford University Press, 1982), pp. 226–7.
44. *Collected Letters*, Vol. II, p. 9.
45. Hardy wrote to Henry Arthur Jones on 16 February 1897, 'I had secretly hoped that *Tess* was going to fall through altogether, as I have been, & am, more interested in other labours.' *Collected Letters*, Vol. II, p. 147.
46. Quoted in Desmond Hawkins, *The Tess Opera* (Taunton, Somerset: Thomas Hardy Society, 1984), p. 6.
47. *Ibid.*, p. 17.

48. *Collected Letters*, Vol. IV, p. 230.
49. Hawkins, p. 9.
50. *Collected Letters*, Vol. IV, p. 99.
51. Marguerite Roberts, *Tess in the Theatre* (Toronto: University of Toronto Press, 1950), p. lxxi.
52. *Ibid.*, p. lxxxii.
53. F. E. Hardy, p. 426.
54. Norman J. Atkins, *Thomas Hardy and the Hardy Players* (St Peter's Port, Guernsey: Toucan Press, 1980), p. 11.
55. F. E. Hardy, p. 429.

Chapter 3: Literary Friendships

1. See, in *Thomas Hardy's Personal Writings: Prefaces, Literary Opinions, Reminiscences*, ed. Harold Orel (London: Macmillan, 1967), Hardy's preface to *Select Poems by William Barnes*, pp. 76–82; two short pieces on 'Dialect in Novels', pp. 91–3; an unsigned review of *Poems of Rural Life in the Dorset Dialect*, by William Barnes, pp. 94–100; and 'The Rev. William Barnes, B.D.', pp. 100–6.
2. *The Literary Notes of Thomas Hardy*, ed. Lennart A. Björk (Göteborg, Sweden: Acta Universitatis Gothoburgensis, 1974), Vol. I, Notes, p. 202.
3. J. A. Sutherland, *Victorian Novelists and Publishers* (Chicago: University of Chicago Press, 1976), p. 214.
4. 'G. M.: A Reminiscence', in *Personal Writings*, p. 151.
5. Florence Emily Hardy, *The Life of Thomas Hardy, 1840–1928* (London: Macmillan, 1962), pp. 61–2.
6. 'G.M.', p. 154.
7. *The Poetry of Thomas Hardy: A Handbook and Commentary*, by J. O. Bailey (Chapel Hill: University of North Carolina Press, 1970), p. 258.
8. Robert Graves, *Good-by to All That* (London: A.P. Watt & Son, 1929), p. 378.
9. *Thomas Hardy's Correspondence at Max Gate: A Descriptive Check List*, compiled by Carl J. Weber and Clara Carter Weber (Waterville, Me.: Colby College Press, 1968), p. 8.
10. Evelyn Hardy, *Thomas Hardy: A Critical Biography* (London: Hogarth Press, 1954), pp. 70–3; *Thomas Hardy's Notebooks and Some Letters from Julia Augusta Martin* ed. E. Hardy (London: Hogarth Press, 1955), p. 73; F. B. Pinion, *A Hardy Companion* (London: Macmillan, 1968), p. 208.
11. F. E. Hardy, p. 287.
12. *Ibid.*, pp. 344–5.
13. *Ibid.*, p. 127; cf. R. J. White, *Thomas Hardy and History* (London: Macmillan Press, 1974), pp. 60–1, 104.
14. *Thomas Hardy: A Bibliographical Study* (London: Oxford University Press, 1954), p. 16.
15. F. E. Hardy, pp. 105–6.
16. *Thomas Hardy's Correspondence at Max Gate*, p. 23.

17. Edmund Gosse, 'Mr Hardy's Lyrical Poems', *Edinburgh Review* 227 (April 1918), 272–93; rptd as 'The Lyrical Poetry of Thomas Hardy', in *Some Diversions of a Man of Letters* (London: Heinemann; New York: Scribner's, 1919), pp. 233–58.
18. *Thomas Hardy's Notebooks,* pp. 104–5.
19. *Literary Notes,* Vol. I, Notes, p. 366.
20. Carl J. Weber, *Hardy of Wessex: His Life and Literary Career* (New York: Columbia University Press, 1940; rpt Hamden, Conn.: Archon Books, 1962), p. 226.
21. Richard L. Purdy, *Thomas Hardy: A Bibliographical Study*, p. 106.
22. F. E. Hardy, pp. 389–90.
    For a fuller discussion of Hardy's symbolic importance to younger novelists and poets, see Patricia Hutchins, 'Thomas Hardy and Some Younger Writers', *Journal of Modern Literature* 3 (Feb., 1973), 35–44. Two quotations may be selected as representative: John Middleton Murry's sentence, in a letter to Hardy dated 3 March 1919, 'In a real sense we desire to sail under your flag', and E. M. Forster's remark, contained in *Aspects of the Novel*, 'Hardy is my home'.

Chapter 4: Kipling and Haggard

1. Ihab H. Hassan, 'The Problem of Influence in Literary History: Notes Towards a Definition', *Journal of Aesthetics and Art Criticism* 14 XIV (1955), 66–7.
2. Carl J. Weber, *Hardy of Wessex: His Life and Literary Career* (1940; rpt Hamden, Conn.: Archon Books, 1962), p. 240.
3. Harold Bloom, *The Anxiety of Influence: A Theory of Poetry* (1973; rpt London: Oxford University Press, 1975).
4. *The Courting of Dinah Shadd and Other Stories* (New York: Harper & Brothers, 1890).
5. Charles Edmund Carrington, *Rudyard Kipling: His Life and Work* (1955; rpt London: Macmillan, 1978), pp. 162–3.
6. *The Personal Notebooks of Thomas Hardy*, ed. Richard H. Taylor (New York: Columbia University Press, 1979), pp. 38–9.
7. *Ibid.*, p. 285.
8. Arthur Young, *A Dictionary of the Characters and Scenes in the Stories and Poems of Rudyard Kipling 1886–1911* (London: George Routledge & Sons, 1913), p. 41.
9. H. Rider Haggard, *The Days of My Life* (London: Longmans Green & Co., 1926), Vol. I, pp. 272–3.
10. Morton N. Cohen, *Rider Haggard: His Life and Work* (London: Macmillan, 1968), p. 181. Hardy's bitter response is contained in a letter to Edward Clodd, dated 4 February 1892; see Purdy and Millgate, Vol. I, p. 256.
11. *The Collected Letters of Thomas Hardy, Volume I, 1870–1892*, ed. Richard L. Purdy and Michael Millgate, p. 235.
12. Haggard, Vol. II, p. 214.

13. F. B. Pinion, *A Hardy Companion: A Guide to the Works of Thomas Hardy and Their Background* (London: Macmillan, 1968), pp. 182–3.
14. Cohen, p. 175.
15. Douglas Brown, *Thomas Hardy* (London: Longmans Green & Co., 1954), Part II, 'The Agricultural Theme', pp. 29–44.
16. Florence Emily Hardy, *The Life of Thomas Hardy 1840–1928* (1928, 1930; rpt London: Macmillan, 1962), pp. 312–14.
17. H. Rider Haggard, *Rural England: Being an Account of Agricultural and Social Researches Carried Out in the Years 1901 & 1902* (1902; rpt London: Longmans, Green & Co., 1906), Vol. I, pp. 282–6.
18. Morton N. Cohen, *Rudyard Kipling to Rider Haggard: The Record of a Friendship* (London: Hutchinson, 1965), *passim*.

Chapter 5: The Dynasts

1. Ellen Glasgow, *The Woman Within* (New York: Harcourt, Brace, 1954), p. 197.
2. Florence Emily Hardy, *The Life of Thomas Hardy 1840–1928* (London: Macmillan, 1962), p. 413.
3. Paul Zietlow, *Moments of Vision: The Poetry of Thomas Hardy* (Cambridge, Mass.: Harvard University Press, 1974), p. ix.
4. Kenneth Marsden, *The Poems of Thomas Hardy: A Critical Introduction* (University of London: Athlone Press, 1969), p. viii.
5. Bert G. Hornback, *The Metaphor of Chance: Vision and Technique in the Works of Thomas Hardy* (Athens, Ohio: Ohio University Press, 1971), pp. 165–6.
6. Hardy always listed the number of scenes as 130, but, as Purdy points out, there are 131, plus the Fore Scene and the After Scene. Richard Little Purdy, *Thomas Hardy: A Bibliographical Study* (London: Oxford University Press, 1954), p. 134.
7. The story of the special trip made by Emma to the British Museum, where she wept as she begged Dr Richard Garnett for aid 'in inducing her husband to burn his vicious manuscript', apparently originated with Ford Madox Ford and was repeated several times by Carl Weber without supporting documentation. Neither Robert Gittings nor Richard Garnett's descendants have found any evidence that Emma made this particular trip.
8. F. E. Hardy, p. 106.
9. *Ibid.*, p. 148.
10. Hoxie N. Fairchild, 'The Immediate Source of *The Dynasts*', *PMLA* 67 (March 1952), 43–64.
11. F. E. Hardy, pp. 284–5.
12. William R. Rutland, *Thomas Hardy: A Study of His Writings and Their Background* (Oxford: Blackwell, 1938; rpt New York: Russell & Russell, 1962), p. 271.
13. See R. J. White, *Thomas Hardy and History* (London: Macmillan, 1974), Ch. 8, 'The Historians', *passim*; Rutland, Ch. 7, 'The Poems and *The Dynasts*';

and Walter Wright, *The Shaping of The Dynasts: A Study in Thomas Hardy* (Lincoln, Nebr.: University of Nebraska Press, 1967), Ch. 4, 'The Substance'.

Chapter 6: Hardy's Interest in the Law

1. *The Personal Notebooks of Thomas Hardy, with an Appendix Including the Unpublished Passages in the Original Typescript of 'The Life of Thomas Hardy'*, ed. Richard H. Taylor (New York: Columbia University Press, 1979), p. 241.
2. *Ibid.*, p. 230.
3. *Ibid.*, p. 70.
4. *Concerning Thomas Hardy: A Composite Portrait from Memory*, ed. D. F. Barber (London: Charles Skilton, 1968), p. 28.
5. *Ibid.*
6. J. O. Bailey, *The Poetry of Thomas Hardy: A Handbook and Commentary* (Chapel Hill: University of North Carolina Press, 1970), p. 534.
7. *Thomas Hardy's Notebooks and Some Letters from Julia Augusta Martin*, ed. Evelyn Hardy (London: Hogarth Press, 1955), pp. 82–3.
8. *Ibid.*, p. 82.
9. *Ibid.*, p. 83.
10. *Thomas Hardy's Personal Writings: Prefaces, Literary Opinions, Reminiscences*, ed. Harold Orel (Lawrence, Kansas: University of Kansas Press, 1966), p. 229.
11. Bailey, pp. 533–4.
12. *Personal Notebooks*, pp. 124–5.
13. Florence Emily Hardy, *The Life of Thomas Hardy 1840–1928* (1928, 1930; rpt. London: Macmillan, 1962), p. 124.
14. G. Stevens Cox believes that the murderer was James Seale, who committed a murder in the little village of Stoke Abbott, near Beaminster, and was hanged as a consequence at Dorchester on 10 August 1858. 'The Dreadful Murder at Stoke Abbott and the Public Execution of James Seale', *The Thomas Hardy Yearbook 1970* (No. 1), pp. 85–93.
15. F. E. Hardy, pp. 28–9.
16. *Ibid.*, p. 153.
17. *Ibid.*, p. 162.
18. *Ibid.*, p. 214.
19. *Ibid.*, p. 255.
20. *Ibid.*, pp. 294–5.
21. F. E. Hardy, p. 317.
22. *Personal Notebooks*, p. 9.
23. F. E. Hardy, p. 107.
24. *Personal Notebooks*, p. 129.
25. F. E. Hardy, p. 392.
26. *Ibid.*, p. 189.
27. *Ibid.*, p. 213.

28. *Ibid.*, p. 454.
29. *Ibid.*, p. 374.
30. Bailey, pp. 419–20.
31. F. E. Hardy, p. 126.
32. *Ibid.*, p. 209.
33. *The Collected Letters of Thomas Hardy*, ed. Richard L. Purdy and Michael Millgate (Oxford: Clarendon Press, 1980), Vol. II, 1893–1901, pp. 15–16.
34. *Ibid.*, pp. 223, 229.
35. *Ibid.*, p. 272.
36. F. E. Hardy, p. 41.
37. *Ibid.*, p. 240.
38. *Ibid.*, p. 227.
39. *Ibid.*, p. 236.
40. *Ibid.*, p. 395.
41. R. J. White, *Thomas Hardy and History* (London: Macmillan, 1974), p. 6.
42. *The Literary Notes of Thomas Hardy*, ed. Lennart A. Björk (Göteborg, Sweden: Acta Universitatis Gothoburgensis, 1974), Vol. I, Notes, p. 287.
43. *One Rare Fair Woman: Thomas Hardy's Letters to Florence Henniker 1893–1922*, ed. Evelyn Hardy and F. B. Pinion (London: Macmillan, 1972), p. 170.
44. *Literary Notes*, Vol. I, Notes, p. 287.
45. *Collected Letters*, Vol. I, p. 290.
46. *Ibid.*, Vol. II, p. 62.
47. Pinion, p. 496.
48. F. E. Hardy, p. 251.
49. *Personal Writings*, p. 34.
50. *Collected Letters*, Vol. II, p. 154.
51. *Dorset County Chronicle*, 18 February 1886, as quoted by Edward C. Sampson, 'Thomas Hardy: Justice of the Peace', *Colby Library Quarterly* 13, 4 (December 1977), 264.
52. Sampson, p. 270.
53. *Dorset County Chronicle*, 5 September 1918, as quoted by Sampson, p. 271.
54. F. E. Hardy, p. 227.
55. *Ibid.*, p. 167.
56. *Collected Letters*, Vol. II, p. 50.
57. Robert Gittings and Jo Manton, *The Second Mrs Hardy* (London: Heinemann, 1979), pp. 123–5.

Chapter 7: *Hardy and the Developing Science of Archaeology*

1. Barry M. Marsden, *The Early Barrow-Diggers* (Aylesbury, Bucks.: Shire Publications, 1974), p. 10.
2. Michael Millgate, *Thomas Hardy: A Biography* (Oxford: Oxford University Press, 1982), p. 90.

3. *Ibid.*, p. 91.
4. *The Literary Notes of Thomas Hardy*, ed. Lennart A. Björk (Göteborg: Acta Universitatis Gothoburgensis, 1974), Vol. I, p. 119.
5. Glyn Daniel, *The Origins and Growth of Archaeology* (Harmondsworth: Penguin, 1967), p. 169. See also Jacquetta Hawkes, *Mortimer Wheeler* (London: Weidenfeld & Nicolson, 1982), for an authoritative survey of British archaeology in this century.
6. Millgate, pp. 244–5.
7. Quoted by Daniel, p. 259.
8. Desmond Hawkins, *Cranborne Chase* (London: Victor Gollancz, 1980), Ch. 11; *Concerning Agnes: Thomas Hardy's 'Good Little Pupil'* (Gloucester: Alan Sutton, 1982), pp. 38–9; and 'The Old General', a script produced in 1950 for the BBC, containing an interview with Sir Mortimer Wheeler in which Sir Mortimer reminisces about the General. For additional biographical material on the General, see Michael Welman Thompson's *General Pitt-Rivers: Evolution and Archaeology in the Nineteenth Century* (Bradford-on-Avon: Moonraker Press, 1977), and the poignant essay by Harold St George Gray, 'A Memoir of General Pitt-Rivers, D.C.L., F.R.S., F.S.A.', in *Index to 'Excavations in Cranborne Chase' and 'King John's House, Tollard Royal'* (Taunton Castle: Somerset, 1905), Vol. V, pp. ix–xxvi.
9. Charles Michael Daugherty, *The Great Archaeologists* (New York: Thomas Y. Crowell Company, 1962), pp. 39–42.
10. Jacquetta Hawkes and Christopher Hawkes, *Prehistoric Britain* (Cambridge, Mass.: Harvard University Press, 1953), p. 156.
11. Hawkins, *Cranborne Chase*, p. 144.
12. Florence Emily Hardy, *The Life of Thomas Hardy 1840–1928* (London: Macmillan, 1962), p. 269.
13. Quoted by Millgate, p. 400.
14. Hawkins, *Cranborne Chase*, p. 144.
15. *Ibid.*
16. 'Maumbury Ring', in *Thomas Hardy's Personal Writings*, ed. Harold Orel (Lawrence, Kansas: University Press of Kansas, 1966), p. 231.
17. *Ibid.*
18. *Ibid.*, p. 226.
19. *Ibid.*
20. *The World of the Past*, ed. Jacquetta Hawkes (New York: Alfred A. Knopf, 1963), pp. 392–3.
21. Quoted by Marsden, p. 49.
22. *Personal Writings*, p. 192.
23. William Archer, 'Real Conversations: Conversation I.—With Mr Thomas Hardy', *Critic* 38 (April 1901), 313.
24. *Personal Writings*, p. 193.
25. *Ibid.*, p. 194.
26. F. E. Hardy, p. 164.
27. William Archer, *Real Conversations* (London: W. Heinemann, 1904), p. 38.
28. F. E. Hardy, pp. 233–4.
29. J. O. Bailey, *The Poetry of Thomas Hardy: A Handbook and Commentary*

(Chapel Hill: University of North Carolina Press, 1970), p. 412.
30. *Ibid.*
31. *The World of the Past*, p. 363.
32. *Personal Writings,* p. 200.
33. Hawkes and Hawkes, p. 61.
34. *Personal Writings*, p. 200.

Index